MW00787486

THE
LAST
RELAPSE

Copyright © 2021 Sathiya Sam

All rights reserved. No part of this publication may be reproduced, distributed, or transmitted in any form or by any means, including photocopying, recording, or other electronic or mechanical methods, without the prior written permission of the publisher, except in the case of brief quotations embodied in critical reviews and certain other noncommercial uses permitted by copyright law. For permission requests, write to the publisher, addressed "Attention: Permissions Coordinator," at the address below.

SMG Publishing – publishing@sathiyasam.com

SMG PUBLISHING
BOOKS THAT MATTER

ISBN: 978-1-7778314-0-0 (paperback)
ISBN: 978-1-7778314-3-1 (hardback)
ISBN: 978-1-7778314-2-4 (ebook)

Ordering Information:
Special discounts are available on quantity purchases by corporations, associations, and others. For details, contact publishing@sathiyasam.com

THE
LAST
RELAPSE

REALIZE YOUR POTENTIAL, RECLAIM INTIMACY,
AND RESOLVE THE ROOT ISSUES
OF **PORN ADDICTION**

SATHIYA SAM

For my parents, Jeeva and Sulojana Sam, who have always believed in me and taught me to value character above all else. I love you both and am grateful God gave me the two of you as my parents.

HELP THOSE IN NEED: 10% of all author royalties are donated to Nalubaale Social Center, an organization that provides startup funding to local entrepreneurs in Uganda through evangelistic soccer tournaments. https://www.nsc.world/en/

Contents

Introduction

I struggled with a pornography addiction for 15 years while being a pastor's kid and eventually becoming a pastor myself. My first exposure to pornography was in the computer lab of my Christian school at the tender age of 11. I was a good kid with good parents and a good life, but those who have struggled with porn know that the first time you see porn won't be the last.

That fateful experience began a gradual decline through my high school years until the middle of my university years, where porn was a daily habit that I needed in order to alleviate the stress of pursuing my education. Porn was a vice, but it was also my medicine. I didn't know how else to cope with the pressures of university. I was hooked.

Ironically, while at university, I found God. Not that I hadn't previously discovered Him (I attended a Christian school, remember?) but it was only in the middle of my degree that I decided to give my life fully to Him. Immediately after, I knew I had to make some changes. I would stop drinking excessively on the weekends. I would clean up my language. And, of course, I had to get rid of porn. The first two habits were easy to address, but shaking pornography felt impossible. No matter how I hard I tried, I could not get "free."

That's when I realized how few resources were available to men like me. Pornography was incredibly accessible (and affordable)—meanwhile there were no resources available to help people that wanted to escape its grip. It was incredibly frustrating. I made a decision there and then that one day I would get free, and I would do everything in my power to help others who were struggling experience the same freedom.

That was a nice idea, don't get me wrong, but following through on it has been anything but easy. Overcoming pornography addiction is a complicated process. There are layers to the experience, and many of these layers are unique to the individual. In other words, just because something worked for me doesn't mean it will work for everyone else.

As anyone who has struggled with an addiction will know, the journey to freedom is a rollercoaster ride. You have days where you wonder if life will ever change, or if you are just fundamentally flawed and have no hope of long-term sobriety. Then you have periods where you are *convinced* you've made it, and that there is no turning back, only to find out a weak moment later that the problem is still there.

It took me five years of earnestly pursuing freedom before I finally achieved it. I spent the first three years trying things that didn't work. They brought temporary results but had little to no long-term effect. I'll explain why in the coming pages.

When I finally got free in February 2016, I had no idea it had even happened. Not because I was oblivious, but simply because it was familiar territory. Previously, I had gone a few weeks, a few months, even a year without slipping, only to fall back into my old habits eventually. Something certainly felt different on this glorious day, but I was not convinced this was the last nail in the coffin of my addiction. I was skeptical, guarded, and pretty sure I was just riding the high of an emotional experience.

Little did I know then that my life would forever be changed. We'll get into what exactly took place later in the book, but just know that I haven't looked at pornography once since. The freedom I felt that day was for real. Since then, I've had the privilege of helping hundreds of men achieve freedom through a weekly newsletter, a daily podcast and a life-changing program.

Given how tumultuous the journey can be, I'm sure you can understand that I waited several years before endeavoring to help other men struggling with addiction. I wasn't going to rush in only to discover I still had work to do myself. I had to be utterly and entirely convinced that I was free before I even *thought* about helping others. Eventually, I reached that place, and I felt a gentle nudge from God to set out and tackle this silent epidemic.

Yes, porn addiction is an **epidemic**. In the three seconds it takes you to read this sentence, the porn industry has made over US $1,000. Its annual revenue likely exceeds the NBA, NFL, and Netflix.[1] Porn viewership has also been shown to increase the likelihood of infidelity. A study reported by *Science* in 2016 showed that divorce rates doubled when pornography was involved.[2]

The average age of exposure to pornography is somewhere between 11 and 13. According to a 2008 study, by the time most boys turn 18, there is a 93% chance they will have viewed porn at least once. For girls, it is 62%.[3]

The impact of pornography on the human body and mind, plus the devastating effects it has relationally and societally, should be enough to sound alarm bells in political, educational, and media arenas. Yet the subject is rarely discussed at these levels. Instead, scores of men struggle every day in silence. Women are struggling too, but for the purposes of this book we will focus on the male experience.

When I first ventured out to start helping other men experience freedom from addiction I found the magnitude of the issue intimidating, to say the least. The main problem was that I didn't know if my own experience was repeatable. Could somebody else just follow the same path I did and obtain the same results? Was it really that simple? What were the factors that helped me anyway? It's a complex matter.

It turns out that not every part of my personal journey is useful for the average man. There were elements of my recovery that were unique to me and quite specific to my life. However, there were also underlying principles and universal tools that have a much broader impact. And the more I shared them, the more impact they had. Young and old, rich and poor, single and married, kids and no kids, it did not matter the stage of life, these fundamentals were helping men all around the world overcome pornography addiction.

As I dove deeper into helping these men, I started to observe that when these fundamental principles were applied in other areas of life—relationships, fitness, finances, and spirituality especially—the results were equal, if not better. That's when I knew I had to write a book. Clearly, this material needed to be shared.

This is a book about how to be a healthy, successful, and godly man, a foreign concept in the 21st century. These life-changing fundamentals have been arranged into a system that I call DeepClean. I have been teaching the DeepClean methodology for several years now, although it is really since 2018 that I formally began coaching men through the process. The goal is to provide Bible-based, research-backed education and empowerment to facilitate freedom in all men, from the hopeless to the healthy.

I've seen the results. Marriages have been restored. Parent relationships have been reconciled. Destinies have been recovered. Men have regained their sense of self. One of my first clients could not pursue the things that God put on his heart because he felt like a hypocrite for struggling with pornography. As you'll see later in this book, that all changed after he went through DeepClean. His story is not uncommon—there are plenty of ways that God has used the DeepClean system to dramatically improve the lives of many men, and we've documented several of them throughout this book. Whether you have struggled for a day or decades, this book will help you. (And if you're inspired by reading success stories, you can reference the appendix where I've laid out several in more detail).

The teachings of this book must be applied with action—they cannot simply be understood cerebrally. If you really want this book to make a difference in your life, it will be essential for you to complete the workbook as well. The workbook is free of charge if you get it from www.sathiyasam. com/recoveryworkbook.

Lastly, I implore you to do something important before you start Chapter 1: you must pray a bold prayer. When my addiction to pornography was particularly rife, I was a single man. Single and hopeless, to be exact. When you have an addiction like this in your life, the idea of bringing someone else into the mix is nothing short of horrifying. Yet when I was single, there was nothing I wanted more than to be with someone else. It was a weird tension to navigate.

Through the wisdom of my peers and a few trusted leaders, I learned that marriage is a magnifier. It does not solve problems, it exposes them. So bringing an issue as severe as a pornography addiction into my future marriage was only going to exacerbate it, and I had no interest in doing that. In response, I prayed a very simple prayer during this time, and I didn't stop praying it until November 2016: "God, until I am free of pornography, keep my future wife from me."

It seems noble now, but it was a royal pain in the butt at the time. It was the last thing I wanted to pray because it put the onus on me to fix the problem. I wanted to believe that if my circumstances could change, then I wouldn't have this struggle. Nothing could have been further from the truth. *I* was the one that had to change.

If you're a fact-checker, you may have observed that February 2016 was my last relapse, but November 2016 was the last time I prayed the prayer. Why the discrepancy? Because nine short months after being free of pornography, I met Shaloma. We dated for a year, were engaged for a year and a half, and in September 2019 we tied the knot. That simple prayer came to pass in what felt like the blink of an eye.

These pages contain the potential for a life-changing experience, so pray bold prayers as you venture into this book. Prayers that put a stake in the ground and say, enough is enough. I'm not going to live life the same anymore. As you partner that boldness with prayer, supernatural will things happen. Inexplicable results will take place. And it will only be a matter of time before you look back and marvel at what God has done.

Take a moment now, pray that bold prayer, and let's get started.

(Note: There are many real-life client stories woven throughout the book. Their names and some details of their stories have been altered for privacy.)

Section 1

TAKING BACK CONTROL OF YOUR LIFE

CHAPTER 1

A New Approach To Recovery

Growing up in a pastor's home, we learned to enjoy life with minimal means. We weren't poor—we always had food on the table and clothes on our backs—but we weren't particularly rich either. However, as my dad's career developed and he was afforded better opportunities, my parents were able to buy a beautiful home on an unusually large lot in the suburbs. I was in high school at the time.

The house was unsuspecting from the front. Quaint and average-sized with a nice front yard. But the minute you stepped inside, it was clear that this home had been renovated and expanded multiple times over the years. Even more exciting for an active and athletic teenager was the massive backyard that boasted a ton of open space and featured an above ground pool. I liken the house to a mullet—business in the front, party in the back.

Owning a property like this as a family was a lot of fun, especially considering that up until then we always rented. Of course, being a teenager in our new home meant that with great fun came great responsibility, including lawn maintenance. Great.

Today I'm the kind of guy who pours my heart and soul into everything I do, even if there isn't much reward or interest. If something needs to be done, I'll do it to the best of my abilities. No questions asked. That's who I am *today*. But 16-year-old Sathiya could only muster that level of diligence if the task at hand involved Xbox or girls (never both, though, as I later found out they are mutually exclusive). If neither incentive was available, then my objective was to get things done as quickly and painlessly as possible.

While about 90% of the yard was lush, healthy grass, there was always a small patch that was primarily weeds. Not big, prickly weeds. Just small, scraggly ones that messed up the grass enough for me to notice, but in my case, not enough to care.

Every time I ran over this small weedy area with the lawnmower, I knew deep down that if I wanted to clean up this area for good, I would have to put on some gloves, get on my knees, and pull those weeds out from the root.

But what 16-year-old has time for that? My Xbox was calling my name. I mean, girls were calling my phone. So, without fail, every time I reached this scraggly area I would run the mower over it just like the rest of the lawn. And when I had done my duty for the day, I would stand on the deck overlooking the yard and admire the fruits of my labor—a clean, fresh-looking plane of grass.

Much to my dismay, only a few short days later, from the same vantage point I would observe that while most of the yard still looked reasonably fresh, the patch of weeds had grown back with a vengeance and was looking rather drab.

"That's for future Sathiya to worry about," I thought to myself. Teens.

So, a couple of weeks later, when it came time to cut the grass again, nothing changed. I continued to cut the grass and the weeds with the same mower, fully aware that the weeds would grow back again and being okay with it. I simply did not have the drive or diligence to do the dirty work.

A remarkable number of people handle their problems in life the exact same way. Their awareness of the issue and pursuit of a solution are thwarted by an unwillingness to commit to hard work.

All behavior is rooted in belief. When you encounter a behavioral issue, such as overeating, social media overuse, spiritual disconnect, pornography addiction, or unmanaged anger, the common response is to modify the behavior. If you're trying to lose weight, you pull out a scale and you start changing your diet. If you're trapped in addictive behavior with your device(s), it means installing an Internet filter or a time limiter.

You get the idea.

We tend to address behavioral issues with behavioral solutions when, in reality, the only way to effectively achieve long-term behavioral change is to probe beneath the surface and address the underlying causes. This is why many who struggle with their weight get excited about a new diet or weight-loss program and stick to it for a few weeks or months, but eventually find themselves back in their old ways. Nothing changed internally— the change of diet and exercise was simply behavioral.

Everyone wants long-term health and success, but few are willing to pay the price. It has to be trendy and convenient. Sadly, anything that fits those two criteria is likely over-focused on external matters and negligent of the internal life.

Now I'm not against behaviorally focused solutions. If you want to try a new diet to lose weight or install a time-restricting app to reduce screen time on your phone, then go for it. I will never disapprove of anyone who is willing to take action toward a goal. However, when that is the sole component of your solution to a behavioral issue, it is only a matter of time before you find yourself back at square one.

External solutions must be accompanied by internal solutions, and we are going to talk about what that means and what it looks like, practically. But first, let's make sure we're on the same page about behavior.

Behavior Breakdown

Let's be real, there are behaviors in your life right now that you know you must deal with. Everyone has them, but let me give you a few examples in case you're in denial.

You may want to:

- Spend more time praying and reading your Bible

- Get in shape

- Stop looking at pornography

- Spend less time on your phone

- Become financially free

- Be more honest in your relationships

- Become a better, more present friend

- Muster up the courage to finally ask that girl out

- Make more of an effort in your marriage

- Start that business you've always talked about

- Step into your creative talents more (i.e. songwriting, creating music, writing a book, painting, etc.)

- Move out of your parents' basement

- Eat healthy food consistently

- Stop lying

- Get out of debt

- Quit smoking

- Decrease social media usage

If you read the entire list and thought, "Ha! I don't have any of those," to prove me wrong, then maybe you need to work on being right all the time. For the rest of us, I'm sure you can agree that there is still work to be done in your life.

Any behavioral change usually starts with **macro** behavior. Eating better, quitting smoking, etc. These are overarching behaviors or behavior patterns that are comprised of several smaller **micro** behaviors.

For example, driving a car is a macro behavior. That macro behavior is made up of several small behaviors like turning the steering wheel, pressing the gas and brake, using your indicator when you turn (depending on how smart of a driver you are), etc.

In the same way, spending less time on your phone is a macro behavior. It will be comprised of micro behaviors like deleting social media apps, activating the screen time limiting function, charging your phone outside of your bedroom, and so on.

As Proverbs 20:11 says, "Even children are known by the way they act, whether their conduct is pure and whether it is right."[4] Our behavior is significant, and the better we understand how it works and how to master it, the more freedom and fulfillment we will experience in life.

Taking a macro behavior and breaking it down into micro behaviors can go a long way when you are trying to affect long-term change in your life. Usually, identifying just a few micro behaviors is enough to hone in on and create momentum toward your targeted behavioral change. But before we start talking about making changes, we should identify another piece of the puzzle.

Behavior Patterns

A behavior pattern is a sequence of actions that are repeated on a regular basis. Every time I get into a vehicle, I put my seat belt on. I don't even think about it. It's pure habit (aka a behavior pattern), a subset of behaviors that always take place, in sequence, with minimal thought or effort.

Behavior patterns are *always* comprised of a series of micro behaviors that eventually lead to macro behaviors. When I step into a vehicle, I put on my seat belt, start the car, check my mirrors, wait until the engine warms up (yeah I'm one of those guys who is willing to wait the 30 seconds), and then put my car into first gear (yeah I'm also one of those guys who drives stick. More on that later.). Only then do I drive.

Identifying your own behavior patterns is so important because it pinpoints the specific microbehaviors you need to address and gives you a clear focus on what you need to change. If you want to lose weight but you can't pinpoint why you've gained so much weight in the first place, you have some work to do before you can achieve your goal. It's one thing to say, "I'm going to lose weight this year." It's another thing to say, "I'm going to stop eating snacks after dinner and exercise twice per week." Once you know the associated behavior patterns that are causing weight gain, it becomes much clearer which micro behaviors are at play. Now you can craft a suitable solution.

So, if you realize that any time you start watching TV you have some sort of salt craving and you always give in, that pattern makes it pretty easy to identify which micro behaviors you need to take care of. Make a game plan for how you handle snacking while watching TV.

In a porn addiction recovery context, you may observe that most of your slips happen at night. You start scrolling before bed and then one thing leads to another. Now we can devise a solution such as turning your phone off an hour before bed.

While identifying behavior patterns is essential, it is not the complete picture. Usually, the issue in our approach to behavior modification is that we do not dive deep enough into the problem to address the systemic issues. As a result, we experience trends and fads instead of long-term change. While identifying behavioral patterns and making changes at a micro behavioral level is good, it is not enough. You will have to dive even deeper to identify the underlying elements of your internal world that are driving your behavior in the first place.

Master of Your Domain

Human beings manage two realms: the external and the internal. We all understand the external realm. It's the things we can experience with our senses. The things we can taste, touch, see, hear, and feel. Since our senses are constantly engaged and we innately pay attention to them, we tend to do all of our behavioral problem-solving at their level.

Behavior exists in the external realm. It is tangible, easy to identify, and even quantifiable. It is for this reason that we are often drawn to quick fixes. We make lofty New Year resolutions or jump on a new fad because we love the idea of being able to solve our behavior problems as efficiently as possible. Greatest results with the least amount of effort. That is human nature, and it is a beautiful thing. This kind of drive for efficient problem-solving has led to some of the most revolutionary innovations in our society today like cell phones and self-driving cars.

The problem is that we are not robots who simply behave. We are humans who feel, perceive, and believe. The complexities of our internal world often prevent us from pursuing and achieving the goals and outcomes in life that we so desperately desire, such as getting permanently free of pornography.

What takes place internally will **always** trump what takes place externally. Jesus said, "out of the abundance of the heart [a good man] speaks."[5] Proverbs 4:23 says, "Guard your heart above all else, for it determines the course of your life."[6] Scripture often pulls on this concept that the external is a manifestation of the internal.

It doesn't matter how well you can cover up your mistakes or live in denial. It doesn't matter how hard you try to mask your feelings or pretend you don't have those troubling thoughts. Eventually, your internal life will catch up with you. What happens internally **will** manifest externally, it is just a matter of time.

Humans hate that notion. We don't like the idea that what's going on internally matters, because it's messy. Complicated. And no one else sees it, so why bother with it in the first place? Then we wonder why every time we make a promise to God to never watch porn again because, "this time it's different," we somehow get discouraged along the way and quit. The issue is not behavioral.

I wish it worked differently, but I'm telling you right now that in your efforts to achieve success and fulfill your calling by getting free of pornography, if all you do is focus on macro and micro behaviors, you will only reach a fraction of your potential. People who emphasize the behavioral component alone focus on counting the number of days clean (Five days free of porn! Come on, baby, let's see if I can do six!), instead of paying more attention to the progress that's happening underneath the surface. The internal realm trumps the external. Every. Single. Time.

Beliefs 101

Let's piece a few things together here. We manage both our external and our internal realms. The fundamental unit of the external realm is behavior. The fundamental unit of the internal realm is belief. The external realm is visible, tangible, and driven by the senses. The internal realm is intangible and centers more around perceptions, emotions, and intuition. The most important work will always be internal because it houses your beliefs.

Beliefs are thoughts with faith attached. Let that one sink in for a minute. It could be any thought in the world, right or wrong, pure or tainted, original or shared. But if it has faith attached, it is a belief. You will have hundreds of thoughts today, but many of them will not stick. Why? Because you don't believe them. There's no faith. It's the thoughts that have faith attached in some form that stick around. This is extremely powerful because most personal issues in life boil down to problematic beliefs. When we really grasp the power that beliefs have in our lives, we are poised to make radical changes that bring major transformation.

Let's keep going with the fitness example. Johnny finds himself out of shape and starting to lose his overall physique. He has put on too much weight, lost his stamina, and is unsatisfied with his overall physical appearance. If Johnny starts to eat well and exercise, and in the process sheds a few pounds and gains his physique back, is he healthy? We don't know. Because true health cannot take place externally alone. It must be accompanied internally.

Turns out Johnny got out of shape in the first place because a girl broke his heart, and he drew the conclusion that he is not lovable. "If I was lovable, she wouldn't have left me," he decides.

It wasn't a big deal at first, was almost unnoticeable. But with time, as this belief started to fester and take root, Johnny's physical health declined. So if Johnny sheds the pounds but still believes he's unlovable, it is only a matter of time before that nasty belief manifests itself again. It might be that poor physical habits return, or Johnny may develop a new way to cope like binge watching Netflix, but mark my words—that belief will come back with a vengeance as long as it has root in his heart.

Is the belief right? Wrong? True? False? It doesn't matter. The point is that Johnny believes it, and that's what gives it place. Faith is extremely powerful, and it only exists in the internal realm. So you can keep running over the weeds of your life with New Year resolutions, lofty promises to God, trends and fads and behavior modification, but if you want to experience long-lasting, deep-seated wholeness, you will have to do deeper work on your belief system.

A set of beliefs (which are thoughts with faith attached) is called a **belief system**. A belief system is like the operating system of a computer—it tells the computer what to do and how to do it. It's the inner wiring of the machine. You have several belief systems in your life, and they all work either for you or against you. Not one of them is neutral.

Belief systems are the driving force of your perceptions, self-worth, relationships, decisions, actions, and lifestyle. Everyone has these belief systems, and most of them are formed without our knowledge or intention. You are the product of your belief systems.

If your computer's operating system is outdated (which is not unusual these days), you can have all of the upgraded, top-of-the-line hardware in the world, and it won't matter. Your operating system does not have the capacity to optimally use your world-class hardware.

You can get in shape. You can quit smoking. You can go weeks or months without looking at pornography or masturbating. You can do all the programs and courses out there to make your life right. But if you don't deal with the belief system that underpins it all, you won't enjoy it. Nothing will ever be quite enough to feel fulfilled and complete. And the fruit will only last for so long. We'll do a deep dive into this subject in Chapter 7.

We often mistakenly pray for God to change our external circumstances instead of praying we become people who are strong and healthy enough internally that we can handle the external circumstances that come our way.

If Johnny takes some time to tackle his belief system, everything changes. Once he works through the emotional pain, gains some perspective, and decides to forgive the girl and move on with his life, he is playing by a completely different set of rules. The operating system is ready for the hardware upgrade. As he digs into his exercise routine and starts eating better, his internal life is now stable and strong enough to support the external changes he makes.

The incredible thing is that when Johnny does work on the core aspects of his identity, such as believing he is a lovable human being, *every* facet of his life is positively impacted. It is no longer about physical health alone. Every part of his life gets better when he makes improvements to his internal life.

There are two reasons most people are unwilling to make changes to their beliefs. One: they simply do not want it enough. It's too hard. It's too much work. It's too messy. I am dumbfounded by the number of people who are not willing to put in a bit of short-term effort for long-term gain. Most settle for convenience and comfort, and continue to live cyclic, miserable lives.

The second reason is that people do not know how to make changes to their beliefs. They lack a system and do not have a competent guide to help them along the way. Unfortunately, these people wind up settling for convenience and comfort, and continue to live their cyclic, miserable lives as well.

Recently, I encountered two people who felt stuck for each of these reasons. The first gentleman was interested in DeepClean so he scheduled a free strategy session through my website. The conversation went well. Generally, by the time people are ready to get on a call with me, they have reached a place where they are prepared to open up and explore viable solutions. In this gentleman's case, he is getting married and wants to deal with things now before tying the knot. A wise move.

Once we got to the time commitment required for the program, his body tensed up, and sure enough, his response was, "Okay that's interesting." Oh no. Not interesting. Anytime someone says that you know they're lying. So I replied, "You seem a bit unsure about the commitment required for the program. Do you foresee that being an issue?"

"Well, it's just that I have a tendency to start things and then quit them as soon as I get discouraged." I love that awareness, but it's hardly an excuse to disregard an opportunity that will drastically improve his future marriage and overall life! I explained this to him, in more professional terms, but to no avail. This gentleman decided that the price he had to pay for getting free of porn was not worth it.

Contrast this with a current client of mine, we'll call him Phil. Part of the DeepClean offering is unlimited group coaching. We open up group coaching calls by asking how everyone did behaviorally in the past week. You might be surprised to hear that given everything you have read in this chapter, but if you read again you'll see that I'm not against behavior-oriented approaches. I just think they're incomplete on their own, and internal solutions must be in the mix as well.

When it was Phil's turn to share about his week, he explained to the group that he had moved house for the second time in as many months, and with all the stressors that came with moving he had had a bad week and messed up several times. About a month prior, when Phil moved the first time, he shared almost the exact same thing. "Yeah, moving was stressful so I had a few extra slips this week." It was almost word-for-word. Without realizing it, Phil was exposing the exact debacle most men find themselves in: solutionless, because they've used external reasons to explain internal issues.

When we gather in these groups, if someone has slipped in the week, they must answer two questions. First, what need was it meeting (internally)? Second, what will you do differently next time you have that need?

The first time Phil moved, he didn't know what the need was. He just knew he was stressed and left it there. By using the changes in his external conditions (moving house) to justify his poor behavior (watching porn and masturbating) the first time, Phil pre-authorized himself to perpetuate that poor behavior the next time he experienced a similar change in his external conditions. In this case, that happened to be a month later because the first place he moved into was a bit of a dud. His roommates seemed great at first, but they were unkind to him (I'd liken this place to a skullet—boring in the front and a mess in the back).

I couldn't let Phil get away with this mistake again, so I decided to push back. "That's what you said last time. What was going on internally?"

"Yeah nah, I think it's just that the move brought a lot of curveballs and things I wasn't prepared for. So I was really feeling buggered from all of the stress." (Phil is from New Zealand so sometimes he says cool things like "yea nah" and "buggered.")

"Yeah, I know, and I totally get that. But that's external. You're telling me about the environment. Moving is stressful, no doubt. What was going on inside?"

Blank stare.

"Can you come back to me?"

It is so easy to go about life explaining away your problems using external circumstances. And let's not kid ourselves—we live in crazy times where justifiable external circumstances are all around. But as long as you continue to justify poor habits, poor decisions, and poor behavior by external means, you will be disempowered to do anything about it. That's no way to live.

To stay empowered for effective change and lasting solutions, regardless of the circumstance, you must understand a few key universal principles that will help you master your internal life. Our friend Phil was about to learn these key principles in a very profound way.

Before moving onto Chapter 2, I highly recommend you complete the workbook material for this chapter at www.sathiyasam.com/recoveryworkbook . It will provide much needed intel for you to fully apply what you read in the remainder of the book.

CHAPTER 2

Freedom Fundamentals

I am an Enneagram Type 3. Of the Meyers–Briggs personality test, I'm an ENTJ. My Life Languages are Shaper-Influencer-Contemplator. My top five strengths of StrengthsFinder are Achiever, Competition, Futuristic, Belief, and Responsibility. I'm a D in the DiSC personality assessment.

Every couple of years there is a new personality test on the scene that people rave about. And it is always the "game-changer." The test that explains all your spousal conflicts and insecurities. The test that reveals why life is so hard and how to make it easy. The test that will cure cancer and end world hunger. Okay, not quite. But you get the idea. People are personality obsessed. We love learning about ourselves.

The danger of personality tests is that they can justify dysfunction. The number of people I've heard excuse themselves from morality and appropriate behavior because, "It's just not my personality," or "I don't feel like doing that," is getting annoyingly high. So hear me loud and clear when I say: principles trump personality.

Your personality will change. It evolves. It's unique to you as an individual. Principles are tried and tested truths that consistently prevail regardless of time or circumstance. In the 21st century, few live by them. These days it's much easier to be caught up in appearance, feeling happy, and doing what feels right, or, much worse, doing what everyone else is doing.

Jesus had several teachings about this, including the parable of the builders. One builds their house on sand. One builds their house on rock.[7] Both appear the same on the outside, until the storm comes, then the truth is revealed.

You may look around and think everyone has a perfect life. You may worry that they know something you don't know. You may lump people together because their lives look the same in some way or another—career, stage of life, geographic location, etc. And so you think you know someone because "all doctors are like that," or "they're just a typical person from the south." But you will not know what those people are really like until they go through a storm.

Living by principles makes you weird, by default. Most people jump on and off bandwagons, keep up with the Joneses, and pursue external rewards thinking it will provide them with internal fulfillment. We intrinsically know this is not the right way to do things, but why?

A lack of principles. To live without principles makes your life shaky and unstable. Moving from one thing to the next, not really knowing where things are leading. It means that one day you might feel a certain way on an important matter but then something else changes your mind and you swing the other way. Then you encounter another opinion and you swing back to where you started.

There is nothing wrong with being open-minded and adjusting your stances on the matters of life. However, some matters should not be malleable. They should be fixed. This is where principles come in. Principles are anchors that keep you grounded. They give you stability in tough times and foster considerable growth when times are good.

The principles outlined in this chapter have one purpose alone: to help you attain freedom. These are not issue-focused principles. In other words, they do not apply under certain circumstances, depending on whether or not you meet certain criteria. These are not even principles that only apply to getting free of pornography. These principles apply *always.* They are tried, tested, and true. And if you learn to master them, I guarantee you will experience long-term success.

It will be tempting to look at some of these principles and say, "Oh I know that already." I just want you to know this: that means absolutely nothing. Knowing a principle is futile. You must *live* by the principle. The extent to which you live out a principle is measured by how well you express it amidst trial. If you only live by a principle when it's convenient, then you do not know yet if you live by that principle. Let's see what happens when times are tough.

So as you read through, even if you have heard of these principles or you already know them, use this as an opportunity to evaluate how well you are living by them.

Also, we are not simply going through a bunch of principles that I think are useful for you. Instead, we are building a **principle stack**. The idea here is that each principle builds on the next and when each principle is in its rightful place it will have the greatest effect. You can pick and choose if you like, but you will minimize your success as a result. These principles work best when they are together and will build an unbreakable foundation in the process.

The order is equally important. You can try to shuffle things around, but it will start to get confusing and the principle stack will lose its synergy. These principles are most effective in the order they are presented. If you skip one or change the order you end up with a bunch of head knowledge and nothing to show for it.

One last thing before we dig in. There is a difference between a principle and a system. Many in the marketplace have developed systems that are predicated on principles, myself included. I'm not teaching you a system in this chapter. If I were then I would expect you to follow everything here to a tee.

For now, we are just looking at fundamental principles that take on a variety of expressions depending on the person. You may apply these principles differently than I have, but as long as the application is true to the principle, your expression is just as valid as mine. That means you can take these principles and develop your own systems. Your own methods. Your own expressions. This is where embracing your personality is beneficial. But you must stay true to the principles.

As you read through, envision how these principles could be applied to your own life and how they might help you solve some of the problems you're facing right now.

Principle #1: Control

A person without self-control is like a city with broken-down walls.
—Proverbs 25:28[8]

You are in control of your life. You have the power. If someone else controls you or has too much power in your life it's because you have given it to them. No ifs, ands, or buts. Both power and control are essential for human success. While that's all well and good in theory, the truth is that many relationships, whether at home, work, or elsewhere, experience control and power struggles.

When someone lacks control in an area where they should have it, that person is a victim. In a legal context, a victim is someone who is negatively affected by a criminal action—a crime, accident, or event that falls along those lines.

When you do not take control in an area of your life where you are supposed to have control, you are a victim by choice, not by force. Huge difference. If your mental health starts to decline because work is consistently stressful, and you do not reach out for professional help, you are a victim of work stress. By choice. You are choosing to not exercise control in this area, and you will deal with the effects of it, for better or for worse. The cause of the stress may not be your fault, but your lack of response is.

What Is Freedom?

Many men reach out to me for help because they have lost control of their lives, or to be more accurate, they have lost control of a specific area of their life that is meaningful. These men have lost control in their marriages, their self-worth, their spirituality, and their sexuality. Falling victim to an addiction is a debilitating experience.

The frustrating thing about being a victim of our own choices is that there is no one else to blame. When you're walking down the street and a crazy guy tries to run you over with his van, you can rightfully blame the crazy guy. But when you are a victim by choice, you are the person walking down the street AND the crazy guy driving the van.

Freedom is the power of choice. When you are a victim, because you have no choices, you have no freedom. The measure of someone's freedom in any area of life will always be measured by the number of perceived choices available to them and their ability to maintain their composure while choosing. In a porn recovery context, someone who is free from porn is able to make a powerful choice even in the face of a temptation or urge. That is true freedom.

In my programs, we do not count "streaks." That is a waste of time. We absolutely track people's progress, but not by simply measuring how many days someone has gone without porn or masturbation. The reason is simple: you can go months without looking at porn and still not be free. The external metrics tell a very small part of the story. The way we track progress is by examining the development taking place *internally*. If a man is learning to gain more choices in the face of temptation, and to reach a place where he can powerfully choose against it, then we know he is making progress.

Recently, one of my clients mentioned that he came home from a hard day's work, took a shower, and began pleasuring himself. As he started, he realized what he was doing and decided to stop. This is very hard to do, but it is the exact embodiment of progress in the recovery journey. It would have been easy to throw in the towel and start over tomorrow. Instead, he gave himself another option in the moment, and in doing so, increased his freedom.

Freedom is not acquired, it is developed. In this moment, you carry a measure of freedom. My guess is you are unsatisfied with that measure and are looking for more, but understand that freedom is not binary, it occurs across a spectrum. The mission now is to steward what you have until it reaches its full potential. This particular client of mine has moved himself further along the spectrum by stopping himself mid-shower. There is still work to be done, but progress has been made.

Out of frustration and despair, I will often hear guys saying, "Man, I wish porn would just go away. Why can't someone just remove it altogether?" This is the tell-tale sign of a victim mindset. Now don't get me wrong, I completely understand the sentiment. It is frustrating to be captive to anything, let alone something as destructive as pornography. And it would be nice if it just disappeared. Kind of.

The implication of a statement like this is: "My problem with porn is the porn industry's fault, not mine. Therefore, if the porn industry were removed, the problem would be solved." Seems reasonable, right? Wrong.

If someone masterfully destroyed the porn industry today, and tomorrow there were no porn sites on the Internet, a majority of porn addicts would still have a problem. Remember, most issues in life are **internal,** not external. An adjustment in the external environment, no matter how significant, does not remedy internal issues.

On the contrary, to experience control you must first accept that there is very little you can control in life. The goal is not to control everything and micromanage every detail in the happenings of our world. Rather, we must simply identify the few areas we can control and manage them to the best of our abilities.

So when someone comes to DeepClean for help, one of the first things we address is control. Another word we often use interchangeably in this context is "ownership." We start to get granular about where the ownership lies, and that can be really humbling.

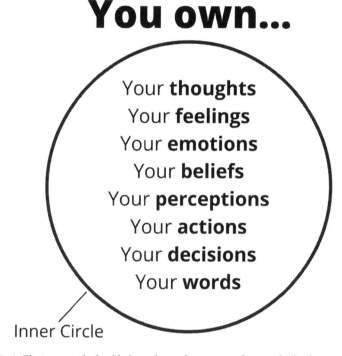

You own...

Your **thoughts**
Your **feelings**
Your **emotions**
Your **beliefs**
Your **perceptions**
Your **actions**
Your **decisions**
Your **words**

Inner Circle

Fig 1. The inner circle should always be a reference point for growth, development, and improvement to ensure you have correctly identified the areas to focus on.

In your life, you have ownership of A LOT. Your thoughts, feelings, emotions, state, responses, actions, decisions, habits, lifestyle, and overall well-being, to name a few. Everything that you own is in your inner circle.

This seems so trivial, right? Obviously you own these things. Who else would? But as you dig further into someone's psychology, it's amazing: you realize how quickly this principle is violated.

Let's take a marital example. A man and his wife set out to have a lovely evening together. It's date night. Their dinner reservation is at 6:30 p.m.

and it's about a 15-minute drive to get there. The plan is to leave the house at 6:15 p.m. sharp.

It's 6:10 and the husband is ready to go, feeling good about himself for being ready in record time. He basks in this good feeling for five minutes, but his pride quickly wanes as he notices his wife is nowhere to be seen. A movie he's seen one too many times.

After some exploration, he finds his wife in the bedroom, frantic, as she has decided to change her dress for the third time. She is talking out loud, trying to make a decision.

"Do I want to go for more of a metro vibe or should I just keep things simple?"

He looks away for a moment to consider how he wants to respond, opens his mouth to give his two cents (on the time, not the dress, obviously) only to look back and see a cloud of makeup. The wife has moved on to her next overdue task.

The clock reads 6:25 p.m., and the husband has made himself comfortable at the front door. Astonishingly, he has held his tongue so far (remember, this is just a story). He gently asks across the house, "Sweetheart, how much more time do you need?"

"Just two more minutes."

His left eye twitches aggressively, knowing that two minutes is not actually 120 seconds in her world. "Great, sounds good!" he pipes back.

Eventually, the wife is ready to go and they hop in the car only to find that their car will not start. Great. A few more turns of the ignition, nothing. In frustration, the husband slams the dash of the car. The wife replies, "Just try one more time. I have a feeling it's going to work."

Oh great, a feeling, the husband thinks to himself. Despite his skepticism, he follows the instruction and, voilà! The car starts. The wife smiles smugly and sits back in her seat, the husband feigns a smile back, and they're on their way.

They get to the restaurant and things start to settle down. The hostess held their table for them, the waiter is friendly, the restaurant is beautiful, and the menu looks fantastic. They place their orders, converse about the happenings of their days, and both breathe a sigh of relief as they can sense that things are better now that they've made it to the restaurant.

Dinner wraps up, the couple pays the bill, and just as they're about to walk out the door, the wife says, "Oh do you mind waiting for a sec? I just want to use the bathroom before we leave."

"No problem, I've been waiting for you all night, what's another two minutes?" replies the husband.

Uh-oh.

The wise wife does not dignify her husband's remark with a response and heads to the bathroom. She comes back a few minutes later, they get in the car, and immediately she asks, "So what was that comment about?"

"What comment?"

"What do you mean, 'What comment'?! You know what comment. You've been waiting on me all night?"

"Oh that. It's not a big deal. It's just, I mean, come on, you gotta admit… I waited on you for a long time before we left the house and we almost missed our reservation."

"Oh, I'm sorry, was I inconveniencing you by taking a little bit of extra time to look good for our date? You know, it takes time to get this all together."

"Well if you know it takes time then why didn't you start earlier?!"

"I would have loved to do that if I didn't have to work, clean the house, and do laundry all while trying to abide by the rules of your regime!"

"You make me feel like I'm some sort of terrible person for having the ability to be ready on time. That's a basic adult skill!"

(Oh no he didn't)

"Well, I'm sorry I'm not mature enough for you. You'll have to figure out what you want to do about that."

The fight starts to get circular and eventually both decide to lay down their weapons due to argument exhaustion. So much for a lovely night out. And the answer is maybe… (I'm assuming you just wondered if this example was based on a personal experience of mine.)

If you want to witness the lines of ownership blur in a hurry, watch a couple duke it out. It's fascinating how quickly the simple principle of ownership gets thrown out the window. Arguments tend to drift toward "right or wrong" paradigms. We feel justified if we are "right" in accordance with the rules, regulations, or expectations. The husband was ready on time, so he was in the "right." Shouldn't that settle it?

Not quite.

The only way we're justified in these sorts of matters is dependent on how well we manage our inner circle. In this case, the husband made a slew of errors. Did you catch him say, "*You make me feel* like I'm a terrible person"? Whose feeling is it? The wife's or the husband's? It's the husband's. Can someone else make him feel a certain way? Nope. It's his feeling, he has to own it. Even if someone else has influenced or evoked that feeling, it's still in his inner circle.

The husband implied that his wife was not an adult. He justified it because his wife was in the wrong. She was late. Even if someone has done something horrendous, you are still the owner of your words. Just because you have behaved correctly or appropriately does not give you the right to speak inappropriately about someone who has not. Own your words.

The reality is, in a situation like this, the wife is also responsible for her words as well as her decisions, actions, and thoughts. If the plan was to be ready at 6:15 p.m. and she was not, she is responsible for her actions and *she* has to take ownership. The husband cannot take ownership of her actions. The wife can be late for the rest of her life and she will have to own it. And the husband will have to live with it. I think there is a better middle ground, but we're just talking about this in the context of control and ownership. The lines have to be clear. At no point is the husband owner of anything in his wife's inner circle.

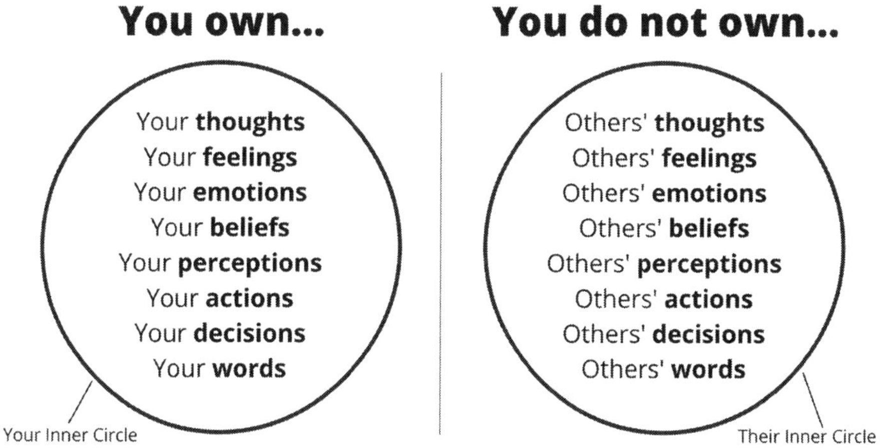

You own...   You do not own...

Your **thoughts**
Your **feelings**
Your **emotions**
Your **beliefs**
Your **perceptions**
Your **actions**
Your **decisions**
Your **words**

Others' **thoughts**
Others' **feelings**
Others' **emotions**
Others' **beliefs**
Others' **perceptions**
Others' **actions**
Others' **decisions**
Others' **words**

Your Inner Circle

Their Inner Circle

Fig 2. When others are involved, do not lose sight of this important concept. You must stay focused on the things you own and trust others to focus on the things they own.

Why does this matter? Because we often justify our own deficiencies and delinquencies using inner circles that do not belong to us. If you have relinquished control of your thoughts, emotions, beliefs, actions, decisions, etc., you will sit around waiting for someone else to spoon-feed you the desires of your heart. If you want to marry the girl of your dreams, start that business, raise a healthy family, get a promotion at work, get free of porn, you will have to start taking ownership.

While it is scary and humbling, it is essential for you to succeed in life. You must accept the things that you *can* control. You must identify the things that *you* own. And then you must relentlessly steward them. You can influence other people and circumstances, but you CANNOT control them. The only thing you can control is yourself. Your emotions, thoughts, beliefs, decisions, actions, and behaviors—those are yours to own and control.

This is the first layer in our principle stack.

Principle #2: Responsibility & Power

He who is slow to anger is better than the mighty,
And he who rules his spirit than he who takes a city.
—Proverbs 16:32[9]

Those who understand control understand responsibility. The word hardly needs a definition, but for the sake of clarity, responsibility is the ability to respond. If your boss hands you a project that you don't want to take on, you can push back. That is within your realm of control. You can explain to him why you're not the right fit for it or why it's not the right time because you're working on a hundred other projects he gave you. But you cannot control his decision. Your boss ultimately decides whether or not this project is yours and you live with it. You get to control your response. This is where responsibility kicks in.

Remember Phil? The guy whose struggle with porn got worse the week he moved to a new place? He reasoned, "I was stressed out from the move, that's why I slipped." Then a month later, he moved to a new place and had another terrible week. Let's pick it back up where we left off—Phil was struggling to find an internal explanation for his external issue.

After some poking and prodding, Phil confessed, "My roommates at the first place I moved into decided I wasn't Christian enough for them, so they started to treat me differently. I was kind of an outcast. In the second move, ultimately, I felt like a victim. Totally powerless. What was I supposed to do?"

What a useful discovery! Before this remark, Phil blamed the external circumstances. The stress of moving, the rush to meet deadlines, etc. All reasonable, but all external. And when poor behavior is justified by external elements, you will behave poorly every single time you encounter those elements.

Narrowing down the internal aspects of a problem is useful because they exist in a realm where you have control. Remember the graphic above.

There is plenty within your inner circle for you to control. Now that Phil has identified a few things in his inner circle, he is able to take responsibility. You're only as powerful as you are responsible.

My job in this conversation was to first help Phil identify the areas he could control and second, to help him identify the options available to him in those areas.

I replied with a question, "What can you control in that situation?"

"Well, I was angry that I couldn't control the situation. So I guess I can control my anger."

Boom. Guess who found his power? No one else owns Phil's anger. It's his. And as the rightful owner of his anger, Phil decided how he would like to respond. Anger is a funny one because the brain's response to anger runs pretty deep. We often think, "This is how I respond to anger. That's just the way it is." But there are other options if you look for them.

This is the key. Once you identify the areas that you control, you become responsible—able to respond. Phil acknowledged that anger was playing a role, which allowed him to decide how he wanted to handle it—he could explore his options. If Phil had not first identified the areas he could control, he might have taken responsibility for things he does not own. Things that are in someone else's inner circle. And that would create unnecessary stress, anxiety, pain, and frustration.

When it comes to personal responsibility, options are everything. I help men get free of pornography. What does it mean to be "free" of anything? Free of sin, drugs, debt, lust, etc.? One simple thing: choice.

The Power of Choice

Freedom is choice. When you lack options, you lack freedom. To gain freedom in any area of your life—mental, financial, relational, emotional, spiritual—you must increase the number of choices available to you. As an example, if your only source of financial provision is your job, then you do not have financial freedom. You have one option only, and there are dire consequences if you do not choose it. Someone with multiple streams of income has more options, and therefore more freedom.

One of the main goals in helping men get free of pornography is to increase the number of viable options they have in a moment of temptation. If Phil is frustrated by his living situation and the stress that comes with moving again, the angst is going to pile up and he will need an outlet. Porn is a viable option for Phil because this is the pattern he has developed. By identifying what's happening in his inner realm—the anger, the frustration, the powerlessness—Phil can access other options to handle the overwhelm. He is now able to respond (response-able). We'll talk about how Phil's responsibility caused major transformation in Chapter 9.

Of course, there are several more layers to porn addiction. This is a bit oversimplified, but hopefully, you get the point. Success and freedom in life begin with acknowledging areas where you feel bound, identifying the things you can control, identifying your choices, and then choosing the wisest response.

Long before I started helping men overcome pornography, I would often find myself having conversations about it with friends and coworkers without even trying. One time I remember a friend opened up to me about his struggles with lust and he said something that I hear quite frequently: "I can't help myself." We were talking about what to do when you see someone attractive walking down the street. His words were, "I can't help myself. I have to check her out."

When you only have one option, you have no freedom. The truth is that my friend could also *not* check her out. He could redirect his attention or use the moment to thank God for creating a beautiful person. Those are real options. But in his head, they are not attainable. As a result he lives bound by lust. No choice, no freedom. Note here that his reality and his perception were at odds, and sadly perception won the day. Sometimes we are bound because we have not identified other options that have existed all along. Other times, we need to create new options.

Explanation vs Excuse

I frequently remind my clients that there is a difference between an explanation and an excuse. We cannot afford to confuse the two. An explanation provides an understanding of why something has taken place. An excuse pardons behavior. The difference is important, especially in light of the conversation around responsibility.

Maybe you made a New Year resolution that you were only going to eat dessert once a week. First week of February, you're feeling a little bad about yourself knowing you're going to be single on Valentine's Day again this year, so you have dessert twice that week. Feelings of remorse and self-pity qualify as explanations for breaking your resolution. They do not excuse you from it.

That might sound harsh, but keep this in perspective. We always want to retain responsibility. If I excuse myself from my goals, ambitions, or standards because of how I feel or because someone mistreated me, or because I faced a curveball I was unprepared for, then how can I expect to reach my targets? Changes to our circumstances give us an understanding of why we fall short, or why we make a mistake. But we must learn from them and not let them reduce our standard.

Be kind to yourself. No one is going to do this perfectly and I am not suggesting that anything short of perfection is unacceptable. But in the conversation around responsibility, ensure that you are not excusing yourself from areas where you should be responsible.

The minute you let explanations become excuses, you surrender responsibility. Think about it. You quit on your New Year's resolution because you were feeling sorry for yourself. Seems reasonable. Then maybe you get back on the wagon and gather some momentum. Maybe someone mistreats you or says something that cuts deep and causes you to feel bad. If you've already been pardoned from your resolution previously when you faced a situation like this, why wouldn't you be pardoned again?

He who holds the responsibility holds the power. If you want to make improvements in your life, you cannot settle for excuses. There is a difference between an excuse and an explanation. Explanations provide intel, and they should enhance your sense of responsibility. Excuses will do the opposite.

The goal is to stay empowered. The more someone assumes responsibility for their life, the more empowered they are to take control and make better decisions. If someone is disempowered in a situation, it does not matter how good their intentions are and how much knowledge they possess. Without the power that comes from responsibility, they will remain helpless. Powerlessness leaves many stuck and it is a tragedy because the solution is within their reach. They must simply take responsibility.

Only when we have retained or reclaimed responsibility, can we begin to dream about the future.

Principle #3: Freedom Bookends

Start With Why

> *The plans of the diligent lead surely to plenty, but those*
> *of everyone who is hasty, surely to poverty.*
> —Proverbs 21:5[10]

I hate buzzwords. I really do. So I'm going to apologize upfront because some of this section will include buzzwords that I have chosen to use (see me taking responsibility?) simply because I could not find a better way to clearly communicate the concepts.

If you want long-term growth, freedom, and success in your life, if you want to leave a legacy for your family and if you want to do things in the way of the Kingdom, you will have to really dig in and ask yourself why? Why do you want to grow? Why do you want success? Why, why, why?

At the time of writing, I have been married for just under two years. Let me tell you something: I do not miss dating or being engaged *one bit*. Those were good years, but marriage is better. In fact, marriage is the best. Dating is fun too. Engagement—it depends. Before I got married, I attended 70+ weddings, so I witnessed a lot of different friends pass through engagement. As a result, I learned a thing or two before my time came. A fascinating thing happens to the average couple when they get engaged: they suddenly become fitness gurus.

"Gotta fit into the dress."

Women diet, work out, exercise, fast, and do anything else within their power to shed those pounds so they can look amazing on their wedding day.

Guys do the same thing. Protein shakes, workout routines, muscle shirts, the whole deal. Skinny Joe weighing in at a whopping 143 lbs spends $300 on a lifetime supply of protein powder and a gym pass. Round Robert does the same. They create a routine. Maybe even hire a trainer. They definitely do some YouTube research.

And all for one reason alone: to look good on the wedding day.

This is the power of **why**. When you have a captivating why it will move you to do great things. Things that you wouldn't otherwise do. Most of the people I know that have made a huge effort to get in shape for their wedding day generally did not care about their physical health that much before. And most of them do not care after.

Therein lies the problem.

If your why is temporal, it is not deep enough. If it only lasts for a season or even a couple of years, it needs work. Remember, truly successful people are in it for the long haul. When your "deep-seated" reason for doing something is the wedding day, then you have no reason to carry on after the wedding. We want a why that is going to stand the test of time. A why that is so deep-seated it could impact just about any area over several seasons and stages of life. We'll look at the meaning and significance of seasons in Chapter 9.

All my clients must go through an exercise early on that helps them clarify their why. It's one of the first steps of the DeepClean program. It's really quite amazing what people come up with when they dig in. Usually it starts superficial.

"Because I want to be free," is usually where they begin. Good start, but it's not a deep enough why. So we do some digging.

"Because I want to improve my relationships and strengthen my spiritual life." Now we're talking. This is heading in the right direction.

Eventually, we end up with something like this: "To be a man of integrity. To be joyful and to give joy." This is a real-life example from one of the first clients I took on. His statement still brings a tear to my eye. It is absolutely astounding how pure-hearted and sincere most men are when you really get to the bottom of their hearts.

You are no exception.

Don't lie to yourself—you have deep-seated motives that drive much of your behavior and decisions. Some help you, some hurt you. Now that you have identified the areas of your life you are meant to control and you are taking responsibility for them, it's time to figure out your why.

Here are the criteria for a solid, deep-seated why:

1. Is it personal?
2. Is it identity-oriented?
3. Is it compelling?
4. Can it be said in one sentence?
5. Could you stay true to it during a painful or difficult season?

I'd encourage you to take some time and work through this exercise. This is a personal mission statement. A summation of why you're on this planet and what ultimately drives the beliefs and decisions that you will make to achieve freedom. (The workbook will help you craft this statement if you need some guidance.)

Cast Vision

Where there is no vision, the people perish.
—Proverbs 29:18a[11]

As well as having a why statement, it is equally important that you have a **vision**—our second freedom bookend. When someone finishes my program and asks how they can continue their success, I usually refer them back to their vision. It's simple. As Proverbs implies, in a leadership context, if the king or ruler did not have a vision for where he was taking his people in his kingdom, the people would not just get angry or frustrated, they would perish. As in, their well-being would deteriorate. That's how important vision is.

The principle applies to your own personal vision as well. Many fear the creation of a vision because they worry that it will be unattainable or that things won't go perfectly according to plan. I can guarantee things will not go perfectly according to plan, but that should not stop you. A vision gives you a destination. How you get there might change over time, but it keeps you focused and heading in the right direction. Without it, you are aimless.

For the same reasons that your why statement should be long-term, a vision should be grandiose. If it's small, then it will breed complacency. I can honestly say that in my own life, things changed dramatically when I started to have vision. I almost felt embarrassed at first. Articulating your dreams feels vulnerable. But I look back on the last few years and realize that I've accomplished way more of my vision in a much shorter time. What felt grandiose and out of reach back then is now starting to look a little too small. I might have to do this exercise again myself.

Here's the deal: the more clearly you can articulate your vision, the better. No one wants to follow a map with blurry pictures. Quite literally, you should print or cut out pictures of the things you envision and create a collage, or vision board. I've helped guys get out of debt, I've helped guys get free of porn, I've helped guys learn how to have a deeper relationship with God, and every single time I always ensure they have a clear-cut vision, and ideally a vision board.

Once most guys have articulated their why, they don't need help dreaming big and envisioning. But almost every guy needs a little kick in the butt to actually write the vision down and create a vision board. So consider this a friendly but firm kick in the butt: Get on it. Go write your vision down. Take 30 minutes and print out a few pictures that capture your vision. And tell someone about it. Your future success depends on it.

Once you can clearly articulate why you're doing this and what you're building, we can move on to the next critical piece of our principle stack.

Principle #4: Delayed Gratification

Go to the ant, you sluggard! Consider her ways and be wise,
which, having no captain, overseer or ruler, provides her supplies in
the summer, and gathers her food in the harvest.
—Proverbs 6:6–8[12]

Mark my words. Nothing will have a bigger impact on your long-term success than your ability to delay gratification. Whether that's your spirituality, business, finances, career, relationships, or anything else that has long-term potential, in order to experience health in these areas you must first master this principle. This is hard to understand in a world where everything is at our fingertips.

I am not a particularly handy person. I'd love to insert an excuse here like, "I'm Indian, we're not handy people!" But the problem with playing the Indian card is that there are over a billion of us on the planet. There is bound to be at least a handful of people who excel in just about any area of life. So even if the majority of Indians isn't handy, there are still probably a couple of million that are. I digress—I'll play the Indian card later.

As I said, I'm not handy. But I was at my friend's new house last week and as we were getting the tour, he showed us his garage which has been converted into a workshop. There was a plank of wood with a bunch of nails in it, some of which were more flush with the wood than others. "Yeah, I'm teaching my son how to set a nail," he said.

I kid you not, that was the first time I had ever heard the phrase "set a nail." I was too embarrassed to ask so I went home that night and Googled it. And that kind of scenario is the beautiful benefit of the information age and our technology culture. We can become educated and informed on a subject in a matter of minutes. Just a few months ago I learned how to clean out the mini sump pump in my dryer by watching a seven-minute YouTube video. How's that for a handy Indian?

Sadly this quick access to content has a dark side. You might think that I'm referring to porn and all of the garbage out there that pollutes the Internet, but I'm not. When you need to find something, you Google it. Then Google spits back the response instantaneously. This was considered a miracle a few years ago, but today, it's the norm. In fact, if Google takes more than just a few short seconds to load, we are outraged.

While quick access to information has made us smarter and more re-sourceful, it has also conditioned us to expect what we want *immediately*. If you don't believe me, go order something from Amazon and tell me whether or not the arrival date factors into your purchase.

We want things, and we want them now. Technology advancement fosters this mentality. The problem is that when you're researching how to clean the sump pump of your dryer, demanding that information imme-diately is no big deal. Totally reasonable. But mentalities are transferable. That same mentality will not serve you well when you're learning how to handle your finances. Or how to handle your sexual urges. Or just about anything else.

A mentor of mine explained it this way. Let's say you and your child are passing by a toy store and they really want a toy, but you say no. They start to whine. You still say no. Then they cry. You still say no. Then they make a big scene in the street, embarrassing you in the process, and you give in and go into the store. The kid learns one thing: If I make enough of a fuss, eventually I can get what I want.

That may not be an issue when they're a child. But if that's how you parent the child as they grow up, then how do you think they'll handle their sex drive when they hit adolescence and no longer have a parent telling them what they can and can't do?

The truth is you cannot have everything you want. Nor should you. There are many things you want that will harm you or work against your goals and purposes in life. You must learn how to delay gratification. You must learn how to manage your own wants and desires. If you don't, your vision board is merely a wish and your why statement has no root.

Part of the equation here is a willingness to make short-term sacrifices to achieve long-term results. If I had told you this at the top of the chapter, before we talked about a why or a vision, you can see how this would be confusing. But now that you've clearly identified why you're here and what you're trying to build, you can begin to make appropriate short-term sacrifices—delaying gratification in the process—to achieve your long-term goal.

In one of my recent group coaching calls, this exact subject came up. Shane was confused about the whole issue of control and how it tied into his goals.

"I get that there are things I can and cannot control. But what happens when you lose control of a situation and you're stuck?"

"Give me an example," I replied (no one asks that question unless there was a recent experience).

"Well, a couple of days ago I was planning to work on the course after work. So I came home, ate dinner, and then opened up the course. But the Internet wasn't working. I take pride in my ability to solve technology-related problems, so I wasn't too bothered. I started to troubleshoot, but I couldn't fix it. An hour later, I was pissed. I couldn't control the situation, so I pulled out my phone and looked at porn."

"Alright, let's go back to the situation. What can you control?" I responded.

"Well…um…I guess, my thoughts. My emotions. And my actions." Shane had learned the first layer of our principle stack well.

"Okay, good. At what point did you lose control of the situation?"

"Once I realized that I wouldn't be able to fix the Internet."

"So now that we've identified what you *can* control, what would it look like to exercise that control if you encountered this situation again?" I had to ask this question because if you don't learn from your mistakes, you will repeat them. A mistake made once is a mistake, a mistake made twice is a choice.

"Oh, I know! Usually, I would go for a walk because being in nature helps me relieve stress. I wanted to go for a walk, but it's winter so I couldn't," Shane replied.

"Do you own a winter coat?"

"Yeah, but I mean it's really cold outside."

"Would you rather endure the sting of a cold winter walk or a slip?"

Shane's eyes widened to the size of dinner plates when I asked that!

"I never thought about it that way. Wow, I'm definitely going for a walk next time."

Shane's experience is not that different from what you and I experience every single day of our lives. We encounter unmet needs and problems. Unmet needs must be met. Problems must be solved. Usually, there is a minimum of two options. One will be more convenient, the other will require more sacrifice upfront with a greater reward later on. If we lack vision, and if we have not understood the value of delayed gratification, we will often choose convenience without considering its long-term consequences.

Nothing has demonstrated this concept better than the "marshmallow test," which was first conducted at Stanford in the 1960s.[13] The experiment began with the experimenter and a child entering a private room and sitting down at a table together.

The experimenter then placed a marshmallow on the table and made a deal with the child. He was going to leave the room. If the child did not eat the sweet treat while he was gone, then he would be rewarded with a second marshmallow. However, if the child decided to eat the first one before the experimenter came back, then he would not receive anything additional.

Essentially, there were two options. One was convenient and meant an immediate reward. The other required a short-term sacrifice for a greater reward later. In this case, about 15 minutes later.

As you can imagine, the footage of this experiment is rather entertaining. Some kids didn't waste any time eating the first marshmallow as soon as the experimenter left the room. Others devised a few interesting strategies to restrain themselves—bouncing, wiggling, and scooting to name a few. Some of these kids eventually gave in to temptation. Others managed to wait until the experimenter returned and of course, they received their well-deserved second marshmallow.

A neat experiment, for sure. But the real meat of it came several years later when researchers collected data on where these kids wound up later in life. The kids who delayed gratification in the experiment went on to have higher SAT scores, lower levels of substance abuse, better physical health, better stress management, stronger social skills as reported by their parents, and generally better scores in a range of other life measures. [14], [15]

Delayed gratification goes a long way. You may look back and realize that delayed gratification is not something you've exercised well enough up until this point. It's okay. This experiment simply illustrates a principle, it does not mean that people cannot change.

The best way to build delayed gratification is to start. Think of it like a muscle. If you haven't been good at this historically, it simply means you have not exercised this muscle enough. In other words, when the resistance became challenging, you faltered instead of pushing through. It is likely that before any given day is over, you will find yourself in a situation choosing between short-term and long-term. Exercise the muscle. Choose long-term, and with repetition it will get stronger.

I could have taken my discussion with Shane one step further and asked, "Is enduring a winter walk worth it for the most important item on your vision board?" The answer to that question is obviously yes, but sometimes in the heat of a moment, our brains do not connect that the seemingly short-term decision has long-term consequences. You can keep justifying slip after slip, but it adds up.

To have long-term freedom in any area of your life, sexuality included, you must be willing to make short-term sacrifices for long-term gains. And you must be willing to do this regularly. This is not a one-off. It must be habitual. When it is, breakthroughs start to happen.

Principle #5: Consistency Compounds

Wealth gained hastily will dwindle, but whoever gathers
little by little will increase it.
—Proverbs 13:11[16]

My wife and I decided early on in our marriage that we would live financially and materialistically simple lives for at least the first 10 years so that we could instill reasonable spending habits and begin investing in our future. That means even if we come into a lot of money or major pay raises, we will keep our lifestyle the same and put the extra money toward our future. With these two things under control, the rewards down the road will be significant.

There are many reasons for a decision like this, but the obvious principle at play here is compound interest. Albert Einstein is known for calling it the eighth wonder of the world and for good reason—to this day it still boggles my mind. Further to the previous section on delayed gratification, it takes little effort to sell someone on the power of compound interest yet, interestingly, few buy in.

Now just to make sure we're all on the same page, compound interest in a financial context refers to the interest that accumulates long enough that it begins to gather interest on itself. See the graph below.

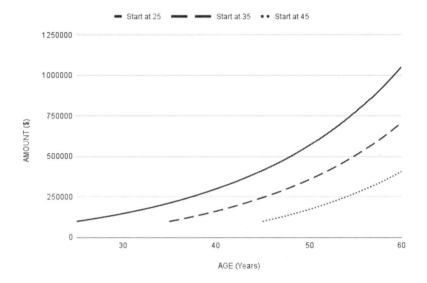

Fig 3. The compounding effect has a noticeable difference when viewed on a larger scale. The key is to start now and stay consistent.

A few things to note here. This graph represents three individuals who start with the same amount of savings and stop contributing at the age of 60. There are only two differences between each person: the amount they contribute and the length of time they contribute. The individual who starts at 35 contributes twice as much each year as the person who started at 25, but they accrue 33% less by 60.

The individual who starts at 45 contributes three times the amount of the person who started at 25. Despite contributing significantly more, they accrue 66% less than the individual who started at 25. This person represents the guy who says, "I'll do it later," thinking the consequences will be minimal when they are actually significant. The amount you contribute does not matter nearly as much as consistently contributing over a long period of time.

In my own research, something that has struck me is how little the numbers have to do with this graph in the long run. I know that sounds blasphemous, but hear me out. There is one thing in common in each line of the graph. One thing that guarantees the three individuals harness the power of compound interest, and it's nothing numerical.

It's not stability in the market. It's not a certain rate of return. There is one thing that each example in the graph above exemplifies: **Consistency**.[17]

The assumption in each of these lines is that the people they represent put away a fixed amount year after year. So is it the interest that compounds or the consistency? If the interest rates stay high for 30 years (an unlikely scenario) but you invest inconsistently, will you still reap the rewards of compound interest? On the flip side, if the interest rates are meager for a long period of time, but you invest consistently, will you capitalize on the compound effect?

The answer is no to the former and yes to the latter. Without consistency, there is no compounding. Period. This is not a book on financial advice, and nothing mentioned in this book should be considered as such. Talk to your professionals. But whether it's finance, fitness, relationships, spirituality, or getting free of porn, you must understand that consistency compounds.

The reason compounding is the final layer of the principle stack is because most men in this world do not have the framework in their own lives to harness its power. How can you consistently invest in something year over year if you cannot delay gratification? Why would you bother delaying gratification if you have no purpose or vision to work toward? If you don't assume responsibility for your life, and you don't take ownership of your finances/freedom/insert-your-desired-area-here, then this conversation doesn't happen.

When the other layers are in place first —when you identify what you can control, take ownership, specify a deep-seated why, make short-term sacrifices for long-term gain—and keep them in place consistently over long periods of time, you become virtually unstoppable.

I gave my life to God in my early 20s. That statement sounds funny to me, but it's the truth. I grew up in the church—my father was a pastor, I went to Christian schools, and lived a relatively Christian life. I wasn't perfect, but I can't say I ever ran away from God. Yet for most of my upbringing, Christianity was so baked into my life that I didn't know anything else. It wasn't until I went to university that I realized Christianity is really one of many viable options.

Studying biological sciences at a large university, you can imagine I encountered a lot of beliefs that opposed the doctrine I learned growing up. I often met people who didn't believe God exists. Sometimes they would even go so far as to mock people for having faith. This is where the rubber hit the road for me.

Remember, these were not random people on the street who had these opposing views. These were my professors and peers. Bright individuals with big brains to back up their theories. Their conclusions on the origins of life, meaning of life, and end result of life were vastly different than what I had learned in my local church and Christian school. Something had to give.

I did a lot of soul-searching, and an equal amount of research, and eventually reached a conclusion. No matter how much my peers reasoned against God, no matter how much evidence was stacked against my beliefs, no matter how "obvious" it was to so many people that God did not exist, in my heart of hearts, I knew He was real. It wasn't the discovery of some breakthrough evidence or anything like that. It was simply that when all was stripped away, I still had faith.

When I reached this point, committing my life to Him was the most obvious decision. This time, it was for real. Previously, my goal had been to become a psychiatrist. Shortly after I made this decision, my goals began to change dramatically. I could feel the pull into ministry—something that I had resisted for nearly my entire life! I used to tell myself I would never be like my dad in that way. Classic.

When I began to accept the calling into ministry, I started to notice that the men and women of God I really admired all had one thing in common: they spent time with God daily. Devotionals and prayer times were not optional endeavors. They were staples to their routine. I deeply admired this and decided that I would do the same in my own life. So at the age of 21, I began to spend an hour with God every day. In fact, the first year or two I was so hungry for God that some days I would spend five or six hours. I was desperate to know Him.

Then I went to ministry school, and I became hungrier. I spent two to three hours with God every day. Weekends included. And the neat thing about ministry school is that I wasn't the only one. I saw others getting up early or staying up late to spend time with God as well. It was incredible to be in an environment where my peers were regularly studying His word, praying, worshiping, and meditating by choice. But anyone can do this for a season. The question would always be what happened after ministry school.

I can't speak for my peers, but personally, I have not relinquished these precious times. I continue to spend one hour with God every day. People who heard my practice early on used to always say, "Oh, just wait until you get a bit older—it gets tougher to do those kinds of things." Or, "Just wait until you get married. You won't have time for that."

That has not been my experience. I'm more enthralled with God today than ever before, and I do not plan to stop any time soon. I look at people whose relationships with God soar when life is good and falter when times are tough. I see some people who are loud and proud about God in public and throw morality out the door in private. Not me.

It's not to say life hasn't had challenges and I haven't had doubts. As you'll find in the pages of this book, life has been a journey for me, to say the least. It's how I've responded to these challenges and doubts that matters. It's not my personality, as some would reason, it's my consistency. Slow and steady wins the race.

Here is the thing I want you to capture: it's only been 10 years. If we're talking about finances, then I would say, "Imagine what it will be like in 20, 30, 40 years when much more time has passed," and that will be true for my spiritual life too. But I'm living for eternity. If I can get the compound effect going during my time on Earth, I expect fantastic returns on my treasures in Heaven.[18]

Consistency compounds. No matter how you slice it, if you want to achieve long-lasting, multi-generational, eternal-imprinting freedom, you will have to learn to be consistent. It's not easy. In fact, it's always the hardest at the beginning. That's why most people cannot grasp the power of this principle. They get to layer three of the principle stack and then quit because they cannot delay gratification. But as you do it over and over again, this amazing compounding effect kicks in.

You might be wondering, "What if I'm more spontaneous and impulsive?"

Not a problem. My wife is definitely the spontaneous one in our relationship. But I have found that in most areas of life, there has to be a balance between structure and spontaneity, in that order.

My wife and I have consistently had date night every Wednesday since we started dating. She does not complain about having date night on Wednesday every week. That structure is useful. She does, however, occasionally make comments about doing the same thing every date night. Cue the spontaneity. Usually, I get the hint and mix things up. Other times, she will take the initiative herself and suggest some different out-of-the-box ideas, and we have the time of our lives. I married a gem.

Structure first. Remember that's what this principle stack is all about anyway. These are just the basics. The fundamental framework for success. You can build whatever you want on top of it. Be spontaneous. Leave room in your life for last-minute changes and impulsive adventures. But implement the principle stack first. These five core virtues *will* propel you toward your goals and, ultimately, your freedom. They are summarized in the graphic below.

The workbook material for this chapter will help you evaluate your strength in each of these principles and give you a chance to solidify your foundation as we get into the deeper aspects of porn addiction recovery.

Fig 4. The principle stack. Think of it as five pieces of Lego that must be assembled in a particular order for optimal structure and maximum effectiveness.

CHAPTER 3

Getting Emotionally Fit

It was January 31, 2018. Shaloma and I had recently celebrated our one-year dating anniversary. I had moved to Toronto about six months prior to start a new position at the church where we first met. The fact that she lived in Toronto was a nice bonus. We'd had a fun first year together. We traveled, went on romantic dates in the big city, and made music together. Of course, in the process we got to know each other and evaluated whether our relationship could work long-term.

One day prior, I found out that Shaloma's father believed we could in fact work out long-term. That's because when I asked him for his daughter's hand in marriage, he replied, "Yeah, mon" (he's Jamaican, so he really could not have replied any more fittingly). I went home that night ecstatic, and also terrified. The checks were all in place. All I had to do was propose.

It was an unassuming Wednesday. As you read in the previous chapter, Wednesday night is date night. When I say unassuming, what I mean is that we did this every week. Nothing out of the ordinary. Furthermore, Shaloma had a nagging cold that had lasted for weeks, so she was not feeling great. To her, this had all the makings of a very average date night, and she was none the wiser. Just the way I wanted it.

I finished up work, grabbed Shaloma, and we went back to my place. I made her favorite dish, fettuccine Alfredo, and we caught up on each other's weeks. After dinner I told her, "So I was hoping we could do something different tonight. I want to play a game."

Until you meet Shaloma, it's hard to fully articulate how child-like she can be. One of our mentors describes her as a "big kid" in the way she approaches life. Innocent, bubbly, and with a boisterous laugh. She's always the fun one in the room. So when the word "game" comes into a conversation, she's in. No questions asked. This night was no exception.

Shaloma and I were long-distance the first seven months of our relationship, so we would write each other letters. Yes, even in the 21st century, people can still write letters when they are in love.

In preparation for that Wednesday night, I had written five letters and scattered them throughout my place, each one leading to the next until the final letter led her to my bedroom door. On the other side, I had candles lit, rose petals on the floor, and music playing in the background that I wrote for her. I still remember the excitement and anxiety I felt as I heard her steps approach the door. She stood at the door for a few seconds—she was soaking in every moment. I was on one knee on the other side, sweating through three layers of shirts.

Finally, she opened the door. I had a little speech planned, but instead I burst into tears. So did she. We gained our composure a couple of minutes later and I managed to squeak out, "Will you marry me?" and she was able to muster an emphatic "Yes" through her sobbing. Other than the botched speech, it was pretty much perfect. Easily the pinnacle of our relationship up until that point. The moment every couple dreams of.

Little did we know our lives were about to dramatically change.

Shaloma had recently finished an internship at our church, moved to her aunt's apartment, and was ready to start looking for work. The internship had been taxing, so her plan was to take two weeks off to rest and catch up before beginning the job hunt. Those two weeks wound up being 18 months.

It was as if the life had been sucked out of her body. No energy. No will. Barely the strength to get up in the morning and make a bowl of cereal. Something was wrong.

Initially, Shaloma's illness had been partially masked by her enthusiasm for our recent engagement, but I knew things were bad when we went looking at wedding venues for the first time. We had three places lined up for the day, but after looking at two of them, I glanced over at the passenger seat to see my darling fiancée flush and weaker than ever. We sat in the car for 20 minutes before she mustered up the energy for the third and final viewing. It was then that I knew we had to get some help.

For the first 12 months, we played medical bingo. Medical bingo is where doctors are as clueless about the cause of your problem as you, so they start to guess. It starts off with the basics—blood work and that kind of thing. Then they start farming you out to specialists. The tests come back negative. So they send you to a different specialist or to someone else of the same specialty for a second opinion. My wife spent as much time that year in medical offices as she spent taking selfies, and that's saying something.

When we had exhausted all physiological options, there was only one option left. It was the option Shaloma had resisted all along, even though she knew it was viable. The first time Shaloma's doctor recommended visiting a mental health specialist, she was hysterical. The second time it came up, she was still resistant. But now, after a whole year of playing medical bingo and losing, it was time to explore the mental illness avenue.

Shaloma's resistance is not unlike many who have stigmas about mental illness, antidepressants, psychiatrists, and so on. However, in other ways her situation is quite unique. Her older brother, Shepha, was diagnosed with schizophrenia at the age of 15. Shaloma was 12 at the time. The diagnosis marked a change of season for her life and for her entire family. Things were never the same as they endured episode after episode, treatment after treatment, and prayer after prayer with seemingly no end in sight.

Growing up in that kind of environment can take a toll on the mind, and when Shaloma finally mustered up the courage to see a trauma therapist, this turned out to be the case. She was diagnosed with complex PTSD. While it was scary to reach out and get some help, this therapist was a godsend and Shaloma began to recover. Her energy started coming back, her personality started to show again, and we finally understood what was going on with her.

Let me just remind you that as a Christian couple, Shaloma and I believe that sex is designed for marriage. We had made mistakes in this area in prior relationships, but both of us were bound and determined to honor this moral. The first few months that you are engaged, you can't help but think about that glorious day when you tie the knot. And by tie the knot, I mean finally get to sleep together. This is natural. Normal. Healthy.

But of course, if you really want to honor a moral like saving sex for marriage, you have to be intentional. Morals do not protect themselves. So Shaloma and I worked very hard to defend it. We set clear guidelines for how late we would be out with each other, we had tight accountability with our pastors and mentors, and we erred on the side of caution when we reached grey areas.

Now all of this is nice in theory. But if you've been in any kind of romantic Christian relationship, you are probably wondering, "But what *actually* happened?" Because unfortunately most Christian couples set out to uphold boundaries and save sex for marriage, but one way or another, for one reason or another, they cave.

When we first got engaged, we realized that things were different between us and we had some clarifying conversations about how we were going to manage this new stage while honoring our morality. Then, not even two weeks in, Shaloma fell ill. She was vulnerable, and in great need. There are moments where you have to put your foot down or you will cave. And I'm proud to say we did not cave. But this was only two weeks in...

The original plan was to get married in the summer of 2018, which was anywhere from five to eight months after our engagement. Some friends advised us to get married more quickly so that we didn't "burn with lust." I'll unpack why that is some of the worst advice you could give later on, but my mantra was more along the lines of, "I've waited 28 years, what's another six months?"

A few months into Shaloma's illness, it became pretty clear that we were not going to get married that summer, and that meant a longer engagement. Great—just what my hormones needed. While it was annoying and not our original plan, it was manageable. And despite the setback and the continuing difficulty of Shaloma's illness, we held our ground and chose to make the most of our engagement instead.

What Is Emotional Fitness?

Everyone today talks about emotional intelligence and emotional health, and it's about time. This area is one of the most overlooked in our society and it has cost us our well-being as a result. However, personally, I am not sold on emotional health as the be-all-end-all of personal wellness. Emotional health is good, but there's more.

In most fundamental areas of life—such as the mental, physical, emotional, spiritual, financial, and vocational—you will have two options in your pursuit: health or fitness. You would be making a heinous error to meld these two concepts together. They are not the same. Health is the absence of illness or injury. Fitness is the ability to adapt or acclimate to changes in circumstances, expected or not.

For many, the journey stops too soon. People build emotional health and call it a day, which is tragic because emotional fitness is actually the end goal. When you are healthy, you go about your day-to-day life with peace and joy. It's a good life. Until something changes in the environment. Then your fitness level is revealed. Can you keep your cool or does your emotional health go out the window?

Most fail this test because they have good practices but no conditioning. If you want to get physically fit, you have to train with resistance. There is no such thing as getting fit comfortably. It's uncomfortable. Painful. But necessary if you want to achieve fitness. You have to condition yourself to persevere through the imposed restraint, which in most cases involves weight and/or time constraints.

When helicopter pilots are trained, they do thousands of simulations in dire conditions because they must train their senses and psychology to respond a certain way if things go south. You can't just trust your instinct in the moment—that will not be enough. You must be fit.

In the same way, you must pursue emotional fitness so that you're able to handle harsh environments or rapidly changing conditions with emotional peace and stability, including sudden urges or temptation. It is not instinct. This is not something you either have or don't have. Some people might have a greater bend toward it, but everyone must work hard to achieve emotional fitness.

When you are emotionally fit, everything in your life becomes easier. No, I'm not trying to sell you on some pie in the sky picture where everything is perfect and problems don't exist. What I mean is that you learn to navigate the waters of life with skill and relative calmness. You recover more quickly from difficulties. And you are positioned for sudden life changes at all times. A must for a life of freedom.

Self-Awareness

Emotions are intel. They are lights on a dashboard letting you know that something is going on under the hood—positive or negative—that needs attention. The emotionally fit still have lights pop up on their dashboard, the difference is they know how to swiftly respond to them.

Emotional fitness cannot happen without self-awareness. You have to be aware of what is going on within you. This is why we've covered the significance of the internal realm already. This is where the power is at. If you can master this realm, you master your life. And to do so, you must develop self-awareness.

It's important to understand that your mental faculties basically operate in three arenas. The conscious (things we are aware of), subconscious (things that are happening just underneath the surface), and nonconscious (things that we will never think about). Self-awareness deals with the conscious arena—termed the conscience.

In essence, self-awareness is recognizing the activities of your conscience. It means finding out how you feel about how you feel and how you think about what you think. Becoming aware of what you're experiencing and how you're experiencing it. This is especially pertinent in the subject of emotional fitness.

To pursue emotional fitness without self-awareness is like Christopher Columbus sailing the seas without a compass. You do not have enough intel to know if you are heading in the right direction. Self-awareness provides valuable information so that you can train and condition yourself to have healthy responses to even the most challenging circumstances.

A great way to build self-awareness is to start asking questions like, "How am I feeling? What am I thinking about? How am I perceiving this situation?" You start to gain an awareness of your tendencies, your perceptions, your attitudes, and so on. In gathering this information, you can make adjustments and improvements, and ultimately become an emotionally stronger person.

The greatest void in men's health is emotional self-awareness. So many men are clueless and we just say, "Oh yeah, you know, that's just a guy thing. Men don't pay attention to feelings. They're just like that." No, they're not. That is hardly an excuse. Men who are "like that" lack self-awareness. No one is born with it; it must be developed. If you do not have self-awareness, that's on you. Similarly, if you want to gain self-awareness, you can.

In my own recovery from pornography addiction, I had to become very aware of people, places, words, movies, and pictures that could be triggering. I also had to become aware of my vulnerabilities—to identify the moments and situations where my thoughts would drift. One of my discoveries in this journey was that when I was in any kind of emotional distress, two cravings would arise. Sugar and sex.

I have a sweet tooth through and through. It's normal for me to experience sugar cravings. In fact, the average person who meets me cannot pronounce my name initially so when I was growing up I had the nickname "Brown Sugar." It worked great. People found an identifier they could pronounce, and my identity became intrinsically linked with something sweet and sugary. Win-win.

That aside, when my sugar cravings intensified, I knew something was going on inside that needed to be addressed. It was a light on the dashboard signaling that something was wrong. With time I built the self-awareness to understand how to remedy the situation. Usually, this involved talking to someone, changing my physical environment (i.e. going for a walk, going to a different room), or journaling. More on journaling shortly.

I finally realized the full power of self-awareness about 10 months into my relationship with Shaloma. I had moved to a new city, started a new job, and was just getting settled into this new relationship. All the adjustments had me overwhelmed, and I knew it. At this point in my life, I had been free of pornography for about two and a half years. On this particular day, while I was at work, I kept thinking about watching porn. This was highly unusual for me so it was a big red light on my emotional dashboard telling me something was wrong.

Knowing that we were going to spend the evening together alone while trying to remain abstinent was like starving a kid for a week and throwing him in a candy shop with the instruction, "Don't eat the candy." We had kept our boundaries perfectly intact at this point, but I was concerned they weren't going to survive the evening.

As we drove to my place, I remember thinking this over. "What do I do? I'm not doing well. My urges are increasing. We're heading to an environment where both of us will be vulnerable. Oh! Of course—talk about it." Took me long enough to figure that out.

We pulled into the driveway and just as Shaloma was getting out I said, "Babe, wait. I need to talk to you about something." I told her everything and ended by saying that I was really concerned about us breaking our boundaries that night if we weren't careful. She understood and said she'd pick up the slack to make sure nothing happened. We had a great date night, and to be honest the simple act of opening up to her dissipated a lot of the pent-up sexual energy.

This experience taught me something about health, recovery, and fitness. I'd rather confess a temptation than confess a mistake. It's better to nip things in the bud before they blossom into something that you'll regret. You can't pull this off without self-awareness. It is man's secret weapon for emotional fitness and a requirement for long-term freedom from pornography.

Emotional Piggy Bank

When I was five years old, my dad took me to the bank to open up my first account. I was so excited. I still remember getting a little blue balance book, a sample check, and of course, a piggy bank. Believe it or not, you can learn a lot about your emotions from a piggy bank.

Truthfully, there are only two types of transactions for a bank account: withdrawals and deposits. Every transaction will boil down to one or the other. Every man has an emotional bank account, and every interaction with the world will boil down to the same categories: a withdrawal or a deposit.

You have a frustrating conversation with a coworker that leaves you agitated. That is an emotional withdrawal. You go home and spend time with your kids who are elated to see you. That is an emotional deposit. Pretty simple—draining experiences are withdrawals, enriching experiences are deposits. Notice the language. We're not talking about positive vs negative experiences. Someone could confront you at work, which could be considered a negative experience, or a withdrawal. However, if they do it in an honoring and healthy manner, then it is more likely an emotional deposit even though the interaction involves some friction. The important question is, how does it impact you? Does it drain or enrich?

A large part of emotional fitness is learning to balance your emotional bank account. When the sum of your withdrawals exceeds the sum of your deposits, you are in debt. This is not advisable. A lot of people mistakenly give too many people an access card to their accounts, leaving them depleted, burnt out, and in serious emotional debt.

You will have to exercise principles #1 (control/ownership) and #2 (responsibility) effectively to properly manage your emotional bank account. In your relationships especially, you will need to identify what is in your inner circle and what is not. The people who access your inner circle should only access it because you give them permission. When people start accessing your inner circle too much, or they start demanding more than what the relationship can handle, this is when breakdowns start to happen.

If you're the guy who's there for everyone no matter what, at every beck and call, I am sorry to say this but you have allowed others too much access to your emotional bank account. You will likely struggle with compassion fatigue and eventually burn out. We tend to justify seemingly good deeds with statements like, "They really need me. If I don't step in, who will?" or, "Oh that's just their personality. It took some getting used to but now I can handle it."

If the sum of your withdrawals in a given day, week, month, or year outweighs the sum of your deposits, you will struggle to get ahead in life, and you will certainly struggle to achieve emotional fitness. This is not permission to be a self-centered, narcissistic jerk who only seeks the betterment of himself. Your accounts should not be closed altogether. All I am suggesting is that you take ownership of your emotional bank account and responsibly choose who gains access and when. Once you can do this, there is a much better chance your emotional books stay balanced.

On the flip side, living with emotional surplus is a nice place to be. It means that even when you have a couple of bad days or a few taxing experiences, you still have currency to play with. We're talking about ideals here, so obviously there will be times where your balance goes negative. I get that. The reality is that as you open up to people and build relationships you will at times find them taxing. They will take a toll. This isn't about guarding yourself so that withdrawals are never made. That is unrealistic. The goal is to live with as much surplus as possible and to build self-awareness of your bank balance so that when these seasons come, you can recover quickly and not run at a deficit for very long. People who experience emotional debt and do not recover eventually become bitter and resentful. They burn bridges, and they shut down.

Now let's clarify something here. There is a difference between the volume of interactions and the sum of the interactions. In other words, the number of deposits does not need to match the number of withdrawals to balance the books. What we are looking for is the overall sum. When you add up the values of each deposit and compare it with the sum of the values of each withdrawal, are the books balanced?

One of the reasons people make poor choices is that they run on empty emotional bank accounts. If your needs don't get met, or you overextend yourself, you become desperate to balance the books. It's an innate function. Whether or not you balance the books in a healthy way is up to you.

Sadly, many men choose alcohol, drugs, pornography, women, video games, gambling, movies, and the like to take the edge off. To feel good again. To temporarily feel like everything is in order and that they are in control. Nothing could be further from the truth. This approach is like using a credit card to pay off pre-existing debt. You resolve the initial debt, but you've also created more debt in the process. Most of the clients I work with have learned this the hard way. A depleted emotional state leads them to engage with pornography to balance the books. Afterward, they feel a hundred times worse. Why? They used a withdrawal to pay off their withdrawals.

To keep the books balanced, you have to be aware of what qualifies as a deposit. This will include finding healthy outlets, making meaningful friendships, having mentors, identifying your emotional patterns, and finding useful ways to process emotions when they arise. This doesn't have to become super touchy-feely, but you do have to start building awareness.

Ask yourself, "What am I feeling? Why am I feeling this way? What will it look like to respond in a healthy way to what I am experiencing?" A little bit of self-inquiry can go a long way.

Validation Cycle

Invalidation

The fundamental unit of the emotional realm is feeling. Contrary to popular belief, men also have feelings. The world has taught us that men should not have feelings or that if they do, to keep them under wraps. As a result, there are a lot of soft-hearted men out there with hard shells that rarely get their needs met because they are so closed off.

The most masculine men have a healthy emotional life. They have built self-awareness, their emotional bank accounts operate at a surplus, and they have mastered the **validation cycle**. The best way to understand the validation cycle is to first look at the invalidation cycle.

Imagine this: There's a man named Peter, and one day he has a feeling (you may have to really use your imagination on this one). Let's say the feeling is inadequacy. Peter feels inadequate about his relationships, his future, his job, and his dreams. Everything points back to Peter being inadequate. This is not a new feeling for Peter. In fact, he has felt inadequate for most of his life, but now it's catching up to him. So much so that his sense of inadequacy is accompanied by sadness and hopelessness.

Peter feels inadequate, sad, and hopeless.

Male tendencies at this point in the emotional experience are: stuff it down, make a joke of it, use a cliché, downplay it, and avoid talking about it.

Let's say Peter has a close friend named Danny.

Danny asks Peter, "How are you doing?"

"Oh you know, I'm good, man. Work is good, life is steady. It's been a bit tougher lately, but God is good, man. I'm good." (Did you catch the cliché?)

"That's awesome, man! But…how are you really doing?" replies perceptive Danny.

"Well, I'm good, like I said. I mean things are a bit tough right now, but you know what's been really tough? Recovering from the pandemic. I can't believe how many people are still struggling." (Avoidance.)

"Yeah the pandemic has really made its mark, but I'm asking about you, man! What is going on? You don't seem to be fully okay," Danny persists.

"Well, okay. You got me. There's a lot going on. I'm miserable, man. I feel so inadequate at work. All my colleagues are getting promotions and moving on, and I'm just stuck in the same old job doing the same old thing. My relationships are all fine, but I want more meaningful connections and obviously I want to meet someone and get married one day. But I just can't muster up the courage to ask girls out. And when I do, it just fails anyway. My nephew in the eighth grade has more game."

"Oh but it's just little old me and my issues. I've struggled with these most of my life anyway, so I don't want to make a big deal now. Sorry, man, didn't mean to burden you." (Downplaying.)

If we are being honest with ourselves, we have all handled our emotions like this at some point in our lives. Emotions are uncomfortable, unpredictable, and unbelievably personal. This conversation between Peter and Danny represents the first and most dangerous part of the invalidation cycle: **Neglect**.

When you neglect your emotions altogether, you become a ticking time bomb. The bomb will either cause an explosion (outbursts, anxiety, obesity, breakdown, burnout, etc.) or an implosion (depression, self-sabotage, addiction, etc.).[19], [20], [21] There is a reason Netflix generates $20 billion+ annually.[22] Men trying to numb their pain is not the only contributor to their massive revenue, but you get my point. It's very easy to tune out and numb out, but it comes with a cost.

When you've merely neglected emotions from time to time, they can still be accessed without much effort. But if neglect persists long enough, eventually you reach **suppression** and after enough time has passed and things remain suppressed, they become much harder to access. To compare neglect and suppression, think of it this way. When you neglect your feelings it's like that one prickly weed growing in your yard that you try to ignore. To tackle that issue, you really just need to uproot the weed, as we discussed in Chapter 1. When you have suppressed your feelings, the weed has begun to multiply. The issue is now buried underground and a root system has developed. The issue has become systemic.

If this persists long enough, you reach **decay**. This is where the suppressed emotion now erodes your quality of life, relationships, sense of self, and so on. For most men who reach this stage, they do not understand why. They draw conclusions that, "This is just how life goes," or, "I guess growing up just gets harder and harder." Not true.

The worst part about the invalidation cycle is that it is cyclical! In other words, as emotions become neglected, then suppressed, and eventually cause decay, it numbs the heart and propagates this neglectful approach. It all starts out innocently by downplaying and making light of a few things, but if enough time passes and you have no solution or system for working through your emotions, things will worsen.

Most of my clients are invalidation experts. Sometimes they will push back on the value of emotions or the role they play in recovering from something like pornography. I will ask them how they've handled their emotions so far in life. Usually, I get a blank stare or an explanation that is a derivative of the invalidation cycle. At the end, I will ask them another question.

"How's that working out for you?"

They're usually more eager to listen to me after I ask that.

So if you have any opposition to what you've heard so far, or you're not convinced that this invalidation cycle is really a problem, or if you acknowledge that the invalidation cycle is an issue in your life and want to do something about it, let me ask you this:

"How's that working out for you?"

Are you happy with where you are in life? Are your relationships thriving? Do you have control in the main areas that matter—mental, emotional, spiritual, financial, social, relational, familial? Do you have an idea of how you're going to get free of pornography?

If your life is perfect and you don't have any room for improvements, I'd encourage you to write a book. For the rest of us, let's carry on.

Labeling

There is good news. The invalidation cycle is only one option. As you'll recall from our principle stack, to stay in control we must assess the options and then make a choice. Therefore, if invalidation is an option, then so too is validation, and that is great news.

Emotions cannot just be felt. They must first be labeled. You cannot simply say, "I don't feel good," and call it a day. What do you call what you're feeling? You must give it a label. Below is a tool that our community of men affectionately call the "Feel Wheel." Make use of it if you need some assistance. Most men do.

The key to the Feel Wheel is to start in the middle. This is usually the extent of our emotional capacity. We can identify that we feel happy/angry/sad/disgusted/fearful/surprised. Remember that emotions are intel. The more detailed our intel, the better our response. When you can branch into the second and third rings of the feel wheel, your intel becomes a lot sharper. You gain more clarity on what is going on inside. As a result, you can take more useful steps in response.

If your emotional dexterity can only go as far as the inner ring, it will be hard to develop emotional fitness. That kind of intel is not conducive to emotional agility. You have to be specific and clear. When you do this, your emotional fitness will skyrocket because you will be able to make wise decisions in response to the clearly labeled emotions. This is a big deal.

The feel wheel displayed below is a simplified version to get you started. Your workbook material has a more enhanced version that both myself and my clients use.

Fig 5. This is a very useful tool for labeling emotions. I highly recommend keeping a printed copy in your journal. Graphic created by Glenn Trigg; https://www.glenntrigg.net/emotions-wheel/

Digestion

Labeling an emotion is not enough. You can't just say, "I feel remorseful," and wash your hands clean of the situation. There is more work to be done. Once you have labeled your emotions, they must be digested. I am occasionally challenged on the use of this word in an emotional context, but I am yet to find a term that better articulates this part of the process. In fitness terms, digestion is anabolic first. In other words, it's about breaking things down. Extracting the useful parts and discarding the waste. Digesting your emotions is not that different.

Any experience of emotions is convoluted with perceptions, mood, assumptions, thoughts, and beliefs. Taking the time to break down labeled emotions allows you to clarify what is really going on. The process of digesting your emotions takes further time. After a heated argument with someone, you may label the emotions within seconds or minutes but find it takes way longer to process and digest the emotions. This is normal.

There is no trick to digesting emotions well. The best way to spur on the digestion process is to continue the activities that helped you label your emotions in the first place. Things like using the Feel Wheel, journaling, talking to friends. Everyone has their own order and system, and some of these will be more desirable than others. Whatever helps you properly work through the emotion in a healthy manner is fair game.

Understanding

An amazing thing happens after enough time has passed: you start to gain clarity. Imagine you get into an argument with someone. You go back and forth, things go a little too far, and you both say things to each other that you know you'll regret. I'm sure you have no personal experiences to go off so really try to get creative with your imagination here.

Let's say that immediately after the argument you call up your friend and talk to them about what happened. What will be the focus of the conversation? Two things. One: all the things the other person did wrong. Two: all the things that you did right. And maybe three: how upset/annoyed/angry you are. Now, granted, you may have a bit more perspective even at that moment, but this is the basis of most initial responses after a heated exchange.

As some time passes and you start to gain more clarity, you might be able to see the other person's side of the story. Initially, this is hard to do in a comprehensive way. Perhaps you understand bits and pieces, but it will be fragmented. However, eventually, you can start to see what was really going on for them. You also start to better understand your side because you've gone to the Feel Wheel, you've done some journaling, and you've been able to digest a little.

Maybe during this process you can identify a few things that you need to take ownership of (Principle #1). And you realize that you did not respond well to some of the things that were said in the conversation (Principle #2).

This is going to dramatically change how you talk about what happened. It might even move you to apologize and ask for forgiveness. Equally, it might help you gain some clarity on what specifically caused you hurt and pain, which can be conveyed the next time you talk. This is what understanding looks like.

Taking time and processing emotions goes a long way. When you have done the work, you will notice the sting has dissipated. Contrast this with the invalidation cycle—if too much time passes and emotion is not validated, it decays. It starts to fester and cause a lot more damage to your well-being and to the relationship if another person is involved.

If enough time passes and you find ways to validate the emotions and work through them, you move through the issues of life with great strength and maturity, learning and growing from each situation that arises.

The important thing here is that you do not jump from having emotions to reaching an understanding. That is a male tendency, but it neglects the vital in-between stages that foster self-awareness and emotional maturity. Namely, validating your emotions, leaning into them, and fleshing them out as necessary. You will know that you've reached that place of understanding when your heart is at rest and your mind is at ease. If you do not have both of those things, you skipped one of the steps or you did not complete one of the steps fully. The differences between the invalidation and validation cycle are outlined below.

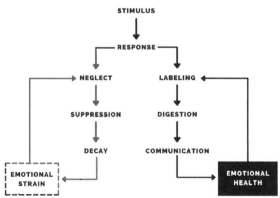

Fig 6. Your response to emotions is the difference between continual emotional health and chronic emotional strain.

Going to the Gym

After a few months of professional counseling, Shaloma asked her trauma therapist if she could handle getting married. The therapist did not even think twice and said yes—the path to recovery was clear and it was only a matter of time before Shaloma would be back to normal. Shaloma and I were thrilled, and we set our sights on a date.

By now it was spring 2019. We had been in an open-ended engagement for 14 months, but things were different. There was stability and a sense of security for the future. We were not hoping or praying things would turn around—we knew what it was going to take for Shaloma to recover. We were looking at the fall of 2019 for our long-anticipated wedding but wanted to run it by our families to make sure it suited their schedules as well before finalizing the date. We were experts at these details by now as this was our third time picking a date.

Then one day, as I was out getting my hair cut, the phone rang. It was Shaloma. "Babe, something is wrong with my brother. They're saying he's not responding and may not have much time left."

Shepha had been hospitalized about a week earlier because he was having some problems with his GI tract. We knew it was serious, but nothing indicated it was life-threatening. We rushed to the hospital to see Shepha for the last time.

That night, on April 26, 2019, Shepha David Judah Webb breathed his last. Shaloma was shattered and I could not comprehend how yet another tragedy had taken place in our lives so suddenly.

The night Shepha passed, Shaloma and I went back to my place at about 2 a.m. Fortunately, my basement apartment was owned by good friends of ours who lived in the upper unit. Understandably, Shaloma did not want to go back to her place that night so we called our landlords to ask if I could sleep in their guest room so Shaloma could have my apartment for the night, and they graciously said yes. When we arrived, they were at the door to greet, hug, and console us.

If there was ever a time to excuse a boundary, this would be it. We would sleep in the same bed, but nothing would happen, not on a night like this. Or I could just sleep in the living room while she slept in the bedroom. Both viable, reasonable options at a time when emotions are high and tragedy has struck. Unless you're emotionally fit. We kept our cool—Shaloma slept in my apartment, I slept in our friend's guest room, and we moved on.

At this point, we wondered if once again we would have to postpone the wedding. We were in a bit of a bind because we still wanted to get married, but we didn't want to add more stress to an already challenging year. I felt it especially for her parents—who wants to bury a child and marry another in the same year?

However, after much prayer and deliberation, we both felt good about getting married by the end of the year. Shaloma's parents were incredibly gracious and more supportive than we could have imagined. It wasn't the conditions any of us wanted, but the wheels were in motion. On September 8, 2019, Shaloma and I tied the knot in front of our family and friends, *finally* completing a 19-month engagement. Rather than party favors, we made a donation to the Center for Addiction and Mental Health in honor of Shepha. It was a day of mixed emotions, but finally we were married.

In the 586 days we were engaged, Shaloma and I did not cross our boundaries. Not once. We came close a few times. Some days were very challenging, but on my weak days Shaloma picked up the slack and on her weak days I held my ground. Moral fiber alone is not enough to pull something like that off. Will power and good intentions won't do the trick either. You must be emotionally fit. You have to cultivate self-awareness, learn to validate your emotions, and then allow the circumstances of life to condition your response.

This is why advising engaged Christian couples to get married pronto so they do not burn with lust is horrible advice. Engagement is the best opportunity a couple gets to lay a foundation for respecting boundaries, learning to control their inner life, and making short-term decisions that have a long-term impact. These are not opportunities you want to neglect. Ever.

If your partner doesn't respect your boundaries when you're engaged, why would they do so when you're married? If you cannot manage your lust when you're engaged and your solution is to run into a covenant, then why would you be able to manage your lust in your marriage? What will you run to when you and your spouse fight? The seasons of life provide us with opportunities to grow that we must harness, otherwise we will not have any emotional fitness.

This same kind of mentality is critical in the porn addiction recovery journey. If you are emotionally healthy, it means that you will regularly be able to manage your thought life (more on this in Chapter 7), process your emotions, and preserve good habits that prevent you from engaging with pornography. All very good things. Emotional fitness means that if you encounter a shock to the system—you run into your ex randomly, you are suddenly tempted, you encounter a change in your environment, your routine is disrupted, or you experience tragedy—you are able to hold your ground and not give in to the lure of pornography or anything else that would work against you.

At this point, most guys wonder how to achieve emotional fitness in the shortest amount of time. I've tried many things over the years, especially when I was first trying to build my emotional strength. I've alluded to things like going for a walk, talking to a friend, creative arts (music, painting, drawing, dance, etc.), all of which are effective. However, I have identified one method in particular that consistently helps the most.

This is not a quick fix, but it is by far the most effective method I've discovered. If you build the practice regularly, you will start to notice dramatic results.

Journaling

Most men hear "journaling" and either love the idea or hate it. Very few are in the middle. As I'm writing this, I'm looking over client notes from two different men in two different sessions last week whose feedback on journaling was almost identical:

"When you first taught me journaling, I pretty much despised the idea. I don't like writing. I'm not a write-it-down kind of guy. I didn't even tell you but I wasn't journaling very much early on even when you told us to. But now I don't know what I would do without it. It's so helpful and I'm so glad you pushed me to do it."

Two different clients said almost the same thing word for word. I think one of the reasons journaling has become so pivotal in my clients' lives is because of the way we teach it. Journaling should not just be rambling. There has to be a degree of structure to truly harness its power. Journaling should have an objective, otherwise, it will fall by the wayside. In this case, our objective is emotional fitness.

When I was working hard to get free of pornography, I journaled a lot. Daily. Sometimes twice a day. I needed it to cultivate self-awareness and work through my emotions. I don't journal as often anymore, maybe just a few times a week. It's still very useful to me, but I'm not dependent on it.

You might say, "I'm a verbal processor, writing just doesn't work for me." I understand the notion, but it's not true. Even if you are a verbal processor, writing can have tremendous benefits. If you follow my methodology, I can guarantee you journaling will add value to your life. It will sharpen your inner man and help you become emotionally fit.

The methodology is not elaborate. In fact, it comprises just two steps and it can be done in as little as five minutes. Or if you have the time, you can spend a good hour doing it. One of my clients journaled 10 pages straight the first time he followed this method. It opened the floodgates. Regardless of your time constraints, you must do both steps and you must do them in the order they are presented.

Step 1: Expression

This is the part of journaling where you get everything out. All the things you are thinking, feeling, perceiving, and believing. We all have things swirling inside of us. Most of it does not need to be vocalized or spoken out loud, but somehow it needs to come out. This step gives you a place to do that.

It means that if you're having an ordinary day, this is the place where you can acknowledge that. You can write about your favorite sports team or the video game you've been thinking about. Sometimes it will be ordinary and seemingly mundane. For more intense times, when you've been dealing with stressors in life or you've had major events take place, Step 1 is the place where you get to process. Write out what you're thinking and write out what you're feeling.

As you express, you want to filter everything through two questions:

1. What am I thinking?
2. How am I feeling?

Guys don't usually need much help answering question #1. Remember that this step is unpolished. You don't have to have a clear thesis and a comprehensive explanation. This is a free-for-all. Whatever you're thinking goes. Write it down.

Question #2 is a bit trickier, hence why an entire chapter of this book is devoted to the subject of emotional fitness. However, you have been given a tool that will help you answer question #2 well: our beloved Feel Wheel.

Use the Feel Wheel to label the emotions you write down. Again, it doesn't have to be pretty, and it doesn't have to be extensive. This is the only area where you want to be as precise and accurate as possible. You should be able to read back this portion of your journal entry and identify the emotions clearly. The language should be obvious because you've used terms from the Feel Wheel.

This part of journaling is easy for some right off the bat (like my client who wrote 10 pages the first time he tried). For others, it's more of an atrophied muscle that needs rehab. In other words, it takes time and consistent practice before you start to experience its benefits. If you try Step 1 and it's hard at first or you can barely write a couple of sentences, that's still great! It's totally fine. As you keep doing it, it will get easier, and you will write more.

Lastly, remember that your journal is private. The goal is not to write something that you can share with the world or even share with loved ones. Sometimes that will happen, but it is not the goal. The main objective is for you to have a safe place to express yourself, free of judgment or ridicule, to cultivate self-awareness. This aspect alone makes journaling a very liberating experience.

Step 2: Reflection

If your journaling experience stops at Step 1, you will never be emotionally fit. You will be emotionally aware, maybe even emotionally healthy to a degree, but never fit. Remember from the validation cycle that after emotions are labeled, they must be digested until an understanding has been reached.

This is where reflection comes in.

In our overstimulated society, we have lost the art of reflection—taking time to listen and ponder. We are usually jumping from one thing to the next. Our written communication is limited to reading a message and then replying instantly. Often, we don't even really think about it, we just reply and move on.

If you aren't careful, today's technology-crazed world will make you an awful listener. You will move from one stimulating thing to the next, without any space to breathe, think, or in this case, reflect. This is why Step 2 of the journaling process is so critical.

After you have taken the time to express yourself and get everything out, put the pen down and reflect. Listen. Learn. Usually, at this point I'll roll my shoulders back, take a deep breath, and leave space.

Two things happen when you do this. First, you begin to connect dots and gain perspective. You start to see things you didn't see before, or you see them but in a different light. There are some things you will not be able to see or perceive until you give yourself space to rest.

The second thing that happens is what sets this method of journaling apart from the rest. In this space of reflection, God speaks. That still, small voice begins to comment on what you shared.

The idea of God seeing our writings from Step 1 is scary to some. If we are going to be brutally honest, then we definitely don't want God to see it! Let me challenge you with two scriptural references. Read the Psalms and you will see that David expresses himself without inhibition all the time. Consider this excerpt from Psalm 6:6-7:

> *I am weary with my groaning;*
>
> *All night I make my bed swim;*
>
> *I drench my couch with my tears.*
>
> *My eye wastes away because of grief;*
>
> *It grows old because of all my enemies.*[23]

He is raw, honest, and unapologetic. He also won such a place in God's heart that the Messiah was called the "Son of David."[24] If brutal honesty helped David connect with God, then it should be no different for us.

Secondly, in Matthew 6, Jesus teaches His disciples to pray. This passage is famous for introducing the Lord's Prayer. Right before Jesus teaches the prayer, He says something rather intriguing:

"For your Father knows the things you have need of before you ask Him. In this manner, therefore, pray…"[25] and He goes on to teach the Lord's Prayer. If God already knows, why pray it? It must be that God is just as interested in the interaction as the intercession. He relishes the times we take to come before Him with the needs, concerns, and aches of our hearts. He is not offended by them. He is endeared and engaged.

In this place where you put the pen down, relax, and reflect, God speaks. It happened to David all the time in the Psalms, and it's happening today to men around the world that have implemented this journaling methodology. What kinds of things does God offer in these rewarding times of reflection? Wisdom, insight, perspective, encouragement, correction, direction, clarification, creativity, ideas, and solutions are just a few.

The most important thing is that you are still. Give yourself the space to hear. I can assure you that when you begin to really dig into this, you will be amazed at what comes up. One of my clients was extremely skeptical of this process before but desperate to experience freedom in his life. To his shock, as he reflected on his writings, things were spoken that were "too smart for him." In other words, he knew that his own brain was not coming up with it. The insights and the profundity of those insights were so sharp, he knew it must have been God.

Most importantly, as these reflections start to come in, pick your pen back up and write it down. These things must be documented because you will not remember everything. Writing it down will also reinforce what is "spoken" in these moments. Hearing it is one thing—hearing it and writing it down is another. Give yourself the space to reflect until the dots start connecting. When that kicks in, write it down.

The more you journal, the more the gap between putting your pen down and picking it back up will narrow. I rarely even put my pen down now. Usually, I express and then I immediately have reflections. Sometimes I even get them before I have finished expressing myself fully. It doesn't take long to reach this place but start by first taking the break in between. It's good for your brain and it will ensure you get clear insights.

Step 1, expression, will help you digest your emotions. Step 2, reflection, will help you reach a place of understanding quickly, and the more quickly you can reach that place of understanding, the greater your emotional fitness will become. For extra guidance, refer to the workbook, which will help you go through this process. If you'd rather try it on your own, here are some tips to help.

Journaling Tips

- **Pray.** A simple prayer of invitation to kick things off can go a long way.

- **Be thankful.** Nothing sets the tone of journaling better than a little thankfulness. Start by writing down at least three things that you're thankful for before you go into expression.

- **Avoid slander.** Do not, under any circumstance, slander someone else's character. When you express, you are welcome to clearly articulate your emotions, and what you write can be emotionally charged, but a line is drawn at someone else's character. Don't let your emotion cause you to speak something that tarnishes the character or personhood of another individual.

- **Find a relaxed environment.** Journal in places that are quiet and distraction-free. Remember that you don't need tons of time to do this well so long as you are in an environment that is conducive to focus and clear thinking.

- **Put your devices away.** You must journal in a notebook. Devices, generally, are distracting. Don't bring them into your journal times. If you need your phone around, put it in "Do Not Disturb" mode (or equivalent).

- **Choose mornings.** If you can, journal in the mornings. Biblically, there seems to be something special about mornings (see Psalms 90:14, 143:8).

Section 2

HEALING FROM YOUR PAST

CHAPTER 4

Making Sense of Your Past

I promised that I would play the Indian card, and as you will soon find out, I am a man of my word. Growing up with immigrant parents in a country that you consider home poses an interesting juxtaposition. I identify with my home and native land (Canada) through and through, but I am fascinated by Indian culture and long to understand it better because I know that as I better understand it, I better understand myself.

In Indian culture, arranged marriages are the norm. In other words, as a young adult, you have a say in who you marry, but it is not entirely your decision. The families are involved. This is a difficult concept to wrap your mind around when you've grown up in North America where the divorce rate is rather high. If people cannot decide for themselves who Mr. or Mrs. Right is, then how could their parents possibly know? The stats in India paint an opposing picture, where around 90% of marriages are arranged and the divorce rate is only 1%.[26] There are several factors these stats do not consider, so I'm not saying arranged marriages are infallible, but the cultural differences in marital arrangements form an interesting paradox for a first-generation North American.

There is a story of an Indian woman who was born outside of her country. She grew up along the east coast of Asia in a small country called Malaysia. Her mom died when she was 12 and to gain more family support, her family moved back to India, where she completed high school and university. At the age of 25, the big moment came when it was time to find her a husband. Cue: the marriage broker.

You read that right. Marriage broker. The same way that an insurance broker helps you find the right insurance company through their many connections, a marriage broker helps you find the right spouse through their network. It's like the pre-Internet version of online dating.

The marriage broker eventually lined her up with a mysterious Indian man who lived in a cold and desolate place called Canada. To make things worse, he was a pastor. Who hired this marriage broker anyway? She had a 10-minute conversation with this curry-loving Canuck, most of which was focused on one topic: If they got married, could she handle sacrificing her positive-temperatures-only life and start over again in Canada? The answer, as it happened, was yes, and 10 days later they were married. Indians don't waste time with marriage.

This brave woman uprooted her life and moved across the world to restart life with a man she barely knew in a cold country that held negative temperatures for half of the year. The newlyweds soon had a daughter. Their lives in Canada were being established as their little family started to grow. After several attempts to have a second child, however, it became clear that something was wrong.

Doctors diagnosed the woman with a prolapsed uterus. Essentially, the surrounding muscles and ligaments were overstretched and unable to support her uterus. It's a pretty serious condition that usually only happens to women after they've had a few babies. Unfortunately, genetics worked against her and she experienced it after her first child. Doctors said she should be able to have a child anyway, so the couple continued to try.

No success.

A few specialists later they tried a second solution that went horribly wrong. Attempting to bypass surgery, the specialist put a solid rubber ring into her uterus to hold the frail walls in place. The ring was not the right fit and it wound up rubbing against the walls as a result. This first caused pain, then it caused bleeding. The bleeding was so bad that she was rushed to the hospital. Had she waited any longer, she could have died.

Conceiving the normal way was not working for them, so the couple started to explore alternative options. The first was adoption.

The second option was surgery to fix the walls of the uterus. All the surgeons agreed this was a viable option, but none was willing to do it because of the risk. Exactly what you want to hear from your surgeons. Eventually, the couple connected with a reputable surgeon who had compassion for them and agreed to do the high-risk procedure. But there was only a 50% chance of success. Do you risk major surgery on your reproductive organs with those kinds of odds?

The woman decided to move forward with the operation after all. It was painful and her hospital stay was extended to make sure she recovered well. She could not lift anything for six weeks and had to wait six whole months before trying to conceive again.

However, six glorious months later, she was pregnant. As you can imagine, the couple was over the moon! Friends and family were let in on the exciting news. The pregnancy was relatively smooth with only a few minor hiccups.

Then the big day came. The contractions were picking up and it was time to head to the hospital. The hospital staff went through the usual protocol, which included hooking the woman up to a monitor to track the baby's heartbeat. This was not standard back then, but they did it because the woman had gestational diabetes. A few hours into labor, the nurse told the couple that the baby's heartbeat has been consistently normal so they could remove the monitor if it was too uncomfortable. They thought about it, and the man suggested they keep it on just in case. Little did they know this would save the baby's life.

Suddenly, everything went wrong. The nurse came in, looked at the monitor, and ran out of the room with a horrified look on her face. She came back and informed the couple that the baby's heartbeat was plummeting. A specialist followed her in and gave the couple two options: wait a little longer to see if the baby's heartbeat picked up or perform an emergency C-section. The specialist warned that after yet another operation on this poor woman's body, there was no guarantee the baby would survive.

With little time to think, the couple hastily agreed to a C-section. The medical staff was frantic. Most were called back from their breaks to attend to the situation. The woman was wheeled into the operating room, yet again. All she could do now was pray that God would perform a miracle. The man stood by in support, white as a ghost (that's when you know an Indian is distressed).

Would the previous operations she had undergone finally pay off? Had the time, energy, and money spent leading up to this moment all been for nothing? Was this family really going to have to adopt a non-Indian child? These are the things my parents mulled over as my mom underwent the C-section. Forty-five minutes later, the specialist pulled out a crying baby.

I was kept in an incubator for a few hours to make sure everything was okay while my mom recovered. Around seven hours later she finally got to see her baby boy, alive and well. The doctors' appointments, medical procedures, and "birthday festivities," as my mom called them, had paid off after all.

As you can imagine, it was hard to write any of this with a dry eye. I read this story over and marvel at my own survival against all odds. This is the power of our past. We can look back and extract useful information about the people we are today. Our past shapes us, forms us, and gives incredible insight into who we are made to be.

Now read this carefully: we are NOT the sum of our past events. Just because something bad happened to you does not mean your life will be bad.

We are the sum of our experiences, which doesn't only mean the events themselves, but the emotions, perceptions, and conclusions that are associated with them.

I do not believe that every slightly negative or imperfect experience in your past needs to be addressed, but I do believe that healing from the damaging experiences in your past can bring tremendous health into your present and set you up for a much better future. How many times do you hear about a person with an angry dad who promised they would never be like that, then they get married, have kids, and become an angry dad? Have you heard of someone who lost their business and "never recovered"? How about someone who lost a loved one and "was never the same after"?

Maybe you remember a time when you were more vibrant, less cynical, and more free to be yourself. You reasoned that part of growing up is that you lose these things. Or you figure this is just the way it is, and that nothing can be done. Maybe you've reached a point in your life where you've hit a wall and cannot progress in certain areas regardless of your efforts. Perhaps your struggle with pornography will not go away no matter how hard you pray and how many different strategies you try to break free.

I'm here to tell you two things. First, your past impacts your present and future whether you like it or not. Second, and much more importantly, your past can be overcome. The goal is to work through the impacts of your past in the most efficient way possible. We do not want to set up camp in the history books—that is futile. Instead, we want to heal from our past so that we can become better versions of ourselves and have a more glorious future of freedom and health. Healing from the past will improve your relationships, mental well-being, spirituality, work ethic, and self-esteem, in addition to playing a vital role in your freedom from pornography.

Ground Rules

When I help my clients with this subject, we always start with a few ground rules to set the record straight. I have seen too many people delve into their pasts without any structure or guidelines and it does more harm than good in the long run. Since I cannot be in a private session with you, it is all the more important that we establish these ground rules and that you follow them if you dare to apply what I will to teach you in this chapter.

Ground Rule #1: We only look at our past long enough to learn. I am not interested in exploring parts of my past that will not make me better. You shouldn't either. Our futures are too glorious. When you explore your past, the goal must always be to learn, improve, and heal. Anything outside of this parameter is high-risk and may not necessarily be beneficial.

Ground Rule #2: Get professional help. I cannot stress this enough. I am a professional coach, but I am not a professional therapist or counselor. I take my clients as far as I can and then, if we reach a certain point in their past that I cannot help them with, I encourage them to get additional therapy. In my own recovery from pornography addiction, outside help was invaluable. To this day, I still see a therapist regularly. I consider it preventative emotional health.

Ground Rule #3: Do not forget Principle #1 (Control/Ownership) and #2 (Responsibility & Power). Identify what you own, then take responsibility for it. Do not reverse the order, and do not exercise one without the other. If you reverse the order, you will look at your past experiences and take unmerited responsibility. This will eventually become a weight you cannot bear. If you only identify what you own in a situation, but do not take responsibility, you wind up overwhelmed and disempowered to do anything about it. Equally problematic.

Now that the ground rules are in place, let's take a closer look at how to overcome your past.

The Triple Threat

About a year into the launch of my practice, I received an invitation to speak on a panel for a woman's TV show called *See Hear Love*, hosted by Melinda Estabrooks. Given the scope of my work and the nature of its content, I was hesitant. I am not one to back down from media opportunities and have done my fair share over the years on several respected platforms, but I wondered if I really had much to offer a female audience. Not to say that porn is exclusively a male issue—women struggle too—but I personally wondered if I was the right person to talk about recovery for women when my work is solely focused on men.

After some prayer and consulting with my advisory council (aka my wife), I realized this was a good chance for me to be stretched and that what I do to help men could provide some value to women as well.

I was asked to arrive at the studio about an hour later than the other female panelists because my makeup and hair took a fraction of the time. Perks of being a guy. We were in the green room and Melinda was talking us through the program, which had a solid subject line: Helping People Overcome Shame, Guilt, and Regret.

I was struck by this grouping. Shame and guilt are often talked about in tandem, but what was regret doing in there? I was momentarily lost in my thoughts when the producer came in and said, "They're ready for you! Let's go!"

We went on set, filmed a wonderful panel discussion in front of a studio audience, and called it a day. I made new friends, found out that women are very receptive to my message and story, and went home, beyond content with how everything went. But I could not shake this shame, guilt, regret grouping. There was something on it.

After some research and my own musings, I have now termed this group the Triple Threat. In my work, I've discovered that collectively, these three sons of a gun are some of the greatest threats that men face when overcoming the past. My tendency is to gloss over things like this so we can move on to the more exciting stuff (aka the things that help you get over your past), but we have to name the enemies first before we take them out. Let's take a closer look at the triple threat.

Shame

I'm happy to say that the subject of shame no longer needs an introduction. Thanks to people like Brené Brown, the American researcher and professor whose TED talks on shame and authenticity went viral,[27] the topic is better understood today than ever before. The research makes it quite clear that part of the reason talks like Brown's have spread like wildfire is because every single person with a pulse on Planet Earth experiences shame. She defines it as an "intensely painful feeling or experience of believing that we are flawed and therefore unworthy of love and belonging."[28] It is the nagging voice that says, "You are not enough," "You should be more _____," "You should be less_____." Shame often sounds like "should" statements.

Shame looks at you, your life, and how you are, then looks at what everyone else is doing. It sees the discrepancy and concludes, "These people must have it all figured out, and I must be out of the loop. I must be missing something."

Shame is not the same thing as guilt, and I will explain why in a moment. But understand this: Shame deals with the identity of an individual. It is an autoimmune identity disorder—an attack on self. Shame says you are wrong, there is something wrong with who you are.

Shame is a bold-faced lie. Its voice could not be any further from the truth. In fact, even scripture tells us that in a new covenant lifestyle, there is no room for shame. Before Christ, we are fundamentally flawed. But there is no condemnation for those who are in Christ Jesus. There is never a good or godly purpose for shame. As men who are pursuing health, we must be vigilant in guarding against shame and its destructive agendas, otherwise we will only become a fraction of the men God made us to be.

Here is how you know if you have shame in your life: hiddenness. If there is something in your life that you are afraid of people finding out, or afraid of God finding out, then shame is in the mix. The primary message of shame is, "Hide! Do not let anyone see your flaws." Shame doesn't just say hide the evidence, hide the aftermath, hide the defects. Shame says, "Hide yourself. Who you are should not be fully seen. If you are truly seen for who you are, you will be rejected. Better to just pull back."

Does that voice sound familiar to you?

Having those thoughts is one thing—giving in to them is another. Giving in to them is much worse. At the end of the day, who really cares if you have those thoughts? What others might think hardly means anything. When *you* agree with them, however, that's when it becomes a problem. When you agree with the voice of shame, you are signing an informal contract to be a fragment of your true self.

The problem with hiding is that after a while, we are no longer able to be seen for our true selves. We are seen for a partial version of ourselves or even worse, a completely different version from who we truly are. There are few worse feelings than being affirmed for someone you are not. Yet it happens every day as people try to be something they are not, to receive acceptance from people that cannot ascribe their true value or worth.

Think about this. A husband is dealing with shame. He has applied for several promotions within his company to advance his career and be a better provider for his family. To no avail. Every application gets turned down. He concludes, "There must be something wrong with me." Now if he said, "There must be something wrong with my work," that's one thing. If he said, "There must be something wrong with how I'm applying for these jobs," that's another. But his conclusion, "There must be something wrong with *me*," is extremely dangerous.

Remember, shame's primary message is "hide." So when his wife asks how the applications are going, he says, "Yeah, they're going alright," when really they are not. But he's too ashamed. He doesn't want his wife to see him struggling or weak. Or maybe he doesn't want his wife to become concerned about whether or not there will be money to put food on the table. They're all valid reasons, but they all stem from shame.

You might think this is reasonable, but if the husband wants a healthy marriage, it is not. In succumbing to shame's primary message, "hide," the man has now created a division in the marriage. The wife does not get to see certain aspects of him and his life. It is understandable why the man would want to hide, but it will not serve him if he wants a vibrant, long lasting marriage.

Situations like this happen every single day. Any man on the planet struggling with porn addiction has also wrestled with the overwhelming shame that comes with it. And as I mentioned already, the voice of shame is annoying, but not the problem. Giving in to the voice of shame is the problem. Acting out of a place of shame is detrimental to our own well-being and to the success of our relationships.

The good news is that shame is *not* insurmountable. It can be overcome, and I believe one day we will learn to live shamelessly. Until we reach that place, research has shown that there is one thing that combats shame better than anything else: vulnerability.[29] The conscious choice to be seen.

I'm going to guess that's not what you wanted to hear. My male brain would much prefer something tangible or an activity that I can do to de-clutter the shameful thoughts. Unfortunately, that won't work. To combat the brutal effects of shame on your psyche and overall well-being, and to find freedom from pornography, you will have to learn to be vulnerable.

Vulnerability does not mean that every time you hang out with people you are a weepy puddle of emotions and pain. It doesn't mean that suddenly you must share all the dirty details and divulge all the specifics of your life challenges. It simply means that when you encounter things in life that tell you to hide, you choose the opposite. You choose to be seen.

The basic rule here is that you should choose to be seen relative to the degree of intimacy you have with the other person. In other words, the options are not "hide everything" or "share everything." Rather, if you are making the brave choice to be vulnerable, you should evaluate the depth of your relationship with the other person and let that dictate the level of vulnerability. If you are just getting to know someone, your attempt to "be vulnerable" about your past might come across as too much because you don't yet have enough relational equity to handle it.

On the flip side, let's go back to our previous example of the man apply-ing for promotions. If he tells his wife, "I'm really frustrated that I'm not getting any of these promotions and I'm scared I won't be able to provide adequately for our growing family," the shame dissipates. It's not necessarily all gone in a moment, but by choosing to not hide, the man has made a powerful step toward healing and health.

Does he risk evoking fear in his wife? Yes. That's scary for her. Is it possible that she changes her mind about him? Yes, but not likely. There are tons of risks and fears associated with vulnerability. That is why it is usually avoided. But the challenges that come with vulnerability pale in comparison to the challenges that come with hiddenness, especially when we're talking about getting free of pornography.

Guilt

While shame is when you feel bad for who you are as a person, guilt is when you feel bad for what you have done. We often lump these two together and assume they're basically the same thing. They are not. Shame is much, much worse because it deals with identity. Anything that addresses your core sense of self is going to have a greater impact.

Nonetheless, guilt is still a problem. A major one, in fact. We've all felt guilty at some point in our lives, probably in the last day, even. Guilt is regular.

Several factors influence whether or not we feel guilt. To list a few: family, culture, and religion.[30] As an example, someone who has no particular faith background will have a different moral compass than someone who grew up in the church. That means if they both use foul language, the individual without a faith background might not feel much guilt for it, especially if it was modelled by their older siblings and/or parents growing up. Meanwhile, the person of faith has a conviction it's wrong and feels guilty for swearing.

Interestingly enough, while there is really never a good time or place for shame, guilt can play a positive role in our lives. Guilt is the thing that tells us we have done something wrong. Sometimes that can be useful.

If you steal and feel guilty afterward, that's a good thing. You *should* feel guilty for stealing because you have done something wrong. It's much worse to steal and not feel guilty. How can you repent, learn, or improve if you do not experience guilt in such a situation?

Guilt can drive you to Jesus. It can help you turn to Him, confess the error of your ways, and catalyze change in your life. Shame cannot do this. Remember, shame says "hide." As long as you hide, you cannot be helped. Guilt says, don't do that again. It can be a constructive emotion.

There are two things that make guilt destructive. First, guilt compounds. It increases with time. Most men do not know how to deal with guilt, so they live under its weight for a very long time. Imagine carrying 20 lbs of weight on your shoulders. Not a big deal, right? It's only 20 lbs. Imagine carrying that 20 lbs for an hour. A day. A week. A year. It doesn't matter how strong you are, eventually you will start to slouch. When we do not address guilt, our inner man becomes a hunchback. We get bogged down by the weight of our guilt and often find it hard to move on and let things go.

The second thing that makes guilt destructive is the conclusions we draw from guilt-inducing incidents. Let me illustrate this with a story that I heard a friend share one time. When she was in high school, she fell in with a not-so-good crowd. These people smoked, drank, and even stole from time to time. One day, she got mixed up in their shenanigans and stole from Walmart (classy stuff). As fate would have it, she got caught.

The security guard arrested her and she was detained. The staff conducted their usual investigation and then eventually called her parents to come pick her up. Do you think my friend felt guilty? You bet she did. She felt awful, and now she had to face her parents. As she was mulling over what she was going to say to them, one of the cops grabbed her attention.

"Hey," he said, "just because you stole doesn't make you a thief."

Those words changed her life. She never stole again, and it wasn't because she was afraid of being caught or because she didn't want to disappoint her parents anymore. It was because she did not harbor any damaging conclusions about herself from the experience. Those precious words the cop spoke changed everything for her.

Imagine if he hadn't said what he did and on the car ride home as her parents chewed her out she concluded, "I'm a thief. I'm a lousy, good-for-nothing thief." Do you think she'd steal again? Of course she would. She thinks she's a thief now. Thieves steal. She would draw destructive conclusions from her guilt-inducing actions.

"Just because you stole doesn't make you a thief."

Do you see how the cop's words drew a very distinct line for her between action and identity? Between guilt and shame? My friend did something wrong, make no mistake about that. But that doesn't mean something is wrong with her. The cop saved her from making a damaging conclusion and it changed her response dramatically as a result. This is the power of combating guilt.

When managing guilt in your life the most important thing is to respond. Inaction will only compound the adverse effects of guilt. Truly, you are left with two choices when you encounter guilt. If it's good guilt, as in you feel guilty about something that you should not have done, then repentance is the best response. If it's bad guilt, as in you feel guilty about something that you were right to do, pull out your journal and find out why you're feeling that way. For example, imagine saying "no" to hanging out with a friend because you would rather be alone for the evening. You have every right to prioritize yourself and spend the evening at home, but bad guilt might tell you that you're selfish. In these moments, you have an opportunity to condition your emotional self by dealing with the bad guilt.

Any time you feel guilty about something when you have done no wrong is an indicator that you are believing a lie. The goal for journaling in this scenario is to identify the lie and replace it with the truth. This is the best way to dissipate unnecessary guilt. If you need some help, you'll get more guidance in Chapter 7.

Regret

Regret is looking at your past without compassion. Remember Ground Rule #1: We only look at our past long enough to learn. Doing this without compassion is dangerous territory.

Regret keeps you locked in your past. Regret is the feeling that if something in your past had happened differently, or that if you were different, your present and future life would be better. Living with regret is awful. Yet most of us can relate to a time where we have had this experience.

Regret robs you of joy in the present and of hope for the future. It stops you from enjoying things in the moment because no matter how great things are, you believe they could be better. You could be making more money, live in a bigger house, have a more functional family, etc., if only you didn't have this nagging problem with porn.

These are common experiences. Men reach later stages in life and then look back and wonder what could have been. All of this falls under regret. Since regret keeps you locked into your past, when you hold on to regret, you do not have resource to dream about the future. Not in a serious way, at least. The future is really a wish, a faint idea. But ultimately, it is out of reach. "Look at my past," says regret. "How could I ever accomplish that? Or become something special?"

The operative term here is compassion. Regret looks at your past through a lens that is unforgiving, critical, and remorseful, all of which can be thwarted by genuine compassion. In this case, compassion is interchangeable with mercy. Mercy is choosing to release someone of consequences they would usually deserve.

Later in this chapter, we're going to look at this whole concept in more detail, but for now, I want you to understand that to truly combat the nasty forces of regret, you will have to develop compassion toward yourself. This is not a comfortable exercise, but what price are you willing to pay for freedom? Success? Growth?

Parental Relationships

At this point, it should be no secret that your childhood, and the experiences you had with people during your childhood, especially your parents, have had a tremendous impact on the person you are today. Nothing is more pivotal and formative in your development as a human being than the relationships you have with your parents.

As men, we don't want to hear that. We like the idea of being strong enough on our own. Not controlled or impacted by other people, let alone our parents. Maybe it's just me. That was certainly my approach to this subject for a very long time. I'm an independent person. I've done alright for myself. So why do my parental relationships matter?

I don't know what kind of parents you had. That's what makes this part of the book a challenge. I wish we could sit down and have a chat about it so that I could hear all the ins and outs of your experiences. No two experiences are the same. No two parents are the same. No two people are the same. You and your siblings may have gone through the same incidents in life but had completely different experiences. For one person it's life-changing, for the other it's just another day. There is a very real uniqueness to this conversation.

It all comes down to this: The number one block that men who follow my programs and coaching encounter is damaging experiences from their childhood. You might be surprised to hear this. How does struggling with pornography have anything to do with childhood? Well, in short, everything.

I do not know anyone who has experienced long-term freedom from an addiction or any other kind of bondage without working through wounds from their parental relationships. Our parents are both invaluable and, unfortunately, insufficient. You might have had the greatest parents in the world, but I'm sorry to break it to you, they were not perfect. And in those areas where they did not meet expectations, damage has been done. It may be minor, or it might seem insurmountable, but either way, it's there.

This topic was a tough one for me for a long time. I have two good parents: My dad has always been present, kind, wise, supportive, and a phenomenal role model. My mom has always been a voice of love and encouragement, and is warm and present as well. I'm not the guy who grew up with a majorly dysfunctional family or only had one parent around to look after the kids. My siblings and I are incredibly fortunate that way—beyond having a functional family and both parents in place, truthfully, we were blessed with very little to worry about growing up.

With that in mind, you can imagine how challenging I found this idea of parental relationships and wounds initially. I had to somehow make the leap and accept that even though my parents are great, they had shortcomings and those shortcomings impacted me. I eventually reached that place, and while it was painful at first, I am so glad it happened. This is where my biggest breakthrough in recovery from porn addiction took place.

Core Needs

Everyone has needs. You have needs. I have needs. We all have needs. This is another one of those things that men tend to avoid. To have needs is "weak." That's what we're taught. You cannot afford to look weak as a man, because then you'll be picked on and seen as "unmasculine." I don't have all the explanations for why men think this way and why these social dynamics exist between us, all I know is that it's wrong.

Men have needs, and those who learn to get their needs met in a healthy way win. A baby's main needs are to be fed, put to sleep, and have its diaper changed. It's a pretty good life if you ask me. The problem when you're a baby is that you cannot meet any of those needs on your own. You cannot get your own food. You cannot climb into bed. And you definitely cannot carry the diaper bag.

As a baby, how do you get what you need? Simple, you make like a professional soccer player when the ref makes a call against their team and you cry. Babies cry. This is healthy in the early stages of life. It's not okay for a teenager to cry when they're hungry. At that point in life, they are expected to have developed better ways to get a snack.

Let's oversimplify this: As you develop you will either find healthy ways to get your needs met or unhealthy ways. One way or another, those needs *will* get met. That's a guarantee. The question is whether or not the methods you've developed are healthy.

When you're hungry, eating McDonald's is one way to get your need met. Is it healthy? No. Did it meet the need? Yes, for about 20 minutes if you ate their chicken, and about 12 minutes if you ate their beef.

When you are a child, you have a say in those dealings. As an adult, you are left to your own devices. Your choice. To use language we all have in common now, it's in your inner circle.

Unfortunately, through shortcomings of our upbringing and imperfections of the world we live in, we develop patterns and habits for getting our needs met that do not serve us well in the long run. We can get by with these faulty solutions in our teens and maybe even our early 20s. By the time you reach your mid-20s, you start to discover the areas that need cleanup. If you put Principles #1 & #2 (Control and Responsibility) into practice, you can do a lot of healing and prevent messes later on. If you don't, then the deficiencies of your childhood will compound.

Over the years I've identified four core areas that cover a majority of our needs. These areas are not all-encompassing, and they are not particularly extensive. But they are, I believe, the closest to the heart and have the greatest impact on our overall development and well-being. If we look at these four needs in the context of our childhood, we can properly assess how they were met (or not) growing up and the areas of our development that might need more attention.

Essentials

Essential needs are food, shelter, and water. They are fundamental for biological survival. Without them, you will not make it. Plain and simple. There's nothing particularly dramatic about them, nothing sentimentally significant. They are foundational needs and must be met for us to survive and certainly to thrive.

This category of need is usually the extent of what most men can identify within themselves. You ask a man, "What were your parents like growing up?"

"Oh good," he says. "There was always food on the table and a shirt on my back."

What we're really saying in this classic response is that our parents looked after our essential needs. There was nothing to complain about. We had the essentials and were able to function normally (relatively) as a result.

When essential needs are not met, several things go wrong. Living without food, shelter, or water will quickly deplete your physical well-being. A person's livelihood becomes limited and their days are occupied wondering where their next meal will come from.

A few years ago, I had the privilege of going on a ministry trip to South Africa with my pastor and boss at the time. The trip had a bit of everything. Hot air balloon rides, unique eating experiences (zebra tastes better than you'd think), wonderful times of ministering in local churches, and a few very notable outreach experiences. These took place primarily in what locals call "squatter camps," settlements with shacks made of wood, tin, cardboard, and other material. A family often has to live in a single shack, which is usually the size of a garden shed.[31]

Many of these children have shelter (barely), and they have water (although it's dirty), but food is hard to come by. Our goal during these outreaches was to bring food to meet their physical needs in the hope it would be an open door to provide spiritual food that would meet their spiritual needs. The looks on their faces were priceless, and we got to pray with many of these young, single-parent families. Experiences like these make you realize how fortunate you are to have the essentials without expending much effort.

Our parents are supposed to meet our essential needs until we become adults. If a child does not have food on the table growing up, he must find other ways to make it happen. He will learn to steal. He is not necessarily a bad kid, but he must eat. This is no justification for stealing, by any means. Rather, I want to illustrate that in this case, the difference between healthy and unhealthy ways of meeting your essential needs can be pretty significant. As an adult it's your responsibility (Principle #2) to get your essential needs met in *healthy* ways.

Safety

Imagine you've just moved to a new neighborhood. You start exploring your surroundings and discover a beautiful park with a trail just minutes from your doorstep. You happen to enjoy exercising outdoors, so a few days later you put on your running shoes and go for a run through the park.

The park is heavily wooded as the trails are engulfed by cedars and oaks that were planted at a time when the average vehicle had 1–2 horsepower max. The trees are tall, that's what I'm trying to say. Now about two-thirds of this park is wooded, but the last third or so is an open field with tall grass.

The path through the park is a straight line, there's no loop. So your running route is simple today. You run to the end of the path and then run back. The first half of the run goes perfectly. You've broken a bit of a sweat, but the sun hasn't risen in full force yet so it's still cool. The birds are chirping. People on the path are smiling. And you think to yourself, "Wow. I picked a good neighborhood."

You turn around and begin your journey back. You're in the tall grass area. You look about 150 meters ahead to where the forested section begins and notice a few dogs sniffing each other out. There are two white dogs and one black. You look around but can't see an owner in sight. Are these dogs lost?

You see that there are now four white dogs that have surrounded the black dog in a semi-circle. You begin to slow down because something doesn't feel right. As you really focus, you realize that those are not white dogs. Those are coywolves, a canid canine that is part coyote and part wolf.

Suddenly, you hear a voice shouting through the tall grass. It's the owner of the black dog. The dog knows better than to turn his back on the pack of coywolves, so he retreats toward his owner by slowly backing up. The coywolves leave him alone.

The question now is, are *you* safe?

What are the chances of this pack of coywolves coming for you next? Hard to say. Not as high as you'd think. Is this scary? Yes, because a threat has been introduced. Before the threat, this was a peaceful run. Now, it's an unexpected test of your physical fitness as you find a new, long-winded way to get home.

In its purest form, safety is the absence of threat, real or perceived. And the answer is yes (I'm assuming you just wondered if the coywolf experience was based on a true story).

Safety is an afterthought when it is satisfied. Think about that one. No one seeks more security when they already have it. It's not like food. If you're hungry, you will eat. But you will also eat when you're not hungry because something entices you. Safety is not quite like that. Once your safety need is satiated, you're not likely to pay much attention to it.

It's only when a threat is introduced that safety becomes priority numero uno. We need safety in our relationships for them to thrive. The underlying question running through your childhood and its accompanying experiences is: Were you safe? The situations where you were unsafe will often stick out the most.

When I was 12, my parents informed me that we would be moving across the country to be closer to our extended family. I liked the idea of being closer to Grandma and Grandpa, and to my aunt, uncle, and cousins, but I was terrified because it meant leaving behind the friendships, communities, and comforts that I was accustomed to. In hindsight, this move was one of the best things to happen to me. But at the time, the move was a threat to my safety and I didn't like it.

Was the threat real? Not really. I soon made friends at my new school and settled in quickly. What more do you need when you're 12? However, the announcement of the move was so jarring to my security that I still remember it quite vividly.

That is why shame, guilt, and regret are called the triple *threat*. They are threats to our security as individuals. They tell us to take cover and stay hidden. They ultimately tell us that something about who we are and/or what we have done is a threat to security within ourselves. That is dangerous territory.

Remember, needs *will* get met, it's just a matter of how. When your parents do not provide an appropriate level of safety during your development, you are forced to find other ways to experience safety. These may be good or bad.

A colleague of mine, Drew Boa, the founder of Husband Material Men, also helps men get free of pornography. He once explained that while growing up, his parents would often tuck him in at night. They would sometimes even embrace him for long periods of time to help him sleep. What great parents, right? The problem is that Drew built a dependency on these safety-inducing interactions to fall asleep. So when he got older and it was no longer appropriate to have these interactions with his parents, where do you think he went?

With a phone at his bedside and pornography a few taps away, he developed a pretty nasty evening habit.[32] As time went on, he built healthier avenues to find safety at night and has now helped hundreds of men overcome pornography as well. This is the power of knowing your needs and finding healthy ways to get them met. Safety included.

Intimacy

Intimacy is the need of all needs. We are all wired for deep, meaningful, intimate connection from day one. If we do not receive intimacy growing up, we become attention and affection-starved adults who make poor choices in life.

Historically, intimacy has not been a comfortable word for men. It seems so lovey-dovey and icky. That was my opinion, at least. But intimacy is fundamental. Innate. Inescapable. It is something that I need, and it is something you need. As is the case with all core needs, your need for intimacy WILL get met. The question is how.

Intimacy was best explained by one of my teachers in ministry school. He said intimacy is "Into-me-see." As in, intimacy is letting people see what is going on within. My favorite definition is that intimacy is being seen, known, and understood. You may recall that our antidote to shame is vulnerability. The conscious choice to be seen. In doing so, carving a path for deep, meaningful connection. Being seen is step one. It means letting people know you exist and letting them see you for who you are.

If this continues long enough, you will eventually be known and then understood. And when you have reached this place in a connection, it is glorious. I only have a handful of people at this point in my life who are close friends, and there is very little that I do not share with them. It's the only way I can experience deep, meaningful connection. I have to take bold risks to be seen, even though it could cost me disconnection, rejection, or judgment.

In all your relationships, you are meant to have a degree of intimacy that matches its strength. The stronger the relationship, the deeper the intimacy. Marriage is the ultimate relationship as it is a covenant, and the level of intimacy required is significant as a result. Sex is the easy part—prior to marriage, that's usually all you think about in terms of intimacy. The daily act of being seen, known, and understood is where the hard work comes in, but it is the only way true intimacy is cultivated. We must have places in our lives where we can experience intimacy.

When you are growing up, intimacy is meant to be experienced with both parents. It is especially important with your mother in the early years, but it is equally important to experience intimacy with your father throughout your upbringing. Someone who gets their need for intimacy met from their parents is more likely to be secure in themselves, confident, and have high capacity for meaningful relationships with their peers.[33], [34] On the flip side, someone who has emotionally disconnected parents or perhaps only one parent growing up may be negatively impacted in these areas.

My mom is an incredible woman, as you know from her across-the-seas-surgery-surmounting experience. She is warm, kind, and caring. She is also quite conservative. A little held back. Growing up, she did not express her affection overtly. I knew she loved me, but sometimes I had to read between the lines to get the message. This affected my capacity for intimacy. It left my emotional bank account at a deficit because I wasn't receiving love from my mom the way I needed it. As a result, when I reached high school, in addition to normal teenage boy activities like obsessing over girls, this deficit manifested itself in secretly looking at porn on a regular basis.

In university, the girl chase slowed down (didn't have enough game), and porn usage went up. That's the telltale sign that porn was not just a vice or some form of escape, it was meeting a need. Simply put, porn is fast-food intimacy. It temporarily satisfies the need in an exhilarating way and then a few minutes later leaves you hungrier than when you first started. Cue the porn addiction.

Most of my clients have major work to do in this area. Even with perfect parents, we usually wind up intimacy deficient. Most of this boils down to one simple thing: no human being has the ability to perfectly satisfy your need for intimacy. The only person who can accomplish this is God. Learning to cultivate intimacy with Him is critical, and something we will explore in more depth later on. Now that you understand journaling, you are already off to a good start in this area.

For now, understand this. Regardless of how you were raised, whether your intimacy capacity is through the roof or you had completely absent parents, everything can be restored. If you feel like you need healing in this area, I'm going to give you plenty of opportunities in this book to do so. Let's keep going to our last core need.

Significance

Few things grieve me more than witnessing someone who believes they are destined for mediocrity. I cannot stand it and it's one of the primary reasons that I do what I do.

Every person who ever lived was born for significance, you included. We have grossly misunderstood what it means to be significant, so allow me to explain. Let's start first with what it is not.

Significance does not mean an extensive social media following. Significance does not mean popularity. Significance does not mean wealth or riches. Significance does not mean six-pack abs and a broad chest. Significance does not mean good looks. Significance does not mean being hyper-gifted. Significance does not mean standing out.

Significance really boils down to one simple thing: personal purpose. The need for significance is the innate desire to be valued for your true self and to know that your true self can meaningfully contribute to something bigger than yourself.

Parents get the first opportunity to instill significance in a child. We often ask children, "What do you want to be when you grow up?" The child usually replies by saying a doctor, policeman, or in my case, a pizza delivery boy (some dream bigger than others). The question implies something that we don't even realize. We are asking the child, "How are you going to meaningfully contribute to this world? What is your purpose? Your life has to go somewhere as you get older, where exactly do you see it going?"

The way parents cultivate this part of a child's development is monumental. My parents were the cream of the crop in this area. They applauded my accomplishments and extended grace in my failures. I still to this day cannot fully put my finger on it, but from a very young age, I truly believed that my life mattered and that I could use it to make the lives of others better. And yes, at one point that meant delivering piping hot pizzas to strangers in record time.

When your need for significance is met, you are not afraid to dream. The minute you stop dreaming is the minute you start dying. Additionally, people whose need for significance is met will often make methodical steps toward their lofty goals. It's easy to say you want something extravagant or grandiose. But if you believe you are significant, you will take steps toward it despite the obstacles you encounter along the way.

To live out your purpose and find fulfillment in life is hard work, and if your need for significance is unmet, it becomes even more challenging. You ultimately make choices that are logical or follow a social trend, but they are not necessarily specific to your unique purpose. You then find yourself in places where you never wanted to be, pursuing things you don't really want. And in response, you say, "Oh well. Too bad." It's the response here that is devastating.

Most of us will find ourselves at some stage of life wondering how we got here. "This isn't what I thought it would look like." That's fine. It's part of growing up and finding yourself in this crazy world we live in. But when your response is apathetic, that's when it's obvious that your need for significance has been severely unmet.

However, if significance was not communicated to you growing up, I have wonderful news for you: that too can change.

Your mission now is to assess. How is the triple threat playing into your life? Have you developed healthy ways for getting your core needs met? What are the areas from your upbringing where these needs were not met? The workbook will help you tackle all these questions and apply the concepts of this chapter.

Remember that understanding your past is critical for you to have a glorious future of freedom. We do not want to dwell here, but we want to ensure that we harness every useful piece of intel from our past and identify areas where there have been contributing wounds. Once we have the lay of the land, it's time to clean up.

CHAPTER 5

Leaving Your Past Behind

The purpose of the previous chapter was to give you a framework for how you view your past. We now have a common language and a basic understanding of the fundamental concepts at play in our past life experiences. It wouldn't be much help, however, if we stopped the conversation here. It is not enough to understand your past. We must resolve the parts of it that have a negative impact on your present. This chapter will continue the conversation as we look at the critical elements for working through your life experiences.

Geysers

Usually, once my clients get settled into DeepClean, they develop an ability to pinpoint parts of their past that are contributing to their present. They can identify certain incidents or dynamics growing up that were problematic or have negatively contributed to their development. It's extremely powerful and I always beam with pride when I see them making these connections.

Not all moments in life are created equal. Think about your favorite birthday celebration. Or one of your most memorable moments with your dad. How about the first time you felt like a man? The list can go on, but you get the point. There are times in our lives that stand out. These examples are milestone moments, which generally speaking, are more memorable to begin with. However, when you dig a little deeper into your history, you realize that sometimes seemingly ordinary moments have had an equal if not greater effect.

The moments where damage was done, because of an unmet need, an unmet expectation, a disappointing outcome, a hurtful action or word, or whatever else, can be reconciled. And part of becoming a healthy and free man is working through the parts of our past that have caused wounding or damage.

For our purposes, we are not interested in digging up every single incident of our past that could have had a negative effect. As Kimberly "Sweet Brown" Wilkins said after escaping a fire in her apartment complex: "Ain't nobody got time for that."[35] There just isn't enough time in the world to work through all of your flawed experiences, even though the perfectionist part of my brain loves the idea. Furthermore, fixing every single incident is not helpful. That's like spending hours working on an assignment that's only worth 1% of your grade in school. You can do it, but in the long run, it's not going to make a notable impact.

Instead, we want to identify what I like to call geysers. Unresolved moments of our past that fester and erode at our inner well-being, sometimes without our awareness. In geological terms, a geyser is a spring underneath the surface that ejects a blast of water. They are quite dangerous and unless you have a map with indicators, you cannot see them.

The reality is that neither your past nor your parents were perfect. No doubt they might have been amazing—I'm not saying we need to start bashing our parents and throwing pity parties for our imperfect pasts. Far from it. What I'd like to suggest is that no matter how great your upbringing, you still had damaging moments that are sitting underneath the surface, ready to blow if they are not resolved.

Marriage has a funny way of exposing geysers. Recently, I did a grocery run. The car took a moment to start but it eventually got there. In the cool of winter in Canada, sometimes the engines are a bit slow to get going, so this was nothing to be concerned about. I carry on, buy my groceries, and go to start the car to begin the journey home. It won't start. I'm not mechanical by any means, which is why I pay for a membership that provides on-demand services to help me with car troubles. I call them up, they send a guy with a truck, and my problems go away. The system works, as was the case on this fateful evening.

While waiting for the guy to arrive, I called my wife to let her know what happened. I don't know why, but it was important at that moment that she could see I was unfazed. I had to be cool about this: It's no big deal. Just some car trouble. It's fine. I'm the man. I got this under control. I'm sure none of you can relate.

The guy arrives within about three minutes and informs me that the battery is dead and the car just needs a boost. How embarrassing. I could have looked after that myself if I'd known. Anyway, he gives me a boost and I'm on my way. I get back to the house and Shaloma is on the couch doing something on her phone. She sees me come in, says hi, and then continues what she was doing as I unload and put away the groceries.

I was livid.

Why? Because I just went through the stress and hassle of working through a car problem on my own. The least she could do was give me a hand with the groceries! Does she normally give me a hand with groceries? No, not really. Has my expectation for her to provide some assistance been communicated? No, definitely not. Did I play it cool on the phone to give off the vibe that I was unfazed, therefore she should not really have to do anything extra to compensate for the situation? Yeah. But…okay fine. I was totally in the wrong here.

This incident began a long fight. And it would be tempting to look back and say that it was all because of my pride. I was too proud to let my wife see me stressed. While that is true, and it did contribute to the problem, it was not the problem. After some trusty journaling, I discovered that my reaction stemmed from a few childhood experiences.

Growing up, neither of my parents ever met my standard for cleanliness and organization. This is partially because my standard was unrealistic and partially because neither of my parents really valued being clean and tidy. Often I would find myself doing way more cleanup than anyone else around the house, and usually I didn't mind. Occasionally I would get in my head a bit and think, "Why am I doing this? My parents should be doing this. Or they should at least help me. And if they aren't going to help me, the least they could do is show a little appreciation."

Ah, and there it is. Feeling valued. Appreciated. It's amazing how sometimes we do things and tell ourselves we don't care if we're seen or noticed, when the truth is that we care deeply. This lack of appreciation was a sore spot for me. Being acknowledged and appreciated by my parents was important growing up, and they generally did a good job of it. This particular area was a different story and years later it played out in this incident with my wife.

These kinds of dynamics are what I call geysers. I didn't know that experience from my past even mattered. It's not something I regularly thought about. But it was there all along and the right set of conditions caused it to blow. I had to do some cleanup. We'll take a closer look at what that looks like shortly so that as you identify geysers in your own life, you can do something about them too.

Pain

A man is only as strong as his ability to face his pain. One of the most defining qualities of a man today is his ability to effectively process pain. I'm not just talking about physical pain. I'm talking about emotional pain. Mental pain. Relational pain. Social pain. Financial pain. Whatever it may be.

Now to be clear, I do not mean someone who doesn't feel pain. What credit belongs to someone who can move past pain they can't feel? That's hardly an accomplishment. Most men develop mechanisms that stop them from experiencing any pain at all and then think they are so strong because they don't flinch in situations that most would find painful. If you were paralyzed from the waist down and I pinched your leg and you don't flinch, does that mean you have pain tolerance? Does it make you strong? Hardly. All it proves is that you cannot feel.

It's the guys who feel pain but still persevere that are true champions. This is why emotional fitness is so critical. I love the story of the late great Kobe Bryant who remembered the song that was playing when his team lost the NBA finals to the Boston Celtics in 2008. He listened to that song every day for the next two years. Why? He wanted the pain of that moment to motivate him. He faced his pain. He didn't act like he wasn't bothered by the loss. He didn't gloss over it. He dealt with it head-on for two whole years and led the Lakers to NBA championships in 2009 and 2010.[36]

Psychologists have theorized for years that the two primary human motivators for behavior are pleasure and pain.[37] In other words, the main reasons that we make decisions are to gain something desirable or to avoid something painful. However, researchers out of Silicon Valley are discovering that avoiding pain is a far greater driving force than a desire *for* something.[38] Our human nature is to avoid pain, and rightfully so. Who actually enjoys it?

The problem is that if you do not experience pain, then you cannot experience gain. They operate in the same avenues. If you block circulation to one, you block off the whole circuit. Many men lose their capacity for joy and a sense of fulfillment because they are unwilling to face their pain. So they medicate. They numb. They tell themselves they are moving on in life when in reality they are simply living in denial. And they white-knuckle their way trying to get free from pornography.

Suppression Catches Up

I know this well because I've done it well. When my parents decided to move our family across the country when I was 12, I had a lot of fears about my new classmates. Would they like me? Would I fit in? Would we have anything in common? Would any of the cute girls like brown boys? You know, standard stuff that an eighth-grade Indian worries about.

I was fortunate to make friends quickly and it helped me settle into my new surroundings faster than I expected. One friend in particular was a guy named Chucky. We connected for a few reasons. We loved sports. We loved video games. And we lived five minutes from each other. By the time we entered high school, it was quite common for Chucky to come over to my place after school, or I would go over to his. We became great friends.

Chucky started life under unfortunate circumstances. Both of his parents were substance abusers and it caused utter chaos and disorder in the home. Eventually, child services stepped in and decided to find a new place for him and his two younger brothers to live. By the time I met Chucky, he and his brothers had been living with a lovely foster couple for more than five years. His foster parents provided the essentials and safety that the children so desperately needed (remember in terms of core needs, these are critical).

Chucky's foster parents also happened to be of Dutch heritage, so the extent of Chucky's ethnic eating experience before he met me was black pepper on his mashed potatoes. The first time Chucky had Indian food at our place, his eyes were the size of naan breads. He was totally enthralled with new flavors and spices he had never tasted before, all in a swirl of flatbreads and buttery rice. He became so obsessed with Indian food that sometimes in class I would look over at him and he would be holding up a strip of paper with the name of his new favorite Indian dish at the time. Once the sign caught my attention he would then ask if he could come over to my place after school and stay for dinner. He was shameless in his obsession, and I loved it. His cheeky demeanor and warmth meant the world to me, especially while I was settling into a new school and city.

Unfortunately, Chucky's rough upbringing caused him tremendous pain. Pain that eventually caught up with him. In high school, it's common for childhood issues to rise to the surface, and this was the case for Chucky. The worst of it came right before spring break in 10th grade. A few months prior, Chucky's foster parents informed him that they were retiring from foster care and were actively looking for a new family for him and his brothers to live with. Chucky did his best to roll with the punches, but it was clear that he was hurt and facing a lot of fear around the situation.

It was the Friday before spring break. I woke up and went to take a shower. On my way into the bathroom, I heard a strange noise from downstairs. I went into the kitchen and saw my dad sobbing. I asked him what was wrong, and through his tears, he told me that the night before, Chucky had taken his own life.

Unsure how to manage the news, I stood still, had a brief conversation with my dad to get some details, and then went back upstairs and took my shower. I will never forget that day. It was no ordinary school day as parents, pastors, counselors, teachers, and peers surrounded our class, and really our entire school, to help us through the difficult news. This was one of the most pivotal moments in my life.

Early in the grieving process, I made a conscious decision that I would not let the pain of the situation get to me. That is a dangerous decision for any 14-year-old. At that stage of life, the patterns for how we manage emotions, pain, and the like are still being formed. Making a decision like this at such a critical time makes for some pretty deep pattern formation. Not letting the pain get the best of me was one thing, but I more or less ignored the pain altogether.

That's not to say I didn't grieve. I spent most nights praying and processing my thoughts to God. I often prayed that God would use our awful circumstances to make something good come out of it. But while I was handling some aspects of the loss, I was bound and determined to avoid the pain.

I became most aware of this when my 15th birthday came around. My parents asked me what I'd like to do to celebrate. I told them, "Nothing." I wasn't interested in doing anything celebratory. Maybe a meal together as a family. That was enough for me. My mom pointedly asked, "Does this have anything to do with losing Chucky?" to which I abruptly responded, "No." Yeah, right.

I know what it's like to suppress pain. To stuff it away and pretend it's not there. We tell ourselves that it will be easier and cleaner if we just avoid it. Little do we know that by doing this, we're creating geysers beneath the surface that will eventually blow.

Of all the men I've worked with over the years, the one thing they undoubtedly have in common is unprocessed pain from their past. Without fail. For some it's major, and they find that being in a safe environment where they can finally work through the pain is a game-changer. For others, it's minor but still has a significant impact.

If you want to be a healthy man you must be able to process pain. You don't have to enjoy it. You don't have to like it. But you have to do it. If you don't, then based on my experience and research findings,[39] here are some of the side effects that you may experience:

- Reduced capacity for joy

- Lack of fulfillment in life

- Disinterest in meaningful relationships

- Sudden outbursts of emotion that "come from nowhere"

- Fear of intimacy

- Fear of failure

- Fear of rejection

- Fear of disappointment

- Hyper-cautious decision-making

- Feeling on edge all the time

- Long-term addiction

- Tyrannical leadership style at home or work

- Uncontrollable anger/rage

- Disjointed spirituality

- Surface-level spirituality

Do any of these sound familiar at all? If they do, you may have some pain to work through. One of the tricky things about pain is that it's not always a bad thing. In fact, pain can be quite useful in the right situation.

If my conclusion from Chucky's passing is that I should avoid building meaningful friendships because it hurts too much, that is poor discernment on my part. It's a damaging response to my pain.

On the contrary, if the pain from Chucky's passing lets me know that there are many things in life I cannot control, and I need to make every moment of my life count, then my pain has helped me. It will prevent me from wasting my life and taking things for granted. It's my responsibility to face the pain, process it, and ensure I am drawing healthy conclusions. Without this level of discernment, pain will wreak havoc on my relationships, spirituality, career, finances, mental health, and overall sense of well-being.

Being able to discern pain's role in any given situation comes with time. That is really a more advanced skill. Most men I meet in my program need to start by simply learning to work through pain, both in the present and from their past.

The good news is that you've already been taught how to process pain in a healthy way. Remember the validation cycle? It's the same application for pain. First, label the pain. Then digest it. Then take time to process it until you reach a place of understanding.

Taking time to process is critical. For guys, it can look like working out, sports, talking to friends, journaling, creative outlets like songwriting, poetry, dance, etc. There is no right or wrong here, but pain must be processed and, generally, that involves something tactile, talkative, or creative.

Once you've worked through your pain, you will begin to reach an understanding. This means comprehending *why* you felt pain and reaching a place internally where you can exercise Principles #1 and #2. You are aware of what you can control (and what you cannot) and are ready to respond to the pain in a useful way.

In my experience with Chucky, it took me a while to get to this place. When I learned about the importance of validating emotions, working through geysers, and processing pain, I realized I had major work to do regarding this incident. For me, it meant identifying that the loss of a dear friend hurt. It meant acknowledging that I felt betrayed because he left me. And then it took time, talking, and tears. Crying about it felt cathartic. It meant that my heart was feeling again, and that is a good thing.

When you are processing pain:

1. **Build self-awareness** of your pain. Learn to identify moments when you feel pain and pay attention to your natural responses. Are they helping or hurting? Make adjustments as needed.

2. **Find outlets** and use them often. Do not wait for pain to go away—proactively work through it. I gave a few examples above, but here they are again: working out, sports, talking to friends, creative outlets like songwriting, poetry, dance.

3. **Involve journaling** in your process. Remember, journaling is our tried, tested, and true method for validating emotions and reaching a place of understanding. This is essential for emotional fitness and working through your past.

4. **Involve others.** I have a few go-to contacts that I reach out to when I'm in pain or going through major life challenges. Having others to chat with is great, not only for verbal processing but

also for thwarting any loneliness that might creep in and compound the pain.

Let's tie everything together now. Your past makes an impact on your present and your future. There are aspects of your past where you need healing—ultimately, areas where your core needs were unmet by your parents or parental figures. The most notable parts of your past that require healing are called geysers. These are major incidents that caused damaging conclusions and unprocessed pain. The pain of these situations must be processed and worked through using the validation cycle. Once you have absorbed this, you are ready for the next phase.

Man's Supreme Solution

If you get nothing else from the book, I hope you will at least grasp the content we are about to uncover. There are few subjects with more significance to your well-being than forgiveness.

To give you an idea, Jesus said, "If you do not forgive men their trespasses, neither will your Father forgive your trespasses" (Matthew 6:15).[40] Paul makes a similar statement to the church of Colossae, declaring that they "must forgive" as Christ forgave them.[41] Forgiveness is not an option. It is a commandment.

There is a myriad of misconceptions about forgiveness, so before we delve any further, let's set the record straight on a few things. For starters, we must always address two aspects of forgiveness: justice and offense.

Forgiveness has little to do with justice, and much to do with offense. In other words, forgiveness has little to do with whether or not someone's behavior was right or wrong. Forgiveness deals with offense, a matter of the heart. If someone has taken offense, whether it's for good reasons or bad, forgiveness will be necessary. Justice has little to do with the equation. The question is *not*, "Do they deserve forgiveness?" The question is, "Did I take offense?" If you did, then you need to forgive.

THE LAST RELAPSE

Let me give you an example. Johnny, Robby, and Bobby are friends. They always spend time at each other's places and have fun together. Robby needs to return an Xbox controller to Johnny's place so one day he swings by to drop it off. Johnny invites him in and they wind up hanging out for a couple of hours. Bobby catches wind that his two buddies hung out without him and he is hurt. He thinks they're trying to edge him out and begins to wonder if he's the third wheel in this bro-triangle.

Did Johnny and Robby do anything wrong? No. Does Bobby need to forgive them? Yes, because he has taken offense. In a situation like this, they can patch things up pretty quickly with a conversation. It doesn't have to be some lavish forgiveness process, but do you see that even though no one did anything wrong, forgiveness is still necessary because offense was taken? Remember this. It will become very important.

Secondly, forgiveness does not justify someone else's misbehavior. If you do a Google search of "murder trial forgiveness" you will see many touching stories where family members of the murdered individual have chosen to publicly forgive the murderer. These are some of the best demonstrations we have of forgiveness as the Bible instructs, regardless of circumstance. But let's make something very clear: The family's choice to forgive the murderer does not make murder okay. Far from it. The choice to forgive is the family's decision to alleviate the offense and not hold it against the murderer.

When Jesus says you must forgive, He is not saying you must be a pushover and tolerate inappropriate behavior. Instead, he is saying that when people treat you badly the best way to move on with your life is to forgive. If you carry that offense, it will not serve you and it removes your ability to be forgiven for your own wrongdoings. You don't have to approve of what they did, but forgive them, and move on with your life.

Lastly, forgiveness is not the same as reconciliation. Forgiveness happens in your inner circle. It is apart from any relationship. Someone may have hurt you badly. You have to forgive them, but you do not have to restore the relationship. If your girlfriend cheats on you, you must forgive her.

Forgiving her does not mean you get back together. Forgiving doesn't even mean you need to talk with her. Forgiveness resides in your inner circle because an offense took place. That is all.

Who to Forgive?

Forgiveness really is the conscious decision to remit. It is not an external process. It is internal. Forgiveness says, "I'm not going to hold this against you anymore." It requires tremendous bravery to forgive. Weak men gain strength from grudges. They would rather find solace in how to exact revenge than face the offense head-on.

Forgiveness is man's supreme solution. It's the best way to reconcile the challenging parts of your past and to release the futile parts that were holding you back. I'm going to show you how to exact forgiveness effectively and efficiently, but I want to make sure you really grasp these concepts. Forgiveness is not just a matter of saying the words "I forgive you." It's a release at a heart level that says, "I will not hold this against you anymore. I'm moving on."

In general, there are three different categories where forgiveness needs to be applied:

1. Others
2. God
3. Yourself

Others is the most obvious. Someone else causes offense, you need to forgive them. Plain and simple. Let's be honest, we get opportunities to forgive others on a daily basis. The world would be a simpler place to live if it weren't for other people.

The idea of forgiving God is more controversial. "If God is perfect, then why would I need to forgive Him?" you may protest. Remember, forgiveness has little to do with whether or not right or wrong was done. All we're asking is: Was offense taken? And you know what, people take offense at

God all the time. Unanswered prayers, unexpected trials, empty promises, world hunger, natural disasters, the list goes on. There is a plethora of reasons to take offense at God. Some are valid, none are recommended. If offense is taken, forgiveness is necessary.

If this sounds strange to you, then I'm glad. It should be jarring. You do not understand forgiveness until you understand that there will be times in life where you need to forgive God. This is why I wanted to first address that forgiveness has little to do with justice and much to do with offense. God never does wrong and I'm not suggesting He does. Right or wrong is not the operative aspect of forgiveness. The only question you need to ask yourself is, "Did *I* take offense?"

Lastly, and arguably most importantly for 21st-century men, is forgiving yourself. When I was working through my pornography addiction, I thought I was one of the few who was unusually hard on myself. It took me a long time to be able to forgive myself for what I had done. As I started to work with more men, I discovered how common this issue really is. So many men out there cannot forgive themselves for the mistakes of their past. I mentioned previously that man's inability to process his pain is one of the greatest stumbling blocks to his success. The inability to forgive oneself is of equal if not greater measure.

These days, I only take on a small number of one-on-one clients because my schedule is filled with other priorities. My team handles a lot of the one-on-one work and we've created several courses and programs to help reach more men who need my services. However, I still take some time for one-on-one clients as I find these sessions to be very rewarding.

I recently worked with a client who reached the subject of forgiving himself and found it extremely challenging. Let me explain. Jim is the kind of guy you instantly get along with. He is warm and outgoing and has a magnetism about him. So it was no surprise when I found out that he was a high-level executive for a burgeoning tech company.

Jim married young, experienced early success in his career, and had a great life. Unfortunately, Jim was cheating on his wife with escorts. Regularly. He eventually got caught and was repentant. Astonishingly, Jim's wife forgave him and agreed to stand by his side while he worked through his stuff.

Jim did exactly that, completing a program that focused on healing from sex and porn addiction. He became the poster boy for recovery in his church community. Everyone knew him as the guy who turned his life around against all odds. Since their marriage survived the trauma, they became a well-respected couple in the community.

After a couple of years of being well, Jim started to slip back into his old patterns. When he reached out to me, he was almost embarrassed to talk about his situation—he was broken, defeated, and utterly hopeless. The good news here was that Jim had not gone as far as hiring escorts again. The issues were primarily concerning porn and masturbation. Not to belittle the issues by any means, but relatively speaking, this was a silver lining.

I was nervous to work with Jim. Most of the guys who reach out to me have never sought help before. It's a bit different to work with someone who already "knows all the stuff." I soon discovered that my own insecurities were ill-founded, as week after week, Jim marveled at the lessons he learned in our system that consisted of principles and tools he had never learned before in a porn recovery context.

Everything was going great until we reached the subject of forgiveness. Jim could forgive everyone who was involved in some of his most significant geysers. While his wife provided incredible support along his journey, she had done a few things over the years that Jim had to forgive her for. No problem.

In reflecting back on his childhood and some of the areas where his core needs weren't met, he was able to identify some of his parents' shortcomings and forgive them too. Not a huge deal.

Interestingly, Jim had some unforgiveness toward God. He felt upset that God was allowing him to struggle again after his breakthrough, and that God didn't intervene and stop him from falling back. Pretty understandable. Let me take a moment again to clarify that God did no wrong in this scenario, but Jim took offense to God's (lack of) actions.

After working through the first two categories, forgiveness of others and of God, we arrived at the third category: forgiveness of self. As we dug in, it became increasingly clear that Jim still had not forgiven himself for cheating on his wife all those years ago. Time does not heal all wounds if you don't have the right tools. We talked it through, and Jim gained some perspective as a result. The session wrapped up and we moved on to the next parts of the program.

One of my priorities when I'm with a client is to get to the truth. This is harder than you'd think. People often say things that sound reasonable or logical, even though they are not completely honest. Humans are SO good at lying to themselves to avoid the truth because sometimes, the truth hurts. And we all know how pain is usually handled if we aren't taught differently. Understanding this dynamic, I've learned to pay attention to the many micro-expressions and micro-movements that pop up when someone is hiding, even in a virtual environment.

On a call a few sessions later, I could tell that Jim was not fully present. I decided to investigate. Sometimes, these little clues of body language and tone are like threads that you have to pull on gently, little by little, to see what else is there.

Jim started talking about the pressure he felt to impress the two main father figures in his life: his own father and his father-in-law. These are reasonable pressures, but the way they were impacting Jim was totally unreasonable. He was becoming obsessed with his investments in the stock market, he was overworking, and he was emotionally disconnected. Hence, the sense of absence on this call.

As we dug in a bit more, Jim said that his 32-year-old brother-in-law just got a huge promotion and it was bothering him because Jim felt he hadn't been as successful at his age. It made Jim wonder what his life would have been like if he had never slept with escorts. How things could be different and better if he hadn't got wrapped up in pornography. He simply could not forgive himself for what he had done, knowing that it hindered him so much in his present life and would likely do so in the future.

That sounds a lot like regret, doesn't it? Remember, regret is looking at your past without compassion. It robs you of joy in the present and hope for the future. Jim had no joy in the present even though his life was on track. He was so caught up in his past that he lost sight of the good things right in front of him. And his future felt bleak because this was "always going to hang over his head." In his mind, nothing would ever be enough to overcome his previous errors. As we'll see in Chapter 9, Jim's errors could be overcome, including his past struggles with sexual misbehavior.

This is what unforgiveness toward yourself looks like. It is the inability to let go of a mistake you made. It blocks you from fully accepting what has happened in your past and accepting who you are in the present as a result. It's the voice that says, "Think about how much better your life would be if you hadn't done that." Every single client I work with has to forgive himself for the mistakes of his past. No ifs, and, or buts. We must all go through this process to become healthy, emotionally fit, and free men. You included.

How to Forgive

How do we forgive properly? Most people's idea of forgiveness is pathetic because we are taught as young kids when we fight with our siblings or peers to look at each other and say, "I forgive you," and then move on. I'm afraid that doesn't work when you're an adult.

Remember that biblical forgiveness is not a cerebral exercise, it is one of the heart. Therefore, the only way we know forgiveness has taken place is a change in the heart. Simply praying a prayer or repeating a few words does not guarantee forgiveness has taken place. This is why we needed to work through all the other layers first before reaching this subject. Building emotional fitness, identifying wounds, and processing pain are all tools that operate on a heart level so that when the time comes to forgive, we are productive.

There are four steps to biblical forgiveness:

1. Identify
2. Specify
3. Release
4. Restore

We're going to go through each step in more detail, using a personal story of mine as an example to demonstrate each step.

In the previous chapter, I mentioned that my mom's way of expressing love was not the way I needed it. For me, words of affirmation and time spent together go a long way, and my mom is relatively quiet and happily keeps to herself. I didn't realize how much this impacted me until I was talking to a counselor one day. It suddenly dawned on me that I had felt neglected by her for most of my life. That was a painful, but significant, discovery.

I'm going to use this story as we go through the four steps, and then you'll see why this became so significant for my freedom from pornography.

Identify is to simply pinpoint the areas where forgiveness is needed. Do you need to forgive others, God, or yourself? Or perhaps a combination of the three? This first step in forgiveness is to simply pinpoint where the offense has taken place and who is involved.

In my situation, it identified my mother as someone who contributed to wounding and pain from my past. It's important here that I didn't just say, "I grew up feeling neglected." That is labeling the emotion, which is good, but it does not identify who needs to be forgiven. Step 1 must clarify the people involved—remember, sometimes it will be yourself.

Specify is Step 2. It is also the most overlooked step. Specifying the offense can be challenging, especially when you are forgiving those you love. It's not always comfortable acknowledging that someone we love has wronged us, but it is necessary. The process of forgiveness should be carried out privately anyway. Hopefully that makes it easier to be specific.

If you do not specify the offense, you cannot truly forgive. Let's say that you and I are going to a basketball game and I, being the nice guy I am, offer to pay for our tickets. Before I buy, you do a bit of research and find a good deal on StubHub and it says you only have five minutes left or the deal expires. I run to my computer to make the purchase but cannot find the deal. The algorithm has hidden it.

Instead, I give you my credit card details so that you can make the purchase before time runs out. You punch in the info, and right as you're checking out, you receive a prompt: Would you like to buy a jersey to wear to the game? You think about it for a second and then think, "Sathiya won't mind. Let's go for it."

Now let's say the credit card number I gave you is for a card that I never use. I don't even check the statements because the balance is usually zero. Knowing this, I ask you, "How much did the tickets come to?" so that I can pay off the balance. You tell me, "Oh, the tickets, they were $50." You don't bother to tell me about the jersey because, technically, I only asked about the cost of the tickets. Well played.

A few months go by and I find out that my credit card balance has racked up a bunch of high-interest charges because of an unpaid balance. How can this be? Because there was unpaid debt. I paid off $50 for the tickets, but I did not pay off the amount for the jersey. I cannot pay off a debt that I am unaware of.

Similarly, when you forgive, you must be specific, upfront, and honest about what you are forgiving the person for. It is not enough to say, "I forgive you for hurting my feelings." That's too vague. Unspecific forgiveness yields minimal freedom.

With my mother, it was identifying that I had felt neglected by her. To be more specific, I felt deficient in the intimacy category of core needs. For essentials and safety, our first two core needs, she was phenomenal, and my needs were met. In the intimacy category, there was a deficiency, and this is where I needed to forgive her.

Now let me add one more point of clarification. When you specify, you must focus on the actions of a person, not on the person themselves. Here's what I mean. I did not forgive my mom for "being a bad mother." I did not forgive my mom for "being neglectful." I forgave her for neglecting me. Do you see the difference? When you specify, you should always be focused on the actions of the individual, not on their character. If you are forgiving someone for a component of their character, then you are not forgiving them. You are covertly judging them. Focus on the actions.

Release is the most essential step. This is the part we all associate with forgiveness. It's the part where you let go of the offense. It's a clearing of the debt. The operative phrase of Step 3 is ,"You owe me nothing." There are no outstanding balances. Nothing has to be paid up or made up. The slate is clean. Sometimes my clients reach this step and realize they are not ready to go through with forgiveness. That is a good thing. We don't want insincere forgiveness. We then revisit the previous stages of geysers, processing pain, and so on until they're ready. When the time comes, it's well worth the work.

In my experience with my mom, this step was massive. Remember that I was in my mid-20s, and I was forgiving her for something that had been going on since day one. This is a dynamic I had combatted my entire life. A dynamic that led me down some dark paths. The feelings of neglect from the mother figure in my life essentially drove me to find female attention elsewhere—chasing girls and a lot of pornography.

Now I am saying, "Mom, you owe me nothing." It means I can't use it as an excuse for my bad behavior anymore. It means that if the dynamic between us stays the exact same, I will move on and not be held up by it. Step 3 was not easy for me but it was necessary, and I can tell you firsthand that when you reach this place, there is no feeling like it. It's as if a huge weight has been lifted off your shoulders. You'll breathe easier and see more clearly. It is glorious.

Restore is the fourth and final step. This is another commonly overlooked area in the process, but we want to end on a high note. Forgiveness should be honoring and seek the best interests of *everyone* involved. Step 4 is the part where you get to pray a blessing over the people you've forgiven. If the wound runs deep, this is often difficult, but it is essential. If you aren't willing to do this step, then I have reason to question whether or not you're doing this at a heart level. A changed heart *will* be open to blessing the people you've forgiven.

With my mom, the biggest key for me was that I let go of my expectations for her to change. Restoring meant that I was praying my mom would become more of the person God made her to be, not more of the person I wanted her to be. It meant blessing her timidness and seeing the value in it, without any animosity or resentment. It was appreciating the ways she did meet my needs as a child and choosing to highlight those instead of dwelling on the deficiencies. This final step is just as healing as the previous three.

The beautiful thing here is that giving my mom permission to be more like herself gave me more permission to be more like myself. I was free to get my core needs met in new and healthier ways. My inner self was no longer longing for that intimacy from my mom in the same way. I was freed to find better and healthier options like meaningful friendships and a deeper relationship with God.

When I finally reached this place where I was able to forgive and release my mom, something shifted in my internal world. Remember that self-awareness is paramount for internal health. My self-awareness radar could tell that a change had taken place. I walked out of my counselor's office a new man. There was no turning back now.

That month was February 2016, and since then I have not looked at pornography. Forgiving my mom turned out to be the final nail in the coffin of my addiction, ending a 15-year battle. I cannot guarantee the same results for those who go through the forgiveness process I've outlined, but I can guarantee results of some kind. Authentic forgiveness is always beneficial.

A few final thoughts. Remember that forgiveness is a process. While I had a pretty major moment in my counselor's office forgiving my mom, I also had many smaller moments in the years leading up to that day. It took time to reach a place of full forgiveness.

Also, when you finally decide to forgive someone that you have had a grudge against for a long time, you don't need to call them up and let them know you've forgiven them. You *can* do this, but it isn't necessary. If you are forgiving people for something that they know was wrong and has clearly caused a rift between the two of you, then calling them to patch things up could be wise. Maybe a friend cheated you out of a bunch of money and never paid you back. Letting him know that you forgive him could be really powerful.

On the other hand, if you're forgiving someone for an offense they may not even be aware of, do not call them up afterward and tell them you forgave them. It will make things worse. "Hey, Mom, just wanted to let you know I have forgiven you for neglecting me as a child."

"What?!"

Don't do it. It just doesn't work.

Finally, I want to leave you with an often-quoted adage that nicely ties everything together: Unforgiveness is like drinking rat poison and expecting the other person to die.

This life is too short to hold grudges. If you're looking for long-term health, success, and freedom, you will need to get really good at forgiving those who offend you. Forgiveness is one of the most powerful tools you will learn in this book, and it is certainly the most effective way to move from your past.

The workbook (www.sathiyasam.com/recoveryworkbook) has a cheat sheet that summarizes the steps of forgiveness and provides our proprietary "Forgiveness Script" to walk you step-by-step through the process. Once this is complete, the fun begins.

Section 3

REGAINING YOUR CONFIDENCE

CHAPTER 6

Building a Bulletproof Identity

You now know most of the story about Chucky, my high school friend who died by suicide when he was only 15 years old. Chucky left behind three siblings—an older sister, and two younger brothers. When I spent time at Chucky's place, I noticed he and his younger brothers interacted differently from how I interacted with mine. They would often tease and taunt each other until one of them wanted to fight, and then they'd wrestle it out. My brother and I were good Indian kids—we fought over who got to play Xbox first after school through a best-of-three round of rock, paper, scissors.

When Chucky heard he and his brothers would be moving to a new home, he took out his fear and frustration on his brothers. At times, I was caught off guard by how he treated them. Sometimes he was verbally abusive, other times it was physical. I only witnessed it a few times, but when I did, I didn't know what to do. All I knew was that Chucky was frustrated and his brothers were getting the brunt of it. When he passed away and

I reflected on some of these experiences, it was obvious that Chucky was hurting and did not know how to handle it.

About five years after Chucky passed, I found myself going through an unusually challenging time. Spiritually, I had made a new commitment to God but I was still figuring the ins and outs of this new life. Vocationally, I was confused. I was in the final year of my degree and could not tell if I should further pursue becoming a psychiatrist or give it all up to become a pastor. Relationally, I was about 14 months past my first breakup and still could not fully get over my ex. Socially, I found out that my best friend and my ex had started dating. As a result, mentally and emotionally, I was a wreck.

I am fairly resilient, so even when life is a swirl of catastrophes, I find ways to keep my head above water. This situation was no exception until I got news about Clay.

Clay was the next oldest brother in Chucky's family. He was a year younger than me. I never got to know Clay much beyond occasionally playing video games at his place and small conversations here and there. When Chucky passed, I remember thinking that the crushing pain would make it clear to all Chucky's loved ones, friends, and family, that suicide wasn't the answer to pain. I was wrong. Clay tragically died by suicide as well, about five and a half years after Chucky. When I got the news, I was stunned. Not again. How? Why?

When Chucky passed, I was sad. When Clay passed, I was mad. Throw in an existential crisis and some relationship drama, and it was just too much.

While this season of my life was not easy, I often look back in awe of God's timing. Had I not committed my life to Him at this point, I'm not sure how I would have responded. But having God by my side through this challenging time was my lifeline, one that I am extremely grateful for. When people close to you decide that life is not worth living, it forces you to ask deep existential questions yourself. When I was faced with these questions, they wound up being pivotal in my recovery journey.

Two Critical Questions

It's human nature to wonder why we are on this planet. Curiosity starts at a young age as we try to find out how life works and where we fit in. Most children at some point reach that annoying phase where they ask "Why?" to *everything possible.* They are not trying to be annoying (usually). On the surface, they are trying to understand the mechanics of life. On the inside, they are wondering where they fit into the picture.

In many ways, we never outgrow these curiosities. We continually ask ourselves how life works and where we fit in. Questions that persist through the different stages of life are fundamental. They must be explored and our answers must be developed. If they are not, life can be confusing, unstable, and unsafe. This is the reason why every man must be able to answer two critical questions.

Firstly, "Who are you?"

This is a loaded question. One that is not easy to answer. You may have an answer, but I guarantee that if we did enough poking around we would find some holes in it. This question is too weighty, too fundamental to simply have a rote response. It must be seriously pondered, wrestled with, and chewed on. It cannot be flippant, or dependent upon external matters. It has to be anchored, permanent, and consistent.

Who are you? What makes you the person you are? Why are you valuable? How do you know if you have value in the first place? These are questions we must be able to answer as men. We cannot simply wonder about them our whole lives. Because if you can't answer this question for yourself, then someone else will answer it for you. Social media, marketing messages, peers, mentors, leaders, bosses, pastors, teachers, friends, and family have no problem telling you who you should be. How you should live your life. The right way to do this, or the wrong way to do that. If you don't know who you are, someone else will tell you who to be.

Man's inability to properly answer this question is the leading cause of moral failure, career breakdown, mindset limitations, physical limitations—the list goes on. The question, "Who are you?" is paramount. Essential. Fun-da-men-tal.

It comes with a sequel that is of equal importance. As you wrestle and work through "Who are you?" maybe you'll reach an answer. You might get there. And when you do, there's a second question of equal importance, "Who told you?"

You see, the person who answers the first question makes all the difference. Are you answering it? Is your mom answering it? God? Satan? We have to know. It's not enough to simply answer the first question. We must then be able to clearly and correctly answer the second.

"Who told you?" is an important question because the answer will cause you to question your response to the first question. You may feel one day like you're on top of the world and you know exactly who you are. You have life figured out and nothing can stop you. Only to find out a few days, weeks, months, or years later that there is more to life than you realized. You may start to question how you answered, "Who are you?"

How you question it will depend a lot on the source of your answer to "Who told you?" If it was a reliable source, it may be able to withstand the doubt and confusion that comes in your search for identity. If the source is unreliable, then how you answered question one will break down in the face of resistance.

The best example we have of this biblically is in Luke's account of Jesus's baptism. The time comes for Jesus to be baptized, and as the prophecies confirmed, it would be done by John the Baptist. This baptism was no ordinary experience. The Holy Spirit descends on Jesus in bodily form like a dove, the heavens part, and a voice from Heaven boldly proclaims, "You are My beloved Son; in You I am well pleased."[42]

Jesus receives an identity statement as He is launched into full-time ministry. Not that Jesus didn't already know who He was, but we all long for public affirmation from our father. The identity statement that Jesus receives is powerful. The Father does not say, "You are a miracle-worker," or,

"You are going to make history." The essence of the statement is that Jesus is a son, and the Father is pleased with Him.

This is significant because it tells us that Jesus's identity was founded on relationship, not activity. If the statement was, "You are a miracle-worker," then Jesus's identity and value is based on His ability to perform miracles. If the statement was, "You are a good teacher," then His value is determined by His ability to teach. The statement here is that Jesus is a son. Therefore, His value is based on a relationship, and to be more precise, a relationship dynamic that cannot change. You cannot change who your father is. You can change the functionality of the relationship, you can run away, but you cannot change the fact that your father is your father.

So these words, "You are my Son, in you I am well pleased," are a big deal, because these are words that we all long to hear from our fathers and they comprise the most fundamentally sound identity statement ever spoken or written. Men are dying to hear these words from their own fathers. They simply want to know that at their absolute core, they are enough. Fathers are supposed to communicate this to their sons. Yet often the message received is the opposite. Men are told they can only be enough if they look a certain way, perform better in school, achieve in sports, etc. More on this shortly.

The point here is that Jesus receives a weighty identity statement from God the Father Himself. Remember our questions: "Who are you?" and "Who told you?" As far as answers go, Jesus got the absolute best.

If Jesus's peers said, "You're the Son of God. He must be so pleased with you." That's not much of an identity statement. They're true words, but they don't cut to the core. If a government official saw Jesus perform a miracle and said, "Wow, you must be the Son of God. Surely God is pleased with you." Well, that means something. But it's hardly an identity statement. In the Garden of Gethsemane, I can't imagine Jesus referencing these kinds of experiences to keep himself encouraged. They would be nice, in theory, but they wouldn't qualify as core identity statements.

The source matters. If you can answer the first question, that's great. But you must also be able to answer, "Who told you?" Is it your peers, leaders, teachers, preachers, friends, family, colleagues, or superiors that are telling you who you are? Because if it is, what happens when they're gone? Or if they change their mind? Are you sure you want to hang your identity hat on their kind words?

In Luke 3, Jesus gets baptized. In Luke 4, Jesus is led by the Spirit into the wilderness where He fasts for 40 days and is tempted by the devil. Then the devil says to Him, "If you are the Son of God, tell this stone to become bread."[43]

Most read this is as: the devil tempted Jesus to turn stones into bread.

Wrong.

That is not the only temptation Jesus faces here.

The primary temptation is to violate His identity statement.

Notice how the devil opens his remark: IF you are the Son of God. Jesus is being tempted to prove His identity when it was already proven at His baptism. This is how the enemy works. He plants doubt. Makes you question and wonder. Did that really happen? Is that really true? What if…?

This is why the way you answer question two matters so much. If Jesus's core identity statement came from his peers, He must fight much harder to ward off the temptations of the devil. But note Jesus's response:

"Man must not live on bread alone but on every word that comes from the mouth of God."[44]

Absolutely brilliant! Jesus uses scripture to show the enemy that He will live by *every word of God,* including the words that were spoken to Him on His baptism day. Therefore, He does not need to prove that He is the Son of God—He does not need to turn stones into bread.

Jesus demonstrates the solidification of identity in the face of temptation. Whether we like it or not, we all function out of our core identity. The beliefs, views, and perceptions of ourselves that we carry drive our decisions, actions, and thoughts on a regular basis. A distorted identity will always lead to a distorted lifestyle. There are men of God all around the world who long to live godly lives and cannot. Again and again, they fall into temptation, they wander, they struggle. And most conclude something is wrong with them. It's a lost cause. What's the point?

Most of them simply have a broken sense of identity. When I reflect on how both Chucky's and Clay's lives ended, I realize that neither of them had much self-worth. The messages they received growing up from their biological parents were that they were worthless. Unlovable. Fundamentally flawed. When you believe these things, the value of life diminishes quickly. I would never want to oversimplify a subject as complex as suicide, so hear me clearly: An identity issue is not necessarily the full explanation for suicide or other situations of that nature. However, in my opinion, it is one of the most important layers of Chucky's and Clay's rather complicated lives that ended far too soon.

You may recall that the belief system of an individual functions similarly to that of an operating system for a computer. It's the wiring that tells the hardware how to perform. Even the greatest of hardware is inhibited by a defective operating system. Your core belief system is no different.

Jesus did not live a flawless life simply because He behaved perfectly. Jesus lived flawlessly because He *believed* perfectly. Every word that came from His Father's mouth, He believed at His absolute core, and as a result it perfectly shaped every facet of His life. His immaculate core belief system led Him to live a perfect life despite betrayal, beatings, controversy, criticism, and death. Most of us cannot endure one of these things without a meltdown.

Jesus shows a better way. When we can answer these two critical questions properly and authentically, we can significantly improve our sense of self. Let's dig in.

The Value Debacle

Reasoning

What makes you valuable? Why are you of any worth to anyone? How can you be sure?

These are questions that every man asks himself, consciously and subconsciously. They must be answered, and if they are answered incorrectly, our sense of value and purpose becomes fragile and eventually fragmented. What makes a person valuable? I mean, let's really think about it. Is it their skill? Talent? Personality? Appearance?

If you grew up in church, I know exactly what you're thinking. "God's thoughts about me make me valuable. That's all that matters." Nice try. I'm not letting you off the hook that easily.

Here's the thing. All Christians know how to answer this question theoretically. We all know the Sunday School answers or the catchy one-liners from a sermon that our pastors created that help us remember the truth. But the danger here is that they teach us how to answer questions correctly instead of teaching us how to correctly *reason* so that we can derive the correct answers on our own.

You see, your answer to these questions matters, but how you reason matters more. If you are spoon-fed the right answers your whole life, you are robbed of the maturity and strength that comes from learning to reason on your own. This does not satisfy the fundamental question of our hearts: "Why am I valuable?"

That's why Jesus was upset when he told the disciples to "watch and beware the leaven of the Pharisees and Sadducees" (Matthew 16:6)[45] and the disciples figured, "Oh dang we forgot to bring bread for the trip." Jesus was upset by their response because of how they reasoned. His words back to them were, "You of little faith, why do you *reason* among yourselves that you have brought no bread?" (Emphasis added.) In other words, He's not upset by the incorrect answer. He's upset about how they got there.

I spoke at an event recently where, after my presentation, we opened up a Q&A. These days I enjoy the Q&As just as much as speaking. I find that after I've shared my story about struggling with pornography addiction for 15 years and discussing all the taboo subjects that come along with it, people are ready to start asking questions they've always wanted to ask but never felt safe to do so before. In this particular session, I had spoken on thought life specifically concerning sexuality, an area that we'll be covering shortly. The question came in, "How do you deal with the root of rejection?"

The common response to this question in church settings is to "pray more," "walk in God's acceptance of you," "understand that God made you acceptable." These answers come from well-meaning places, but on their own, they are useless, even if they are true statements. Why? Because usually, they come without an explanation. There's no reasoning behind them.

So I replied, "I cannot answer your question. Only you can. But let me help. The truth is that you are accepted. You don't have to believe it yet. You don't have to perfectly live it out, yet. First, you must accept in your mind that it is true even if your heart doesn't believe it. Then, you must answer the question, 'Why?'"

The disciples knew how to spit back what Jesus told them, or the answers that they had learned along the way. When you start your faith journey, you are measured by how well you can answer questions. You are measured by knowledge. To reach greater levels of maturity, you must be measured by your ability to reason. That means sometimes you will get things wrong. That's okay. It is less about getting correct answers and more about understanding the process that leads to them.

What does this have to do with the value question? Absolutely everything.

You may answer that what gives you value is that you are a child of God. Or that you are talented. Perhaps it's your riches and wealth. Maybe it's your calling and your sense of purpose. You might think that what gives you value is having dependents in your life—children, elderly parents, relatives with disabilities, etc. Maybe you derive your value from how many followers you have on social media.

None of these responses is inherently right or wrong. But what is the reasoning behind the response? A professional model is valuable because of his or her appearance. That's what gives them professional value. So what happens to a model if their appearance diminishes because of age or unforeseen circumstances? Are they still valuable?

A father is valuable because he provides a home, food, and care to his wife and children. That gives him value. So what happens if the husband and wife split up? What happens if the father makes a mistake parenting one of his kids? What happens when his kids grow up and no longer depend on his provision? Does his value change?

You see, answering these questions is only half the battle. It's how you reason that really matters. If the way you reason is superficial, externally driven, or unscriptural, you are primed for a very up-and-down life. When things go well, you'll be on top of the world. When things go south, you will cower in a corner holding on for dear life. That might be a bit dramatic, but people who struggle often with their sense of self-worth and sense of belonging cannot answer the value question with much substance. What they say is superficial rhetoric that sounds right, feels good, and brings no inner transformation. Our reasoning must be solid.

Balancing Act

The value conversation is really a value equation, and the value equation always balances. You cannot distribute value to the lives of others if you do not have any value yourself. On a regular basis, I see people trying to encourage others through their struggles, offering advice, and saying the right things. This is an innate response when we become aware of someone else's challenges. It's a good thing. But you can always tell when someone is providing encouragement with authority—when they intrinsically know they are valuable and not simply saying the right things—because they are able to bestow value to another person.

Similarly, the person without authority is one who knows all these things in their head yet struggles to truly live them out in their hearts. When they share, it will sound encouraging but there will not be a value exchange because this individual has no value to give.

The way we reason our answer to "What makes me valuable?" reflects the sources we extract our value from. If your answer is related to net worth or how much you have in savings, then money is your primary source of value. If your answer is activity or action-driven, then performance will be your primary source of value. Many cultures place a high value on career and vocation, so if you have a prestigious job, you have greater value.

Understand that the source you extract value from is *everything*. Not only in how it impacts your sense of self but also in how it impacts the value you can provide to others. There is a vertical dynamic here. How you receive value (up) determines how much value you can give (down). So the person who finds their self-worth in their career will look at others through that lens and evaluate whether or not they are valuable. This will always be the filter by which they evaluate and ascribe value to others.

The irony is that we are innately wired to provide value to others. It's something we long to do, and we know our lives are better when we do it, but we do not always learn the best ways to do it. Those who can reason why they are valuable and extract value from unlimited places provide the most value to those around them.

Being the middle child in my family, I saw this vertical dynamic play out regularly in my own life. My sister is five and a half years older than me and my brother is three and a half years younger. Growing up, I was the younger child in my sister–brother relationship and the older child in my brother–brother relationship. All this really meant is that when my sister teased, tricked, or taunted me, I would waste little time wallowing in the pain of it and instead would find my little brother and use the same tactics that I had just learned from my sister against him. The circle of life is a beautiful thing.

We often extract life lessons and even our reasoning from the people we look up to. The people whose opinions we care about the most. We ought to choose wisely.

Your source of value is your god. People, relationships, romance, money, cars, houses, status, followers, fame, fortune, wealth. We search high and low looking for value because it is our wiring. We know that it's there to be discovered and that in and of ourselves, we are limited. If you do not understand the power of the vertical dynamic, you will either fall into the trap of thinking that you simply decide your own value or you will stay oblivious to the primary sources that define your worth. Mark my words: there is always a source.

Performance

The ways in which you receive affection and affirmation growing up are key factors in your identity formation. If you grow up in a Christian home, your parents will likely applaud and celebrate your early efforts to pray, read the Bible, and engage in spiritual activities. This affirmation reinforces that engaging spiritually is worthy of praise and this is what being a Christian looks like. These are good things.

School is another great example. You go to school where you are evaluated on how well you understand material and how well you can complete assignments, tests, and the like. In some homes, parents may focus more on your effort and less on your grade. As long as you tried your best, that's all that matters. These homes are not Indian homes. Indian households care deeply about academic performance from a young age. I would proudly return 98% test scores to my parents, to which they would half-jokingly-but-not-so-jokingly reply, "What happened to the other 2%?"

Everyone grows up differently, but regardless, we are quick to draw conclusions about how to receive worth and value because our identities when we are young are wet cement. They are malleable and moldable, constantly changing based on our experiences and environments. Some boys learn that doing well in sports is the best way to garner their parents' attention.

For others, it's woodworking or being able to clean up around the house. In making the discovery that certain activities please their parents, boys incorrectly conclude that their value and worth are only found in these places of approval.

When your value is anchored in something that you can do well, be it academically, athletically, or otherwise, it is called performance. You may know the word "performance" as an indicator of how well something was performed. An athlete performs well at a competition, or a race car driver performs well on the track. They are high-performance individuals. In these contexts, performance is a good thing. However, for our purposes, performance means that your value as a person is equated with how well you can accomplish something. This is dangerous.

For me personally, I grew up believing that the better I performed in school, the more value I had. This was an excellent incentive to achieve at a high level for most of my academic career—I skipped second grade, had a 95% average in my last year of high school, and graduated with a first-class honors degree by the time I was 20. But while this value was useful for academic achievement, it was not as helpful for my identity formation. In the fourth grade, I cried because I got 74% on a math test. I'm embarrassed to write that, but it's the truth. That's how wrapped up my identity was in academic performance and it's a problem that I have had to work hard at resolving.

For others, performance manifests in arenas like athletics. Boys compete on fields, courts, and rinks to gain the approval and affection of their parents, especially their fathers. The better you perform, the more approval you receive. Sometimes, it's relative. Your parents don't want you to be the best, they just want you to be better than that entitled punk who lives down the street and whose parents drive a nicer car. The dynamics here vary from household to household, but one thing is clear: without excellent parenting and deep spiritual foundations in godly identity from a young age, boys will one way or another draw the conclusion that their worth is based on their ability to perform.

A performance mindset is a house of cards. When things are going well, everything is awesome. Things are stable, safe, secure. When things go south—you have an off game, you mistreat your sibling, or you get a 74% on a fourth-grade math test—you have a meltdown. It's hard for boys to identify these destructive mindsets while growing up because they do not know any better. When your identity is forming, you will take anything you can get to feel valuable and worthy. It's not until adulthood that men reflect and see the damage that was done.

Performance Breakdown

One of my clients, we'll call him Barry, came to me struggling with anxiety, in addition to pornography addiction. The two often go hand in hand. When we started to dig into his situation, it was clear that Barry was operating with a deeply rooted perfectionist mindset. He was taught at a young age by his mom that everything must be perfect always. Everything must be perfectly put away in the house. Everything must look neat and tidy at all times. The food must be perfectly cooked and served. Everything must be perfect.

In a house like this, there is no room for error. So the pressure mounts as you walk on eggshells day and night, knowing it's only a matter of time before something cracks. And voilà, my dear client Barry had developed brutal anxiety as a result of this perpetuated thinking. He was talented, compassionate, and intelligent, but had hardly tapped into his potential because he was so crippled by fear of failure. That is hardly a way to live. To make matters worse, Barry was married and struggling with porn, with a baby on the way.

As we dug further, it was clear that doing things "correctly" was the only way Barry could receive affirmation from his mom. She showed love in other ways as well, but the main message that came across was, "Do things perfectly, or there will be consequences." Now, over a decade into adulthood, he could not cope with real life. Barry was drowning in the shame of porn addiction and the disarray of major anxiety.

Someone who has placed their identity in their performance will hide, blame, defend, accuse, or break down if they come up short. Someone who has learned healthy and godly identity will not. They will be able to maintain their composure, internally and externally, despite the mistake. That is the true mark of godly identity.

The truth is that the mindsets we acquire through our upbringing are projected onto our relationship with God. Our parents build a model for relating, attaching, connecting, and receiving love that we then transfer to God as we become adults. However, if you learned growing up that things must be perfect for you to be accepted, then when you start building a relationship with God you will think the same way. Or if you learned that you must perform well to receive affirmation, you will read your Bible, pray, and engage spiritually from a place of fear, not desire, because "you must perform well."

The preachers teach that you are a child of God and that God is a good father. As soon as you use familial terminology, you are now subject to the patterns, conclusions, and experiences that you experienced, or did not experience, with your physical family. This is why simply hearing good sermons on a Sunday morning is not enough to walk in the fullness of our God-given identities.

You don't have to look too far in the church to find the propagation of performance mindsets. I am all for spiritual disciplines, and I am all for righteous living, as you will soon find out. I'm not saying we shouldn't do these things. I am saying that if we do them only to gain God's approval, then it is likely that we have taken the harmful mindsets we learned in childhood and transferred them to our relationship with God.

Furthermore, the problem is not solely the limitations of our upbringing, although they play a role. The problem is not just the societal norms that applaud high achievement and performance, although that dynamic is clearly at play as well. The ultimate problem lies with the conclusions that we draw from these experiences, as they often tell us that our value is tied to our behavior. These faulty conclusions are harmful as we enter adulthood and experience the harsh realities of life, but they become fatal when given a place of influence in our relationship with God.

Barry's relationship with God was a perfect example of these dynamics. His early experiences with his mom caused him to subconsciously create damaging conclusions about himself and his value. As he progressed in his spiritual walk, the same thoughts and mindsets were transferred to his relationship with God. He believed that things had to be perfect, or God would not accept him.

These mindsets cannot be changed in a day. I wish they could. I wish I could tell you that Barry used a simple three-step process, and that his life was perfect again. It doesn't work that quickly. But remember Principle #5 (Consistency Compounds): we are in this for the long run. If you instill good practices in these areas, with time you will notice dramatic improvements.

We chipped away at some of these paradigms. We had to work through the damaging experiences first, and then, with consistent effort, we reached some really remarkable places. Once Barry had hurdled a few mother wounds, we tackled his relationship with God. Again, this was not a perfect process, but we made major progress using some of the strategies I'm about to show you. With time, an incredible thing happened. Barry found comfort in his own skin. Being himself. Embracing who he was. Establishing his core identity.

In the last 70 days that Barry and I worked together, he looked at porn once. A dramatic turnaround from when he first started with me just a couple months prior, where porn was at least a weekly occurrence. We'd set the wheels in motion, and as Barry continues down the path of recovery he will look to porn less and less to get his needs met.

An experience like Barry's may seem far-fetched if performance thinking is deeply ingrained into your mind. Maybe the idea of being okay with yourself despite a mistake, error, or flaw is inconceivable. While that may feel like a stretch for you now, let me be the first to tell you that it is possible for every single man to achieve. You are not the exception. It is not complicated. It is not easy either, but it can be done.

All the topics we've addressed in this chapter culminate with just a few keywords from Barry's recovery: feeling comfortable in your own skin. This is the mark of a rooted, firmly established, godly identity. This is the goal. It is the pinnacle. And it is fundamental. There are many different terms for this concept, but for our purposes, we'll be calling it self-acceptance.

Self-Acceptance

I didn't write this chapter just to be provocative and give you a few nice philosophical discussion points. We need answers. I had to set the stage first before arriving here, otherwise, this section would simply become a feel-good pep talk without much substance. Thanks for reading this far—now that I've exposed all your problems, let's start solving them (I joke, kind of).

When you boil it all down, our ultimate quest in life is to be accepted. We long to hear from our parents, authority figures, peers, leaders, mentors, teachers, pastors, and family: "You are acceptable. You are accepted." Of course, these words are rarely spoken out loud, and even if they were, it would not fully satisfy the desire.

Instead, it's the actions, body language, and other significant, yet subtle, clues that tell us that who we are and what we are doing is accepted and acceptable. As far as we know, the Father only spoke audibly to the public about His Son twice: his baptism, as we discussed, and on the Mount of Transfiguration (Matthew 17:5). Even for Jesus, the message of acceptance from His father rarely came audibly, yet Jesus lived His entire life on Earth knowing with all His heart that He was accepted by the Father.

The challenge with our innate need for acceptance on a social level is that we become prone to conformity. We shape and mold ourselves into something that we have been taught will garner acceptance by people whose opinions we care about. Social media is the ultimate example of this, as millions of users curate their profiles and content to project a persona that gains follows, likes, and comments. In short: we crave social acceptance.

It requires little strength to present yourself in a way that matches social norms. It's hardly worth applause. Anyone can do it even without a fiber of courage because when you fit a social mold already, you are guaranteed acceptance before you put yourself out there. But it requires unbelievable amounts of courage and strength to put yourself out there when you know you may *not* fit with popular opinion or the like.

You may think that these kinds of bold moves are reserved for the few that have the courage to pull it off. Nothing could be further from the truth. Every single person with a working brain is wired to fully express their unique selves. However, few choose to do so out of fear of rejection. The irony is that when we act out of a fear of rejection, we eliminate any possibility of being authentically accepted. Instead, the only option we give ourselves is to be accepted for someone we are not. This is not acceptance at all.

Ultimately, you will not walk into your calling, or achieve your potential or any level of freedom until you reach a place of self-acceptance. A place where you have come to terms with your flaws, failures, strengths, and successes without guilt, shame, or condemnation. Self-acceptance is the place where man has confronted the uncomfortable parts of himself and his life and has found comfort in the process. It's a place where he can look at himself, look at his life, and feel at peace. It's the place where manhood is born.

What Do You See?

In my mid-20s I had the opportunity to attend a renowned ministry school as my final step toward a career in full-time ministry. I was excited and nervous, but I made up my mind that I was going all-in for this experience. No holding back, no hesitation. I was ready to grow in my spiritual life, build a better relationship with God, and get the training I needed to begin my career as a pastor. I was excited.

It would take a whole book to articulate my experience in ministry school and how deeply it impacted me. I am not the same person I was because of the transformation that took place during my time there. Between the lifelong friendships, incredible experiences with God, and world-class teaching that I still apply regularly in my day-to-day life, ministry school was everything I hoped for and then some. While I hold a fond collection of meaningful and impactful moments, one of my peak experiences came in a rather unsuspecting way.

The program I signed up for was structured so that every week focused on a different module. Topics varied from basic theology to hearing God's voice and everything in between. Without a doubt, one of the most popular weeks, if not the most popular, was a week on the subject of identity. There are many reasons for its popularity, not least of which was The Mirror. The instructor would pull a student out of the crowd, bring them to the front of the class, and stand them in front of…The Mirror.

What was so special about this mirror? Absolutely nothing. It was just an ordinary mirror. But it brought about extraordinary experiences.

The Mirror on its own was not powerful. It was the question that the instructor would pose as he and the student would stand side-by-side facing it while the rest of the class watched that was powerful. There wasn't anything fancy or elaborate about the question. It was simple. Sometimes simple things strike deepest.

It's always a little disconcerting to be in a group where the instructor, at any given moment, could point you out and call you up to the front. But ministry school is about transformation. It's about becoming the man or woman of God you were made to be, and there has to be some risk involved to fully achieve that. Confronting the uncomfortable often catalyzes the greatest growth, and The Mirror was no exception.

The greatest demonstration of The Mirror's life-changing impact that I witnessed during identity week was when my friend Adam was called to the front.

"YOU!" the instructor exclaimed. "Come on up."

The room was silent.

"Him?!" everyone whispered. "This should be interesting."

Adam was the quiet one. The one you barely knew a few months into the school term because he was so absent and unseen. In an environment where you are literally making friends for life, Adam kept to himself and chose to withdraw. He was from Mexico, so some reasoned that he was just adapting culturally. But this was an international school with people from all over the world—no one else used their country of origin as an excuse to pull away. Somehow the instructor knew that Adam needed shaking up, but we had no idea just how shook up he was going to be.

First came the awkward moment: the instructor gave a direction and the student refused to follow. Adam was resistant. He shook his head profusely. His English wasn't great, but his body language did all the talking. Adam was not interested in participating. No Mirror. Not now. No way.

The instructor had clearly encountered this kind of resistance before. He remained unfazed and held his ground. The tension eventually broke as Adam caved and agreed to come to the front.

Students erupted with applause. "Yeah, Adam!" but the room quickly fell silent again as the instructor and Adam stood in front of The Mirror, side-by-side, the class looking on to see what would happen.

Then, the question came.

"What do you see?"

Adam was rubbing his hands together, looking anywhere but at himself.

"What do you see?" the instructor repeated, snapping Adam out of any self-induced trance he may have attempted to put himself in to escape the awkwardness.

The room was silent for what felt like five minutes (it was probably 10 seconds), and then came the tears. Adam broke down as he quite literally confronted the man in The Mirror. Some of the most atrocious things I've ever heard someone say about a person came out of Adam's mouth. He wasn't crude or vulgar, but he was not kind to himself at all. Years of self-hatred spilled out. Adam was finally coming to terms with his life after years of being abused and blaming himself.

You see, there is no self-acceptance without confronting the man in your own mirror. You cannot simply declare that you are accepted. You cannot simply hear it from a stage and assume it to be true. Self-acceptance must be *experienced*.

Most men learn to suppress. Whether it's feelings, pain, regret, sexuality, or something else that's internally fundamental, we are taught to keep it under wraps. Be strong. Don't let it get to you. This isn't strength at all. True strength is being able to look at these parts of you head-on while holding your ground.

The incredible thing is that you already have all the tools you need to pull this off. You have a journal and you have learned to forgive. The essence of self-acceptance is embracing the inner world and forgiving the self for shortcomings and mistakes.

The message of Christ on the cross is not simply "You are forgiven." It is "You are accepted." For us to be forgiven of our sins means that we become acceptable in God's eyes. Similarly, when you forgive others, you are accepting them as they are—flaws, failures, and everything else. Most relevantly, when you forgive yourself, you are accepting yourself for who you are. To not forgive yourself is to devalue the price that Christ paid on Calvary.

Allow me to illustrate. Imagine you get to test drive one of two luxury cars, but you don't know any details about them. You don't know the make, model, year, or anything. The only information you are given is this: one of them costs $100,000 and the other costs $200,000. Which one would you drive? Obviously, you would choose the car with the higher cost. Why? Because the greater the cost, the greater the value.

So if a perfect, flawless, unblemished, and sinless life was paid as a ransom for your salvation, then how valuable are you?

Adam went on to be one of the most popular students in our school. Everyone knew who he was after The Mirror experience. He began to sing on worship teams, write songs with other musicians, and eat lunch with everyone else in the cafeteria! He was a new man because he finally confronted the uncomfortable parts of his life and reached a place of forgiveness and self-acceptance in the process.

This is a good moment for you to assess what is stopping you from experiencing self-acceptance. Is it a past mistake? Something about your body or appearance? Is it an addiction? Lustful thoughts? Incompetency or deficiency? What is holding you back from fully accepting yourself for who you are?

The amazing thing about the story of Jesus in Luke 4 is that the words the Father spoke over Him are the same words the Father speaks over you. Paul wrote explicitly in Romans that the Spirit of God testifies that we are sons of God (Romans 8:16). As one of my ministry school teachers profoundly stated: Jesus, the son of God, became a son of man so that the sons of man could become sons of God. While we are works in progress and certainly not at the caliber of Jesus, the work of Christ on the cross ensures that as we walk in the forgiveness of God, we also walk in His acceptance. You are His beloved son and in you, He is well pleased.

This is powerful because the defining quality of sonship is a relationship. In other words, there is no element of works or activity associated. The words of the Father are based purely on the relationship, eliminating any opportunity to fall into performance thinking. It is not measured by how good a son you are, it is measured simply by whether you are a son. When relationship is the defining quality, our value is simply anchored in God choosing us. Nothing more, nothing less. If you find value, acceptance, worth, and identity in places other than the Father Himself, your life is a house built on sand.

Self-Care

Most men shy away from the subjects of self-acceptance and self-care for two reasons. One, they are uncomfortable. It's much easier to focus on others. Second, it could be viewed as selfishness. I'm not sure what your culture is like, but in Christian Canadian culture, most of us learn a healthy fear of conceitedness from a pretty young age.

The danger with side-stepping these self-focused syndromes is that in our noble efforts to avoid selfishness, we neglect ourselves too much and shoot ourselves in the foot. We diminish our God-given value out of a fear of being viewed as conceited or self-absorbed. The folly of this thinking is proven both scientifically and in scripture. Research shows that those who can demonstrate compassion toward themselves are much more likely to have similar levels of compassion toward others.[46] It is possible to have compassion toward others without having compassion toward yourself, but it is not sustainable. People who live this way eventually burn out and become resentful.

Scripturally, when Jesus was asked, "What is the greatest commandment?" He said, "'Love the Lord your God with all your heart, with all your soul, and with all your mind.' This is the first and greatest commandment. And the second is like it: 'You shall love your neighbor *as* yourself'" (Matthew 22:37–39 [emphasis added]).[47] Note the keyword here: "as." You can only love others to the degree you love yourself. If you cannot value yourself, look after yourself, and have compassion toward yourself, it will be very difficult for you to provide any of these things to others in a sustainable way. You are worth taking care of, as we've already discussed. Furthermore, you must take good care of yourself if you want to take good care of others.

Let me give you an example so you can see what this might look like. At the time of writing this, I am doing some pro bono work with a young man whom we'll call Luke. Although Luke is young, he already has an extensive history with women. For many years, he was involved in online forums that would share secrets and strategies for picking up girls. Luke became well versed in these methods and knew how to get exactly what he wanted out of any woman he met.

Fast forward a few years now, Luke has given his life to Jesus, wants to get married one day, and realizes he has some cleaning up to do. When

Luke and I first started meeting, he had just broken up with a girlfriend. They weren't right for each other and so he ended things. He explained that during his internship, now that he was single, he mainly wanted to focus on God. He had found a lot of his own value in other women over the years, jumping from relationship to relationship, and it had left him unsatisfied. Now that he was committing his life to God, he wanted to find his identity in Him instead. No dating for a while. This went well for a few weeks, but on our third call, Luke had news to share. He had met someone.

His face lit up like a Christmas tree as he talked about her devotion to God, how beautiful she was, her great personality, and of course, how they seemed perfect for each other. "I've never had a connection like this before," he said. I asked about some of the desires he had laid out when we first started meeting: finding value in God, staying single, etc. All of it was thwarted or somehow less relevant now that he had met this woman.

Sadly, after only two months of seeing each other, the woman decided that she did not want to go any further in the relationship. Luke was crushed and came running to me. He was upset with her and he was upset the relationship failed so quickly, but in his heart of hearts, Luke was upset with himself. Here he was, back in the exact same place he was just a few months ago. Single, alone, and feeling worthless.

The beautiful part of this moment was that Luke made a firm decision that he was not going to make the same mistake again. He was going to be single for real this time, no exceptions. He now realized how much work needed to be done for him to rewire his sense of self and he was ready to commit to it. It was time for our bi-weekly meeting just a couple of days ago and we hit the ground running.

"Bro, I need your help," he said. "I'm craving female attention and I don't know what to do."

For starters, Luke deserves *huge* props for having enough self-awareness to identify his underlying need. This is a skill that everyone is born with to some extent—but it requires work and development. So we started there. I told him I was proud of him for cultivating that kind of self-awareness and explained that because of it he had an opportunity to do something about the issue at hand. Then, I asked for him to elaborate a little more.

"I don't know, it's just that I need to have a girl show interest in me. If girls aren't showing interest in me, I don't feel good about myself. This lack of female attention is killing me. I watched a girl playing the piano on Instagram for seven minutes yesterday. She wasn't cute or anything like that, but I just needed to have that feeling of being around a woman."

In moments like these, I am always tempted to set the record straight and offer advice, but usually when I do, although I feel good afterward and the person on the receiving end might nod their head in agreement, they then walk away unchanged. For people to really make a change in their thinking, they have to make discoveries themselves. So instead of advising, I said, "Wow. This is clearly a very deep need for you. Let me ask, if you were to give yourself advice on how to respond, what would you say?"

Silence.

"I have no clue, bro. I guess when I think about it, it's not even about needing a woman's affection. It's just their attention. I just want to be noticed. And it's been really cool because even though I'm wrestling with this need, I have found other ways to get it met. I've been hanging out with Wesley (his roommate) a lot more. We've been watching movies and working out together, it's been great. And I've been trying to talk to God about it too. It's helping, but I still feel unfulfilled sometimes."

"When have you felt the most fulfilled in your life?" I replied.

"Easy. Good grades and getting girls. My parents always applauded good grades at home, so that made me feel good about myself. And you know my history with girls—having them around makes me feel good about myself too."

"That's it?" I asked, a little surprised.

"Honestly, that's it. I can't think of any other times in my life I've felt fulfilled."

At this point, it was clear that Luke had little to no sense of true fulfillment in life. When the only way you've experienced fulfillment as a young adult is through good grades and girls, you are left with very few options once you graduate school. No wonder Luke's needs were sky high. Without the opportunity to get good grades, girls were his only option, but they were the one thing he had given up.

I explained to Luke that this was a season for him to develop new avenues for feeling fulfilled that didn't involve a romantic relationship. There were two ways to do so. One was to cultivate a deeper relationship with God using some of the methods we'd already looked at. The second was to get curious. Rather than trying activities that had worked for me or other clients, I wanted Luke to be exploratory.

I encouraged him to try a couple of new activities between sessions to see how they impacted him. If they didn't help him find fulfilment, he could move on and try other things. If they worked, he could try to integrate them into his life regularly. It could be working out, music, joining an extracurricular club. There was no right or wrong.

This is self-care. It is identifying your needs and finding healthy ways to get them met. It is the essence of mastering your inner circle, cultivating self-awareness, and developing a strong sense of self. When Luke is ready to date again, he will not just be looking to get something out of it. He will have plenty to *give*. That is the difference between someone who settles for external solutions and someone who is willing to do the messy inner work. It's the difference between someone who has cultivated a sense of godly identity and someone who can simply give the rote responses.

Mirror Therapy

When I started to make some progress in the porn addiction recovery process, I made an important discovery. I realized why Adam had such a profound experience in front of The Mirror. He was looking at himself. Seems obvious, but it really struck me. Adam was standing face-to-face with himself as he confronted the deepest parts of his self.

When I understood the principle underlying The Mirror experience, I realized it could be applied in my own life as part of reforming my own identity, regardless of whether there was an audience. This was a game-changer for me, especially as I was breaking free of pornography. It is a compound principle, meaning that it combines two different principles in one and I believe this is one of the most effective weapons in your arsenal for overcoming pornography.

The first principle is this: Your eyes are the window to your soul. Jesus taught this in Matthew 6:22–23 when He said, "Your eye is like a lamp that provides light for your body. When your eye is healthy, your whole body is filled with light. But when your eye is unhealthy, your whole body is filled with darkness. And if the light you think you have is actually darkness, how deep that darkness is!"[48]

The second principle, based on Proverbs 18:21, is that life and death are in the power of the tongue.[49] If I can speak powerful words of life into my soul, something good is bound to happen within me. This is why when Adam stood in front of The Mirror and looked himself in the eyes, he spoke darkness. It was all he could see. It was all that he allowed in. But bringing in his classmates around him to speak the truth and to speak life was healing. Not only because they were powerful words of truth, but because they were looking at him in the eyes (through The Mirror) while they spoke.

If that's what made The Mirror so powerful for Adam, then I could have my own powerful experiences with The Mirror as well. So when I had a bad day and caved in to the lures of pornography and masturbation yet again, afterward I learned to look at myself in The Mirror, square in the eyes, and speak one or two things about my identity. "You are enough. You are going to get through this. You can do it."

Doing this immediately after a slip became pivotal for curbing my thoughts and shaping how I responded. I condemned myself less and I bounced back more quickly. Moreover, as I kept doing the exercise, along with healing my heart and cultivating self-awareness, I noticed I was gaining more control. My brain was starting to change. We're going to talk about thought life extensively in the next chapter, but for now, I want to invite you to try something that I have my clients do. I call it mirror therapy.

Mirror therapy is exactly what I've described above. It's standing in front of a mirror, looking at yourself square in the eyes, and speaking the truth into the depths of your soul. Standing in front of a mirror is not too hard, we do that every day. For some of you, looking at yourself in the eyes might be enough work to start. It certainly was for me. I felt so much shame and humiliation about who I was that I could not bear to even look at myself at first. But as I confronted the discomfort, that's when I really learned to love myself. It's very healing to look at yourself in the eyes and find a place of peace. It is not easy, but it is worth the effort.

Finally, you need to speak your own truth into your soul. I am going to provide a few statements to get you started. These are basic affirmations that anyone can use, however, I strongly discourage using these alone. It is much more powerful for you to craft your own statements and add them to the mix. This is what I have my clients do and they love it. The workbook material for this chapter will walk you through how to craft your own customized affirmations so you can start declaring personalized truth into the depths of your soul.

To give you an idea of how powerful this can be, let Gerald's story inspire you. When Gerald was young, he was made to believe that he was not strong enough. He was the small, skinny kid who was constantly picked on. The experiences he had growing up led him to conclude that he was incapable, and could not stand up for himself. He believed that he wasn't strong enough to get his needs met, enjoy his body, have a healthy relationship, and step into his God-given calling. Those are some major obstacles to face from one pesky core belief!

As Gerald went through the exercise of crafting new truths through journaling to give him some mirror therapy material, he received two life-changing statements. First, God said to him, "I was always your strength when you were weak, and I always will be. You owe nothing to anyone. I make you strong enough each day." Powerful, right? Imagine hearing these words from God as He speaks the truth about who you are.

Then God said to Gerald, "You are stout-hearted." What? I was worried Gerald had heard from something other than God when we got to this part. I had never heard the phrase "stout-hearted" before. And I thought to myself, "The poor guy is already struggling with his sense of strength and might, and then he hears God call him stout!"

Turns out I was the fool here. Stout-hearted means courageous and de-termined, and has a biblical basis. Psalm 138:3 says, "When I called, You answered me; You made me bold and stout-hearted."[50] Now imagine if Gerald tried to tackle the lie he told himself of not being strong enough without the mirror exercise. It would have led to statements like, "I am strong enough," or, "I can do all things through Christ who strengthens me." Nothing wrong with these. But Gerald heard something that was specific to his unique identity from God. As a result, these words mean so much more to him. He could embrace them with all his heart, soul, mind, and strength because they carry so much more weight.

These scripture-based affirmations below are a great place to start, but nothing will have a greater impact than affirmations that are personally customized to you. I help you create these in the workbook. Visit www.sathiyasam.com/recoveryworkbook. This is how your identity begins to transform.

1. I am beyond condemnation. I am enough. (Romans 8:1)

2. I am holy, blameless, and above reproach. (Colossians 1:22)

3. Freedom is mine. (John 8:36)

4. I am worthy of love. (John 3:16)

5. I have the mind of Christ. (1 Corinthians 2:16)

CHAPTER 7

Renewing Your Mind, Rewiring Your Brain

As I've grown older and worked with more people, I've observed that much of life is about choosing the battles you are willing to fight. Some men choose to fight crime and become police officers. Others choose to fight injustice and become lawyers. Several of my university friends chose to fight sickness and became doctors. These examples are on a vocational level, but there are other arenas where men can battle.

Some choose to fight fatherlessness and focus on raising their family. And yes, some men choose to fight the Flood as supersoldier Spartan Master Chief in the Halo franchise (I told you video games were a big part of my life back in the day).

King David is a great example of someone who chose his battles carefully, both literally and metaphorically. As the leader of the Israelite army, David frequently assessed a situation before deciding whether to engage in battle. In 1 Samuel 30, the Amalekites raided David's city while his army was out fighting. They set it on fire and took their families captive. The entire army was affected, and they were upset with David—when in doubt, blame the leader. David was greatly distressed. Not only was his own family taken captive, but now the men he was leading were ready to turn on him. Cooler heads prevailed and David inquired of the Lord. The Lord replied and told him that He will deliver them into his hands. This is a great example of someone wisely choosing their battle.

Things go wrong when you avoid the battles you are meant to fight. While David is a shining example of someone who wisely selected his battles, unfortunately, he also neglected battles that he was supposed to fight. In 2 Samuel 11 we learn that at a time when kings would go out to fight with their armies, David sent everyone else out and stayed at home. One day, he wakes up, walks to the roof of his house overlooking the city, and notices a beautiful woman bathing. Bathsheba is her name. David inquires about Bathsheba, has messengers send for her, and they sleep together.

We don't know the nature of this relationship. Was there much connection prior? Was it consensual or did David exert his powers as king to make this happen? It's not totally clear. But this experience is not that different from that of a 21st-century man struggling with pornography. He gets stimulated, thinks about what he needs to satisfy the arousal, pulls up his phone, and acquires it. This kind of approach to handling temptations and urges is dysfunctional and severely degrades the value of those involved.

In the last few years, we are seeing this dysfunction in full force as moral failure amongst prominent male Christian leaders has become more prevalent. Not only moral failure, such as adultery, but sexual abuse. While it's easy to read King David's handling of Bathsheba at a distance and disconnect from some of the harsher realities of the story, we see this story play out consistently in modern day Christianity. Make no mistake, this biblical example is one that we must carefully learn from if we are to live lives of freedom.

To complicate King David's situation, Bathsheba conceives. This is a problem because not only is David on the hook for a child outside of his marriages, but he has impregnated the wife of Uriah, an elite soldier in his army. To cover up, David pulls Uriah out of the war and brings him home, in hopes that he will sleep with his wife. This ought to mask David's error. The problem is that Uriah is a man of integrity and abides by a code—that you do not lay with your wife during battle. David tried to corrupt Uriah in several different ways, which included getting him drunk, but to no avail. Uriah would not sleep with his wife while his army was fighting. So instead, David sends him back to war and manipulates his army's commands so that Uriah is guaranteed to die in battle.

Bad things happen when you avoid battles you are supposed to fight. While we may read David's story and scoff at how someone could be so foolish, the truth is that an alarmingly high number of men worldwide behave exactly as David did. Men are refusing to engage in the very battle they are supposed to win, hoping to either fight some smaller battle that has less significance or waiting for someone else to fight the battle for them. As a result, men are failing. Falling into temptation. Covering up their mistakes. And repeatedly avoiding the battle they are destined to win.

There is no greater battle in this life than that of the mind. Your mind is the greatest battlefield you will encounter in your lifetime. There are some battles you can ignore with little to no consequence. You may not be that interested in fighting world hunger. Your choice to avoid that battle has little repercussion for you personally if you have enough means to put food on the table. One could argue that not fighting world hunger has repercussions globally, but we will leave that for another day. You may not be that interested in fighting the fatherlessness of our generation. That's also fine, as long as you don't plan to have kids. These battles are options. You can choose whether or not to engage.

The battle of the mind is not optional. It is for all. You have a mind, therefore you have a battle. If you do not fight in the battle, catastrophes result. You cannot exchange your mind for someone else's. You cannot choose to fight some days and take it easy other days. The battle of the mind is an open invitation, and it will only end when you breathe your last.

The good news is that we have been set up for success. There are principles and practices that you and I can apply in our regular lives to not only fight this battle, but win it consistently. God does not send you into battles you are not positioned to win. If he did, He would be no better than King David leaving Uriah alone on the frontlines. Winning is possible, we must start there. We don't know exactly why David retreated and stayed back while his army fought. All we know is that his choice to avoid a battle he was meant to fight cost him and those involved, and the same is true for you.

One of the biggest lies you can believe about pornography consumption is that it only affects you. Nothing could be further from the truth. The people on your screen have hearts too, and some of them performed on camera in abysmal conditions to put food on their table. I had a conversation with a former porn star who at one point was extremely popular online. She told me that, in her experience, many porn stars are addicted to drugs, forced to engage in sexual acts without consent, and living paycheck to paycheck. She said that porn viewership lines the pockets of the swindlers who run these operations, leaving pennies for the people you see on camera.

Also, remember that your life is not your own. The decisions you make impact your relationship with God and your relationship with others. Sexual misbehavior impacts all involved in your life, the same way that David's fornication not only tainted his kingship but also ruined another family. All the more reason to get your thought life sorted out.

Before we dive in, I want to make it clear that the concepts outlined in this chapter are ideals. We cannot live them perfectly, nor should we try. Ideals help us set a target. They give us direction (Principle #3). Something to aim toward and measure up to. Ideals are not meant to shame or condemn, they are simply meant to set a standard. If you struggle with a mental illness, exploring ideals can be a deflating experience because the concepts seem impossible and out of reach. If you fall into that category, I want to encourage you to have lots of kindness toward yourself as you read this chapter.

I also want to set you a challenge: As we explore the battle of the mind, consider how the principle stack and tools we've talked about can help you. Let that be your lens instead of wondering why it's all so hard or disqualifying yourself before you try. The battle of the mind is meant to be won. It may be intimidating or scary or hopeless. I personally have had seasons of my life where I felt trapped in my own mind, wishing there was a way out or that I could shut it down for a few days. I can assure you that whether this battle excites you or exhausts you, the content we're about to explore will sharpen your arsenal and strengthen your armor. Let the battle begin.

Origins

Not every thought you have is worth your time. In fact, few of them are. Romans 8:1 says, "there is therefore now no condemnation for those who are in Christ Jesus,"[51] yet how quick are we to condemn ourselves for having bad thoughts? Doesn't seem scripturally sound to me. We often have a sexually oriented thought and go into panic mode because it's a terrible thing to think when it is merely a thought.

I'm not downplaying the power of a thought, far from it. In fact, thoughts are so powerful that I have dedicated an entire chapter to the subject. How you think determines how you live. What I mean is that you have a say in the matter. You are not a hostage to the thoughts that freely enter and exit your mind. You are border control. You get to decide what comes in and what has to go.

There are four sources of thought:

1. God
2. Self
3. Others
4. The enemy

A thought inherently reveals the nature of its source. The greatest skill in this battle of the mind is being able to identify where a thought originated. Did it come from God? Self? Others? The enemy? Perhaps more importantly, how do you know? This kind of discernment is extremely important and is essential for winning the battle in your mind.

Only when you've identified the source of a thought, can you decide what you want to do with it. If it's a thought that will serve you and your purposes, engage with it. Entertain it. We're going to explore what this looks like practically. If it's a thought that will not serve you in the moment, or ever, then you can respond accordingly. Personally, I will reply to these thoughts with one of the following: "No," "Not now," or "Nice try." You'll see how these responses play out in the next few paragraphs.

If you skip the step of identifying the origins of your thoughts, you remain powerless and will then take ownership of every thought, even the ones that originated elsewhere. So first things first, we must identify the sources of our thoughts.

God

If we look at our previous example of Jesus's baptism, it's clear that the voice of the Father is one of love and acceptance. This doesn't mean that God will not correct us, because He will. But he will never condemn us (remember Romans 8:1). No one's thoughts matter more than God's. We must become aficionados at detecting the thoughts of God. They enter our minds every single day, but if we do not recognize them as God's thoughts, we will dismiss them. This is the beautiful power of life on Earth in conjunction with the Holy Spirit. He was sent to counsel us.

The voice that encourages you and gives you hope and strength—that is the voice of the Holy Spirit. Those are His thoughts. The voice that gives you wild, crazy dreams that seem impossible to accomplish on your own. That is the Holy Spirit's voice. The thought that says, "You know the way you handled that wasn't quite right. You need to go back and apologize," is the Holy Spirit. We must always be looking for His gentle whisper. These thoughts are critical, and they are not for the select few. Everyone has a chance to experience godly thoughts.

The problem is that we ignore them. They are too good to be true or too kind. So we pay little attention to them and we miss out. It's like God handing you a rifle for a gunfight and you saying, "No I'm good. I'll just duke it out with my fists." You have thoughts from God enter your mind every single day and each of them should be latched onto with every fiber of your mental being. Learn to recognize them and embrace them.

Self

Early on in this journey to understand the mind, I swung a bit too far on the God thoughts idea and concluded that every thought is either from God or Satan. It's not a horrible conclusion, but it's not accurate. You and I have thoughts of our own as well. We were given brains that are trained to think a certain way from a very young age. Some of our brain functions are innate and genetic, but many of our thinking patterns are learned.

Understand that some of the thoughts you think and ideas you have are most definitely your own. Remember that we're not talking about emotions or feelings—those are yours, and we looked at those in great detail already. We are talking about thoughts now. You may feel angry about the cold temperatures you're experiencing in your cold country during the winter while others in the world are enjoying sunshine and beaches, but the idea that it would be so nice to live the colder half of the year in Florida is yours (to use a completely hypothetical example that definitely is not based on any of my own personal experiences).

God did not tell you to move to Florida. The devil is not trying to detract you from your calling to a cold country. You are cold and you saw others experiencing warmth. So your brain found a way to solve that issue.

Your own thoughts should be encouraged when they serve you. Thoughts like, "Hey, I think I'm starting to get the hang of this!" and, "I really am learning to become a better man. Still not perfect, but making progress."

Similarly, you will initiate thoughts that really aren't worth your time. The thoughts that cause you to second-guess yourself, hypercriticize your decisions and behaviors, etc. Anytime you encounter those thoughts, the response should be "No," "Nice try," or "Not now." I love saying "Nice try" to my brain when these errant thoughts come up. It's very empowering. Sometimes I can tell that a thought is not necessarily worth my time at that moment but could be useful later. That's when I will say, "Not now." These are often thoughts that have some emotions attached or insecurities that I need to dig into a bit more. They don't need to be disregarded altogether, but they don't need to become front and center in the moment either.

Remember that if you do not take ownership of a thought (Principle #1), then you cannot master it. Learning to identify your own thoughts is an important part of winning this war and developing discernment. Once you discover a thought was your own, you must assess if it will serve you or not. If it will, keep it. If it won't, dismiss it.

Others

We are social creatures, and that means that we are influenced by the thoughts of others. These days, it's very easy to access the thoughts of other people through social media, news outlets, blogs, podcasts, movies, music, etc. There are so many avenues for sending and receiving messages, it has become overwhelming. No matter how strong you think you are, you are affected by the thoughts of others.

This can be a positive thing. A mentor or leader may speak into your life and give you perspective on a matter that you could not have found on your own. Maybe your parents have taught you a thing or two over the years that you didn't really appreciate at the time but later on in life have discovered that it was valuable. You may hear a sermon that really challenges the way you think about a subject or a podcast that gives you a new way of viewing something. The thoughts of others can be useful.

Similarly, the thoughts of others can be harmful if they communicate bad advice, ungodly world views, jaded perspectives, etc. There are many ways that the thoughts of others can enter our minds and have adverse effects. We are naturally influenced by others—that is a given. So we must learn to discern when the thoughts we entertain in our minds originated from someone else. Then we can decide whether or not they are serving us. If they serve, we engage. If they don't, we reply with "No," "Nice try," or "Not now."

The Enemy

One of the most dangerous notions in Christianity today is that there is no devil. I know that may sound ridiculous to you, but many today are preaching a message that negates the existence or the influence of the enemy. Now let's be clear, I'm not into over-glorifying a fallen being who was permanently defeated 2,000 years ago. I don't believe we need to fret the activity of the enemy in our lives. Similarly, we cannot deny the level of influence he can have if we are not careful.

The enemy comes to kill, steal, and destroy (John 10:10).[52] Thoughts that are critical, destructive, and devalue a person, either yourself or someone else, are from the enemy. The voice in your head that says you'll never amount to anything and tries to steal your hope of any success or confidence in the future is the voice of the enemy. He will do everything he can to take you down and have you think poor and ungodly thoughts.

In fact, over the years the enemy has realized that overt operations in western cultures have little to no success. We are quick to identify overt expressions of evil. Blatant seduction, over-the-top marketing tactics, and outright demonic oppression are easy to spot. Instead, the enemy tries covert tactics to trip up believers and non-believers alike, having them believe lies, think small, and devalue one another. Look out for these thoughts.

When these thoughts come, we must dispose of them quickly. They are not worth our time, attention, or effort.

James 4:7 says, "Resist the devil and he will flee from you."[53] In case you didn't know, he isn't talking about a physical fistfight. Resisting the devil takes place in the unseen world. There is no better feeling than identifying a thought of the enemy—a lie, an alluring temptation, or a scheme—and responding, "No." Sometimes I'll even be sarcastically polite and tell him, "No thanks." It's not that different from how Jesus responded to the devil in Luke 4, as we explored in the previous chapter.

The best way to recognize the thoughts of the enemy is to learn the thoughts of God. God's thoughts are the real thing. The standard. Bank tellers undergo extensive training to handle money. The idea is that they must become so familiar with authentic bills that they can immediately identify a counterfeit because something *feels* different in comparison to the real thing. You would think a teller would identify a counterfeit first by seeing an inconsistency, but that is secondary.

Do not waste your time in the enemy's camp. Instead, make it your goal to become so familiar with God's thoughts that the counterfeit thoughts of the enemy become easily recognizable. This skill alone puts you miles ahead of the average person in winning the battle in your mind.

Get Your Garden Gloves

Human nature leans toward judgment in areas we understand well, and toward amazement in areas we know little about. For example, I am a communicator. I love speaking and writing and anything that involves communicating. So naturally, I am quite critical of communicators and communication in general. I pay close attention when someone speaks, especially if it's in a formal setting like a speech or a sermon. I notice the intonation and cadence, the word choice and conjugations. It's a blessing in some ways, but other times it's a curse. My wife and I have got into fights because I get nitpicky about her word choice in an argument. Not my greatest moments as a husband, to say the least.

On the flip side, I am a horrible gardener. I couldn't keep a palm tree alive in Cancun. I don't know what it is, but anytime someone has asked me to water their garden while they're on holiday or look after an office plant, it dies. I'm like the Grim Reaper of gardens. It's just better if I don't touch it. And it's for this reason that I marvel at my wife who is the complete opposite. She is a pro gardener. She knows the names of hundreds of plants and flowers and she knows how to take care of them properly. Even if a plant is dying (because, for example, the Grim Gardener laid his hands on it), she knows how to nurse it back to life. I simply watch in amazement. Who said opposites don't attract?

While I am amazed, I am equally grateful that I'm not the one with gardening skills. Gardening is hard work. I'm the guy who ran over the weeds with the lawnmower, remember? Sixteen-year-old Sathiya had no interest in uprooting the weeds in his parents' backyard. Much easier to just run them over. Sathiya today has not changed much on this front as far as lawn care goes. But I love that I've married someone who enjoys gardening because the end result of my wife's labor is glorious. Our yard looks clean and the house feels fresh.

My aversion to gardening is how many men approach thought life. Too much hard work, so why bother? Most men haven't been told that they are the gardener of their minds, and if they're not careful, their thoughts will start to bear ugly fruit.

Every thought is a seed. It takes root when you agree with it, grows as you repeat it, and bears fruit when you act on it. Read those last two sentences again to make sure you got it. We have been given a responsibility (Principle #2) to govern our thoughts in such a way that our mind becomes a lush garden.

If you have not assumed responsibility in this area, your garden is probably a mess. Gardens do not stay nice on their own for long. Regular maintenance is required. This is why if you sit around waiting for a preacher or a quick fix to magically heal your mind, you will be waiting until Kingdom come. You may have breakthrough moments where your mind is clear and it feels like everything has changed, but without a follow through and regular maintenance, those moments of mental clarity will be short-lived. If your thought life feels messy it might be because you haven't been gardening.

You entertain many thoughts in a day. They are merely seeds. Potent, but not planted. If you entertain the thought, now it has taken root. You have made agreement with it. Agreement is not the same as acknowledgment. Agreement is a partnership, whereas acknowledgment is an acquaintance. I try to acknowledge my thoughts as much as possible. Even the ugly ones. It's better to look them in the eyes than to run away. To agree is to engage. Most thoughts you have in a day should be acknowledged and disposed of immediately afterward. Few are worth your engagement.

At an early stage of agreement, little damage (or benefit) has been done. The thought is simply unpacking its potential. However, as you dwell on it—meditate on it—think on it— the plant starts to grow. Now the thought is gaining influence, and with continued repetition, it will gain prominence. Anything you dwell on becomes magnified.

The enemy knows that if he can get you to entertain a lie long enough, the rest will take care of itself. The recurrence of ungodly thoughts is usually instigated by the enemy, but fueled by our inability to govern our thoughts. As a result, damaging thoughts begin to wreak havoc. Similarly, godly thoughts begin to abound when you identify the truth. This is the covert nature of thought development because we sometimes entertain thoughts without realizing the downstream impact. Learn to catch thoughts early in the process and you will have much more success preventing ungodly thought patterns and encouraging godly mentalities instead.

The longer a thought sticks around, the more likely it is that it will result in action. Eventually, the plant bears fruit as you act on the thought. Action is the greatest reinforcer of thought. It is more effective than motivational speaking or affirmation or authority or anything else. To act on a thought is to solidify it. Furthermore, just as fruit carries the seeds of reproduction, so do thoughts. As you act on them, you increase the likelihood of repeating those thoughts and accompanying behaviors, especially if the outcome of the action was rewarding in some way.

One of the biggest lies the enemy wants us to believe is that our small actions don't matter. What's a little white lie? Or a little fudging of the numbers? They do matter. Actions reinforce beliefs. If you have a good belief system and you start to behave outside of it even slightly, you will either have to correct the behaviors or change the beliefs. The incongruence will not last. This is why we must remain in control (Principle #1) even in the most distressing moments. We will often justify poor behavior or decisions because we were having a bad day or we were feeling really strongly about something. Regardless of circumstance, ultimately those behaviors will reinforce belief. Choose carefully.

Now let me be clear, we want to validate the emotions. Those are totally justifiable. But the ensuing actions should stay aligned with your personalized truth. If you give yourself permission to deviate from your truth in weak or challenging moments, then you don't fully believe it. You just enjoy reaping its rewards when it's convenient. Your actions matter and the goal is that our lives reflect and regularly reinforce our truth in our attitudes and action.

The Truth

If you only believed the truth, your life would be immaculate. Your emotions would be stable. Your decision-making would be clear. Your relationships would be healthy. Your spirituality would be enriching. Porn would be a nonexistent issue in your life.

The greatest cause of our deficiencies and inefficiencies in life is nothing other than the influence of lies. When relationships break down, when spirituality strains, and when you struggle to make wise choices and manage your internal realm, it all points to one thing: there are lies at play.

The truth is absolute. Ground zero. Cannot be shaken. Fundamentally infallible. When you discover the truth, you'd better hold on to it. That's why Proverbs says, "Buy the truth and do not sell it" (Proverbs 23:23).[24] Pay whatever price you can to acquire it, and don't you dare let it go once you have it. Truth is meant to shape our sense of self, the world, God, and others. When we believe the truth, incredible things happen in our lives. When we do not, we suffer.

The truth is not the same as a fact, though they are similar. Facts are empirical and case-specific. An investigative journalist may research an event that took place to gather the facts and figure out what really happened. The individual aspects of the case they uncover are all facts. They are not truth, per se. Facts are cerebral. They demonstrate logical, rational, proven elements of a story or situation that stand as true. Facts generally stand the test of time, but not always.

Centuries ago, Charles Darwin theorized that the development of adults affected the genetic content they passed down to their children. In other words, if an adult started studying music and became a good piano player, they would now have stronger piano-playing genes to pass down to their children, which the scientists termed gemmules.[55] That theory did not last, for obvious reasons: it was untrue. My dad is a phenomenal piano player and I'm still waiting for my gemmules to catch up.

Facts can change, but that aspect alone is not what separates them from truth. The reason facts and truth are not interchangeable is that facts are a matter of the mind. Truth is a matter of the heart. You may know the facts, you may know the correct details of a situation, but you can still deduce lies about it.

The goal is for you and me to live lives that are predicated on truth. We want to abolish lies and their influence on our thinking. In doing so, we begin to walk in greater levels of freedom, sexual integrity, and godliness.

Truth is hard to come by these days. With so many opinions flying at our craniums a mile a minute, we are bombarded with a variety of perspectives and perceptions. If we are not careful, we will look to unfit places like social media and news outlets to find truth, places that can only offer facts (on a good day). To find the truth, we must look deeper at the heart of Jesus. This is the only place *true* truth exists. However, it is not enough to know the truth. You cannot just find it. Proverbs instructs us to buy the truth. We must invest, commit, channel our resources toward it. Ultimately, we must believe it.

There are four criteria I personally use to identify if something qualifies as the truth:

1. **Is it biblical?** Truth must be in the Bible. If it cannot be backed by scripture, it is not truth.

2. **Does it align with the character of Jesus?** A slight distinction from the first point. Some things might not be overtly written word-for-word in the Bible, but they should align with the person of Jesus that is depicted in the Bible. For example, the truth is that you are worthy. The Bible doesn't say that outrightly, but the teachings and life of Jesus demonstrate that He saw us as worthy.

3. **Does it have conditions?** Truth is unconditional. It holds its ground regardless of circumstance or situation. Facts may change based on conditions—truth does not.

4. **Is it clear?** Truth cannot be convoluted. It should be crystal clear. Its expression might have some complexities, but the truth itself should be easily discernible. If it is unclear, it is not the truth.

You're going to see why these criteria are so important when we began to dig into our own belief systems. The reality is that you will have areas in your heart that are influenced by lies. They must be addressed before you can experience long-term freedom. As long as those faulty beliefs linger, you will struggle. Uprooted lies should be replaced by the truth. Bear these four criteria in mind as we delve further into properly managing your thought life while simultaneously pursuing freedom.

Thought–Belief Continuum

Now that we have a basic framework to understand thought life, we can get into the nitty-gritty elements. Thoughts are the singular units that collectively comprise our minds. They form the patterns, pathways, and perceptions that shape every single moment of every single day.

A thought is simply an idea. As you've read more of this book, you might have wondered, "Does this guy do anything other than watch sports in his spare time?" That is a thought, and a fair one at that. But thoughts mean little on their own. It's the meaning and value we ascribe to them that matters. Just because you felt tempted to look at an attractive woman hardly means anything. Jesus was "tempted in every way" (Hebrews 4:15).[56] But if you respond poorly to the thought, it can create a lot of problems.

A thought with faith attached is a belief. Beliefs are everything. Thoughts are a dime a dozen—they come and go. Beliefs stay. Beliefs are embedded. You cannot simply turn a thought into a belief. Many gurus out there paint a picture of identifying magical phrases and truths that will revolutionize your belief system. It doesn't work that way. Just because you have a nice thought doesn't mean you can suddenly believe it. Work must be done. Specifically, the work of faith.

You see, thoughts and beliefs exist on a continuum, the same way that temperature exists on a spectrum. We often use terms like "hot" and "cold" to describe weather or food, when really those are non-specific terms. If you heat up a frozen pop tart for 10 seconds in your microwave, is it hot? Probably not. But it got warmer, right? That's a continuum. It's not one or the other, it's a measurement of degree. There are two ends of the spectrum (hot and cold) and a deciding factor that moves things along the spectrum in either direction (temperature).

Similarly, thoughts exist at one end of this continuum. On the other end are beliefs. You may have a thought that resonates with you. Hopefully, something you've read in this book so far has stuck with you and you've thought, "That makes sense." Having a little more confidence in the thought moves it along the scale toward belief. When something becomes a belief, it is a thought that has solidified itself in our thinking. We then know it as truth.

There is only one thing that moves a thought along the continuum to eventually become a belief. The same way that heat moves something from cold to hot. That thing is *faith*. That's the secret sauce.

Thought ————————————————————————▶ Belief

FAITH

Fig 7. Gradual increases in faith develop thoughts into beliefs. We must not only guard our thoughts but also guard our faith.

In this conversation, we are more concerned about the heart than the head. You cannot simply believe something in your head and expect everything to fall into place. Faith is a matter of the heart, and it's the only thing that drives thoughts into beliefs. So what does this mean for you and me? Simple. Our goal must be to increase our faith in thoughts that we know are true. With time they become beliefs, and our belief systems will serve us instead of hurt us.

Belief Magnetism

Men will often ask me, "How do I get rid of dirty/damaging/dangerous thoughts? I don't want to think them anymore." There are lots of answers to these questions, but I haven't found anything more helpful around this subject than **belief magnetism.**[57]

The basic premise is that your beliefs act as magnets for thoughts. They dictate which thoughts stick around and which ones pass through. If you have lingering thoughts or patterns of thought that you cannot shake, it might be an indicator that there is an underlying belief at play that needs to get addressed. Sometimes we fall into these thought traps and conclude something is wrong with us for having these terrible thoughts when it is our beliefs that are causing the trouble.

On the flip side, healthy and godly beliefs will attract healthy and godly thoughts. You will be prone to dwelling on the truth when your belief systems are intact and aligned. In my personal life, I have struggled with thought life the most when I am struggling to believe the truth about myself. Similarly, I have excelled in my thought life the most when I believe the truth about who I am. Remember, this is a battle. It is not one and done. There is always work to do, which is why reinforcing the truth into our belief system on a regular basis is vital for our well-being and long-term freedom.

Let me illustrate. Imagine little Timmy and little Tommy are struggling with eighth-grade math. The concepts are just a bit too complex for them to wrap their minds around. Timmy and Tommy are in the same class, with the same teacher, and about the same level of ability in mathematics. The only difference is their belief system.

Timmy has been encouraged and given unconditional acceptance at home. He fundamentally believes that he is loved and that he is enough. Meanwhile, Tommy gets a very different message at home. His parents are distant and not emotionally present. The only identity statements he has heard from them are, "Why are you such a pain in the butt?" and "What's wrong with you?" He fundamentally believes that he is a screwup.

The teacher asks Timmy and Tommy to stay back after math class to get some extra tutoring. Immediately, their belief systems kick in. Timmy is not thrilled about having to stay back, but he is resilient and wants to conquer his issue with math. "I'll find a way to do this," he thinks. Meanwhile Tommy is dreading every single minute of the extra tutoring. "Great," he thinks to himself, "more proof that I'm a failure."

Thankfully, the teacher is extremely positive and encouraging as he coaches Timmy and Tommy through their math struggles. He says to them right off the bat, "Guys, I know this is not easy, but trust me. You can do this, I think you are both good at math, you just need a little guidance."

Timmy's face lights up as he hears positive, encouraging words from his teacher. These kinds of thoughts are attractive to his belief system. They stick and even resonate. Timmy is full of faith and confident that he will sort this out.

Tommy is unsure. He hears the words and wants to believe them, but he concludes, "Oh he's just saying that. He doesn't really mean it."

The outcome here is obvious. Timmy will hurdle the obstacle. One way or another, he'll figure it out and will probably improve. Tommy likely will not. Instead, he will struggle. Not because he is bad at math—they are equally skilled on the subject. But the differences in the belief system are too vast for them to have the same outcome in this situation, and ultimately in life.

Beliefs not only matter because they drive our decisions and behavior, they also affect the thoughts we entertain and how we process them. The same thought can enter two different people's brains and yield different outcomes because of their different belief systems. One brain identifies the thought as useful and sees alignment with its beliefs. The other brain sees no use for it and dismisses the thought. Belief magnetism regulates what sticks and what doesn't.

If you want a clear mind that is regularly occupied with the truth and aligned with the mind of God, then you will have to work diligently to establish healthy beliefs. Many of my clients wish they had learned this earlier in life because they realize how much their faulty beliefs have cost them. They were trying to fight bad thoughts instead of addressing the beliefs that were drawing them in.

The good news is that our belief systems are malleable. They aren't fixed. We are constantly changing and adapting what we believe and why we believe it. Even if you have a shoddy belief system, there is no time like the present to uproot those bad beliefs and replace them with the truth. We're going to take a closer look at how to do this properly so that you can enjoy and thrive on a healthy, truth-based belief system.

Rewiring

The million-dollar question at this point is, "How?" How do I put everything into practice? What does it look like? Can my brain actually be rewired or are these just nice concepts? Can I truly change? Could my thoughts really improve? Is any of this really possible?

I get it. At least 80% of my work is helping clients overcome these mental obstacles as they pursue their goals. Yes, it is possible, and even the most convoluted and corrupted minds can be healed through the concepts and practices we are about to explore. You deserve a healthy, truth-based belief system just as much as anyone else. In fact, it is a part of your inheritance. 1 Corinthians 2 explains that no one could know the mind of God before we had the Holy Spirit.[58] Now that believers have received the Holy Spirit, we have the mind of Christ. I consider it my responsibility to help you walk this out.

However, I will make it abundantly clear that I cannot do this work *for* you. To put the principles of this subject into play, you will need to do the work yourself. It is *your* belief system and it is *your* journey to freedom, breakthrough, and a better life. I am going to facilitate the process as best as I can in the remainder of this chapter.

Uprooting

You will never have a more mixed feeling than when you discover a lie that you've believed your whole life. In some ways, it's infuriating as you realize this stupid thought from the pit of hell has been holding you back. In other ways, it's like finding the missing piece of a puzzle you have been trying to assemble since birth. I *love* the look on my clients' faces in these moments where a lie is exposed.

You see, until you identify the faulty roots that are in your heart, you cannot uproot them. On the flip side, if you rush into uprooting faulty roots without doing the necessary work to loosen them, you will only be partially successful. That's why there is a process of cultivating emotional fitness and working through issues of the past before we get to this point. By the time you are here, you're ready to uproot.

The most powerful part of uprooting a lie is simply identifying it. Until you acknowledge a lie, you cannot deal with it or replace it. First you need to label faulty roots. There are several ways to do this, but my number one encouragement would be to journal. If you already know some of your roots from counseling or other experiences, that's great, you can continue on. If you don't know where to start, the workbook will guide you through a very simple process for identifying the core lies that must be uprooted for you to move forward.

Remember, a thought is a seed that takes root when we agree with it, grows as we repeat it, and bears fruit when we act on it. Where does the problem begin? Seed, root, growth, or fruit? It's not at the seed level because seeds are harmless in themselves. They carry potential, yes, but the mere existence of a seed is not problematic. By the time it bears fruit, the problem has blossomed—it's too late. It's when a thought takes root that the problem really develops. This is where we want to pay special attention.

By agreeing with a thought, you create a partnership with it and give it ground in your garden. If it's based on truth, then we celebrate because the growth of this thought will lead to better decisions and behaviors. If it's a lie, then it's only a matter of time before it wreaks havoc. This is why when you identify a lie, you must uproot it by breaking agreement. It is not enough to simply state the opposite of the lie and hope that the new happy thought will take root. First, we have to cancel the original partnership made with the lie.

This can be done by reading through a simple script in the workbook material that ensures you cover your bases once you've pinpointed the lie. Don't forget you have to be able to clearly label and articulate the thought behind it first. Only then can you uproot it.

Identity

There is a reason we talked about core identity before we talked about thought life. Identity comes first, then thoughts. Not the other way around. How you view yourself matters deeply. Identity is the rudder steering the ship. Who are you? Who told you? What makes you valuable? Those are the questions we long to answer, knowing that if we answer them with faith, they will solidify in our belief system.

We worked hard in the last chapter to get some answers to these questions. Not just blanket answers that work across the board, but personalized and customized answers that are specific to you. Your mission now is to take these answers and apply the faith factors. This is like adding gasoline to your core identity flame. It will not be enough for you to declare those statements while looking in the mirror. That is a really good start, don't get me wrong, but not enough on its own. We must continue to push these thoughts along the continuum by increasing our faith in them until they become settled and solidified beliefs.

There are four factors that enhance our faith in the truth: authority, social proof, repetition, and action. What would it look like to apply these factors to the answers you came up with in the last chapter?

Authority: This really goes back to, "Who told you?" Preachers, teachers, and speakers have a huge responsibility. They are people with authority and influence, and we are more likely to take their word for it as a result. People of authority can make a huge difference in solidifying a belief.

Journaling is the best way to answer the more provocative identity-based questions because it's a proven way to consistently hear from God. There is no better authority to deliver the truth than God himself. If He speaks it, it must be true. The words of the Bible can be greatly cemented in our belief system when we hear the whisper of God speak them to our hearts. It's why the statement, "You are my Son in whom I am well pleased," is so powerful. Jesus already knew this, but now that He is hearing it freshly spoken, something is solidified. Faith is enhanced. Not only for himself but also for those around Him.

Continue to ask God bold identity questions in your journaling. Come at the subject from different angles. Make it your goal to get more comfortable hearing His words of love, affirmation, and correction. Yes, correction is a part of this as well. Nothing demonstrates love better than correction. If He corrects you, it is because He is looking out for you. With time, as the leading authority in your life continues to affirm your identity, your faith *will* increase in the truth of His words.

Here are a few sample questions to journal:

1. God, what were you thinking when you made me?

2. God, what is my purpose?

3. God, what do you think of me?

Social Proof: I wish this one wasn't true, because sometimes our social instincts are counterproductive. Social proof enhances faith, that is a reality. If you are unsure about a restaurant or a store, chances are you will check out reviews before you make a decision about going there. The experience of others will determine whether or not you trust the vendor. Similarly, witnessing others who believe in something can be a compelling reason to believe the same thing ourselves. Be careful here. Just because something is common doesn't mean it is true. This is why first we must identify what is true, *then* we aim to increase our faith in it.

If you want to grow in your identity and sense of self, pay close attention to the people you spend time with. Do they encourage you? Do they have your best interests in mind? Are they secure enough to genuinely celebrate your successes? In 1 Corinthians 15:33, the Apostle Paul quotes the Greek poet Menander, "bad company corrupts good character."[59] The implication here is that even if you do all the right things to establish a healthy internal life, it can be nullified by bad company. It will be a challenge to solidify your identity and establish a healthy belief system if you are surrounded by people who do not ascribe value toward you.

Remember Adam? The guy who stood before The Mirror, in front of the entire class, and was then asked by the instructor, "What do you see?" Well, after he answered the question with some pretty dark and sad sentiments, the instructor looked to the class and said, "What do you guys see?"

One student after another came up to the front, stood on either side of Adam, looked him in the eyes, and told him the truth. They spoke of his character, kindness, gentleness, and on and on they went. Nearly half the class took a turn to stand beside Adam and proclaim the truth over his life, and this is why he was never the same afterward. Faith was imparted in that moment to transition those distant truths into a believable reality. This is the power of social proof.

I'm not suggesting you only find friends who are super positive and ultra-encouraging. The question here is, "Do they value you?" Does the way they treat you and handle the relationship communicate value? If it doesn't, I would suggest you look for other people to share your time with. You don't need to abandon the current friendships (unless they are toxic or abusive), but it might be wise to find others who will help you increase your faith in the truth about who you are.

Repetition: Repetition, repetition, repetition. Marketers in the 21st century understand the power of repetition better than anyone else. If you simply talk about a piece of clothing you want to buy or a renovation you're planning for your home, the minute you get on the Internet you will start seeing targeted ads for those exact desires. Marketers know that if you see something enough, you'll move toward buying it. Similarly, if you hear a thought over and over again, you'll buy it too. That's why Proverbs says to buy the truth. Repetition of the truth is a powerful way to increase our faith in it.

There is something about regularly seeing, hearing, and experiencing a message over and over again that cements it in us. Being exposed to the truth on a consistent basis goes a long way to transitioning thoughts into truth. Think about Timmy and Tommy. If Tommy continues to struggle with math, he will inevitably start to lose his confidence and the struggle will worsen. In this case, repetition is decreasing his faith and not giving him any chance to believe that he has any mathematical ability. If Tommy finally gets back a good test score, he may breathe a sigh of relief, but he will need many more good test scores before he starts believing in himself. Repetition is key.

This really just boils down to Principle #5 (Consistency Compounds). When you profess the truth consistently through affirmations. When you regularly journal and hear identity statements from God. As you spend more time around people that affirm and encourage you. These things all collectively increase your faith in the truth, converting thoughts into rooted beliefs.

My biggest tip here is that when you find something that increases your faith in the truth—journaling, affirmations, meditation, studying the Word—do not depart from it. Make time for it on a *consistent* basis. Don't let it be a fad or phase—treat it like your belief system depends on it. In many ways, it does.

Action: Nothing is more solidifying of the truth than acting on it. As we already discussed, this is when a thought "bears fruit." Actions reinforce the beliefs of your heart. As you work hard to change your belief system, you cannot just stop and say, "I believe this now." It must be demonstrated in your actions. That is when you will truly know it has become a belief.

Your behaviors reinforce your beliefs. If you believe a lie and act on it, that is going to cause problems. So what happens if you act on the truth instead, even though you don't believe it? Well, this creates a dissonance in your brain. There is a conflict between belief and behavior. One will have to give. Either the belief you have needs an adjustment or that new behavior you attempted will have to go. Creating these moments while you are rewiring can be very powerful because it has the potential to forge a new avenue for the truth in your belief system. Your actions are that important.

Let me use a story to illustrate. One of my clients, let's call him Raj (you knew it was only a matter of time before I used an Indian alias) has found the emphasis of my program on emotional well-being especially impactful. He has found himself again after a season of feeling lost and apathetic. While doing DeepClean, he has also been seeing a counselor. About two months into the program, his counselor remarked that Raj's emotional agility had dramatically improved. This was proven when his girlfriend broke up with him and rather than turning to pornography in his time of great need and distress, he chose to lean into his emotions, process them, and stay clean.

In a recent group coaching call, I asked everybody, "What subject or area are you most focused on in your recovery journey right now?" Raj said something that struck me.

"I quit my job the other day." Poor guy! Lost his girlfriend and a job in the span of a month. I was ready to comfort and console him. "I had this amazing moment as I was quitting," he continued with notable enthusiasm. "I was really unhappy with the working conditions. Too much isolation was negatively impacting my mental health. My usual response would be to just quit and peacefully leave to save face. But then I realized I had always been afraid of telling the truth.

"So in the exit interview, I opened up and I was honest. Not rude or hurtful, just up-front about some of the issues I had run into. It wasn't received that well, but it didn't matter because I stood up for myself. I've never done that before. Not in that manner. It felt so good."

Faith has increased in the truth. Raj behaved in a way that contradicts a lie he believed for a long time. A lie of powerlessness and not having a voice. A lie that says he does not have the right or worth to speak up. In that moment, Raj didn't have the time to journal and validate his emotions, but he was already doing that work behind the scenes. And it primed him to take a stand and act in accordance with the truth, even though it was unfamiliar. By taking action, Raj gave himself an experience with the truth and it felt good. He will need to continue to stand up for himself, and as he does, faith will increase more and more until those thoughts of worth, power, and positive self-esteem solidify as beliefs. You'll read more on how Raj's freedom developed in Chapter 9.

In essence, this is how you plant the truth in your belief system. Once you've done the work of uprooting lies, it's not as simple as declaring the opposite of that lie until you believe it. If you discover you've been believing the lie that you are not enough, you cannot simply declare "I am enough" and hope it replaces that lie. Remember, lies are not the opposite of truth. They are distortions. This is why we work hard to break the partnership with the lies, acquire the truth through journaling, scripture, and the like, and then start acting on the truth. When you begin to do this, in the context of emotional fitness, a recovered past, and pursuit of godly identity, this is extremely powerful. Everything you have learned so far is consolidated in the rewiring process.

When I was in ministry school, I had a moment that really demonstrated the significance of integrating these concepts. I was interning as a small group leader, which was an incredible experience. After having had such a transformative experience as a student myself, I now got to play a role in facilitating transformation in the lives of a new batch of students. At the same time, as an intern, I got to learn the operations and behind-the-scenes elements of ministry. It was a very rich time in my life.

One of the key factors that made this season particularly enjoyable was my fellow interns. It's fine to have these experiences on your own, but much better to do it with others. Everything is more fun with a group.

During our internship, the other male interns and I got up to the typical guy shenanigans like playing sports, talking about girls, and forming a band (we called ourselves "Back on the Market" because we were all single at the time and clearly forming the band to attract girls). But we also got to experience major heart-healing and identity formation collectively.

We all agreed that The Mirror was one of the most effective ways for people to experience transformation, but none of us had had the experience as students (due to the nature of the classes, only a few get called up to the front). So we agreed that one evening each of us would take a turn in front of The Mirror, except it was the mirror of our bathroom instead of the one in the auditorium.

When my turn came to stand in front of The Mirror and answer the question, "What do you see?" I could not believe what came out of my mouth. Words of love, hope, encouragement, and kindness. Statements of belief, faith, and self-trust. If it were not in front of trusted friends, I would have felt embarrassed. I wasn't trying to say the right things or forcing things to come out a certain way. I just looked at myself, started talking, and out came these incredible value-filled statements.

This is what happens when you begin to experience the truth. It's one thing to profess it— that's a good start—but things go to another level as you start to transition those thoughts along the continuum into a place of belief. The truth was coming out because it was finally taking root. You can have experiences like this too if you put these concepts and principles into practice.

It is also worth noting the power of being in a group. I cannot overstate the synergy that takes place when you bring men together for a common goal and purpose. In fact, this is why all DeepClean programs include a group coaching component. Belonging to a greater group is a critical part of recovery.

Brain Circuits

The brain is a beautiful thing. I do not believe we are in a fight against our brains. I do believe that sometimes we have conditioned our brains to function in ways that work against us. Your brain is extremely malleable. The clinical word is plasticity. Your brain can be trained and retrained over and over again. We think that is obvious, but until the 1980s, most thought the brain was dry cement once you became an adult.[60]

When you run into difficulties in your life—a struggle with pornography, bad habits with money, poor diet—the brain feels like enemy #1. If only your silly brain would stop thinking about women provocatively, things would be so much easier. No doubt, the brain is at play here and it definitely needs to be rewired, but remember that you are in control (Principle #1). Not your brain.

The truth is that our brains serve us, and they serve us well. Your brain is not perfect, but a majority of the time its functioning is helpful for you. It's important that we do not wage war on ourselves like an autoimmune disease. The writings of Paul make it clear that our fight is not against flesh and blood, ourselves included. We are to embrace our brains. Love them. Nurture and value them. They are not the enemy.

Positive appreciation of our brains must be the starting point for this part of the conversation because if we incorrectly label our brains as the enemy, we will engage in the wrong battle. Your brain *can* work for your good and be on your side, but not by default. You must train it. And that is really what this book has been doing: explaining the concepts, principles, tools, and experiences required for your brain to improve and function in your favor on a regular basis as you pursue freedom.

However, in our consumer-driven society we frequently make mistakes when it comes to brain rewiring. In the 21st century, where data and information are king, it's commonly believed that taking in good content and useful information is enough. If we listen to enough podcasts, watch enough sermons, hear enough motivational speeches, then we should be good. Osmosis kicks in and the information starts to change the way we think. Knowledge is power, right? Nothing could be further from the truth.

Knowledge is potential. It primes the pump, so to speak. Knowledge positions you to make better decisions because you have more information. However, in and of itself, knowledge only does so much to the circuits of your brain. I personally detest this fact because I am an information junkie. To give you an idea, in my YouTube home feed on my TV, about 70% of suggestions are motivational speakers like Tony Robbins and Dave Ramsey. I would like to think that if I expose myself to the wisdom of these geniuses, eventually my brain will start to connect the dots. There is some truth to this, but it's not enough.

To combat bad patterns and wiring in your cranium, you have two options. You can create new pathways by building a healthier belief system and behaving in accordance with the truth. This is primarily what we've explored. However, the second option is that you change the pre-existing pathways. To do one or the other will have some impact, but to do both together is extremely powerful.[61]

Let's say you have a struggle with pornography and masturbation. You cannot kick the habit no matter how hard you try. You go a couple of days, maybe even a couple of weeks, but something always sucks you back in.

So you take a course and learn about how to handle temptations and make better decisions that encourage sexual health. You get a system. You learn principles. You're given tools. And at the end, you are given the pep talk to go change the world one clean day at a time. All of this is great. You are now loaded with valuable resources, some of which have forged new paths in your brain. But they have not addressed the old ones.

So maybe for a month, you stick to the program. You journal regularly. You declare affirmations and walk in your identity. Things are going well. But then your old circuit starts to feel neglected, so it pipes up. You see a post on social media where a girl is showing just enough skin to get you thinking. Or you see someone in the mall with a nice figure and you look just a little too long. Your old wiring has been activated, and now you have choices. You can select new wiring, change old wiring, or continue with old wiring.

You see, while you were following a program with all the excitement and momentum during that first month, it wasn't a big deal. You could make those adjustments to your life with ease. This is usually how far people get in the transformation journey. They make some changes, the momentum carries them for a while, and they celebrate their success. But at this point their old habits kick back in. The mistake is thinking that just because you created new pathways, the old ones are suddenly gone. It doesn't work that way. You must neglect the old ones entirely or change them, in addition to forging new ones.

Please make note of what I am about to say. You can only change a brain circuit when it is active. Read that sentence again if you have to—it's very important. When you've done the "hard work" of ingesting information, you have just begun. It's in the moments when your old wiring comes back, that is when you *must* put into practice what you have learned or you will revert to old habits.

I see this dynamic play out with my clients all the time. They watch the course content, do the worksheets, give themselves a pat on the back, and carry on with their days, not realizing that until they are tempted to watch porn, the hard work has only just begun. The reason you take in useful content and increase your knowledge is so that in those moments when you're tempted, or you're caught between a rock and a hard place, you are equipped to change the narrative. Remember, thoughts are malleable. Just because you had a thought means nothing. How you respond is everything.

That is why knowledge is potential, not power. Knowledge *with action* is power. When you start acting on knowledge, both to form new pathways and to modify old ones, you become unstoppable. It requires effort initially, but once the momentum gathers, it's only a matter of time before you notice dramatic changes.

As we wrap up this chapter on thought life, I'd like you to consider times where this dynamic has played a role for you. Can you think of an occasion where you had a real issue, got some helpful information, and then stayed stuck? Do you remember the confusion and the disappointment of falling back into old habits?

What about the other side of the coin… Can you think of a time where you had an issue and you resolved it? Can you identify specific moments where old wiring kicked in and you chose against it? Do you remember what that felt like?

This is a weighty chapter with some significant topics. I strongly encourage you to go through the workbook online so you can get the most out of what you learned. The work of ingesting content and fleshing it out through activities and exercises is extremely valuable—it's what initiates the rewiring process.

Section 4

BECOMING A NEW MAN

CHAPTER 8

A Thriving Relationship with God

When I was in seventh grade, one of my teachers rototilled part of our school's field. Now when I say "part," what I mean is about a 200-square-foot plot. It was a significant portion of the field. For several days before and after school, he was out in the field rototilling away. When he was done he moved on to the next step, flooding. This beautifully tilled ground was about to become a slimy mud land. He sprayed gallons of water onto the ground, perfectly muddying everything up.

Why would he do such a thing? He was preparing the battleground for a school-wide tug of war, of course. (When you attend a private Christian school, this is the kind of thing you get up to for fun.)

The big day came. After a morning of classes, we ate lunch and began buzzing about the afternoon's festivities. We changed excitedly into our most raggedy clothes and braced ourselves for the field. You could practically taste the excitement in the air. A few students got in on the action early, building little mud balls and throwing them at each other. Classic. Now, we just had to wait on our opponents.

Not too long after, our worthy opposition took to the field, each and every teacher sporting their own set of clothes that they probably should have disposed of a few decades prior. They were few compared to the students, but they were mighty. The stage was set: the students vs teachers mud tug of war was ready to begin.

Generally, tugs of war on this scale take time and this one was no exception. The students heaved, the teachers pulled harder. Back and forth we went for what felt like hours until finally, the teachers started to pull away. The students fought. Dug their heels in the thick of the mud. But it only delayed the inevitable. The teachers were stronger and had more stamina. They were declared the winners.

Many men believe they are in a tug of war with the authorities of their life, God included. I'm amazed at how many Christian men believe God's arm must be twisted for them to walk in integrity and freedom. They think that growing spiritually or shaking off bad habits of porn and masturbation means going to war with the Big Guy. Pleading their case. Apologizing for falling short. Begging for another chance, desperately hoping God will throw them a bone.

The journey to freedom and holiness is not a tug of war with God. You are on the same team. In fact, you are a member of His team. The Author of freedom and holiness has invited you to join forces with His mission. At no point in this journey of spiritual growth do you become enemies. You were enemies because of sin. You are not any more thanks to the shed blood of Jesus.

This sounds basic but pay close attention. God is on your side. He is for you, not against. He is more excited about your freedom, sexual integrity, and holiness than you are! He does not hold your past failures against you. He is not waiting for you to get your act together or to prove yourself before He accepts you and helps you out. As a good team captain, He is willing to do everything He possibly can for you.

In my search for freedom from pornography, this was hard to believe. As far as I was concerned, my track record of porn viewership, empty promises, and messed up thought life were all valid reasons to disqualify me from God's support. Why would He help someone like me?

Maybe you've felt that way too at some point in your life. You look at your mistakes. You look at the times you swore you wouldn't do it again. You see the areas of your life where you aren't honoring God but you cannot bring yourself to make a long-lasting change. Maybe you're still watching porn. Maybe you still have outbursts at your spouse or you yell at your kids. Maybe you're still fantasizing about other women.

It does not matter what you've done. Where you've been. Who you are. If you have accepted Jesus into your heart and have repented of your sins, God is on your side. Bear this in mind as we deep dive into the spiritual elements of manhood. Remember that there is no condemnation for those who are in Christ Jesus. That means there is no condemnation for you. God is not condemning you, neither should you.

Scripture says in several places that you are made in the image of God. You reflect a part of Him that no one else can. Every human being on Planet Earth collectively forms a reflection of the living God. Not a complete one, mind you, but a reflection. We are all made to uncover the part of God's image that we represent. If you really believe this, you would become very careful about how you speak of yourself and others. If you slander yourself, and you are made in God's image, then who are you really slandering?

This is what I mean when I say that He is on your team. He made you in His image! He is eager and willing to help you become more like Him every single day. God doesn't tally up the ways in which you fall short. He is much more interested in helping you reduce your shortfalls and step further into the man He made you to be.

We must start here as we explore the spiritual realm because if you make the mistake of coming at this like a beggar and hoping you can find some way to get into God's good books, you will be disappointed. Everything we are about to uncover comes from an understanding that you, me, and God are all on the same team working together to achieve greater levels of freedom, holiness, and health.

Build Your House

Some have questioned why my methodology leaves the spiritual matters for the end. "Spirituality is the most important, it should be first." I agree that there is no greater realm than the spiritual realm. If you want to have any kind of success, fulfillment, or health, you must address the spiritual parts of your life. That is the truth. It's equally true that the spiritual arena of life is of greater significance than the emotional, mental, physical, social, financial, and vocational arenas.

The reason we do not address spirituality directly until the end is because of a lesson I learned in the first grade. I was at the birthday party of my friend Julian. For reasons that are well beyond my understanding, Julian's dad was my #1 fan. He was always so supportive and encouraging. He would buy me expensive gifts for my birthday (I still remember that gloriously noisy, top-of-the-line firetruck he bought when I turned six) and when Julian and I would hang out, he was just as supportive of me as he was his own son.

Julian wanted to go mini-putting for his birthday, so off we went. I had an awesome time, not only because I was hanging out with my friends and playing mini-putt, but because I got a hole in one! I didn't even know what that was, but Julian's dad was so excited for me that I figured it was a good thing. He explained to me why it was so special and used the moment to encourage me and cheer me on. Julian's dad was a quality man.

Since Julian's dad was such an encouragement to me at such a young age, I listened when he spoke. After we finished mini-putting, we went back to Julian's place for pizza and ice cream. Being a kid was the best, man. I filled my plate with a few slices of pepperoni pizza and balanced it with a couple of slices of cake, as one does at a six-year-old's birthday party. I looked around and saw that many of my friends had bailed on pizza and gone straight for cake! I missed the memo, apparently.

I was caught in a dilemma. Do I bail on the pizza too? I am very methodical, so even though I knew I *could* eat the cake first, that's not how you do things. You eat pizza first because it's the meal. Then you have dessert after. It was so simple to me. But now my methodical ways were putting me at risk of social rejection.

Julian's dad could see my struggle, so he asked me, with a slight smirk on his face, "Which one are you going to eat first?" His interest alone was empowering enough for me to stick to my guns.

"The pizza!" I exclaimed.

"Good!" he said. "Remember to always save the best for last."

Principle #4 (Delayed Gratification).

This moment marked me. I have lived much of my life with this mindset, wanting to save the best for last whenever possible. It's not just a nice idea, it's a proven principle. There is no greater example than eternity. Our lives here on Earth are just warm-up. God is saving the best for last—when we are fully and perfectly reunited with Him forever. And it's for these same reasons that I address the spiritual elements after everything else: I'm saving the best for last.

In scripture, your personal life *and* your belief system are often equated with houses. Jesus warns about building your life on sand and instead encourages you to build on rock.[62] He wants to see you and your belief system strong enough to withstand the storms of life. A life built on external pursuits like money and fame, and a belief system built on lies, is a house on sand. It is only a matter of time before it breaks down.

Jesus also uses the house metaphor in Matthew 12:43–45 when he explains casting out demons. "When an evil spirit leaves a person, it goes into the desert, seeking rest but finding none. Then it says, 'I will return to the person I came from.' So it returns and finds its former **home** empty, swept, and in order. Then the spirit finds seven other spirits more evil than itself, and they all enter the person and live there. And so that person is worse off than before. That will be the experience of this evil generation."[63] (Emphasis added.)

Notice that Jesus equates a person's internal and eternal life with a house. If your house is left empty and unoccupied, there is room for demons to re-enter with their friends. Not a good look. Instead, we want a house that is built on truth and full of the knowledge of God. That's why Proverbs 24:3 says, "Through wisdom a house is built, And by understanding it is established; By knowledge the rooms are filled."[64]

I find that many address the spiritual elements of life with effective spiritual tools, but do not know how to build their house on rock. The spiritual elements can clean the house, pray a deliverance prayer, or get some ministry from trusted elders. That stuff is good, and it helps. But if all they're doing is cleaning out a house built on sand, it will not have a long-term effect.

The work of the previous chapters was to dismantle any parts of your life that might be built on sand and rebuild them on rock. We look after these things first so that by the time we address spiritual matters, we can be confident that even if anything ungodly were to return and try to take you down, there would be no room in the house because its foundation is firmly established on rock and its rooms have been filled with the knowledge of God.

Three-Dimensional Humanity

Earlier in the book, I mentioned that we exist primarily in two realms: the internal and the external. I'm not saying that I lied to you, per se, but that wasn't fully true (yes, I'm confessing my own sin in the chapter about holiness and integrity). There is a third dimension: the eternal.

The eternal is the spiritual realm. It is everything beyond what happens in our inner circle and in our visible world. The nuances of life that cannot be explained by physical means. Scripture rarely talks about the internal, external, and eternal collectively. Instead, it usually draws comparisons between two camps: the internal and external, which we looked at already, or it groups the internal and external together (non-eternal) and compares them to the eternal.

Allow me to demonstrate. Luke 6:45 says, "out of the abundance of the heart, his mouth speaks."[65] Jesus was saying, what goes in (internal), comes out (external). He is creating a contrast between the two. But both the internal, and the external are non-eternal.

In Matthew 16, Jesus asks the disciples who they think He is. Simon Peter replies, "You are the Christ, the Son of the living God,"[66] and Jesus is delighted with his answer. In reply, Jesus says to him, "Blessed are you, Simon Bar-Jonah, for flesh and blood [non-eternal] has not revealed this to you but My Father who is in Heaven [eternal]."[67]

You are an eternal being. This is important to understand because we are exploring a subject that exists in the eternal realm. All spirituality must transcend the non-eternal world. While God exists primarily in the eternal realm, you and I exist primarily in the non-eternal realm (for now). However, there is a way that we can access the eternal realm, even now while we are on Earth: our spirit.

We are spiritual beings. It's the reason we are able to have a relationship with an eternal God. It's the reason we are able to hear His whispers when we journal. And it's the reason we have a responsibility to manage our spiritual world effectively so that we maximize our relationship with God and the resulting freedom.

The spiritual realm is both critical and invisible. The enemy wants you to believe it is less important because it cannot be seen or heard. Nothing is further from the truth. When Christ comes back again, the physical, visible non-eternal realm will hardly matter. Eventually, this story ends in the eternal realm, so we ought to pay close attention to it.

Dismantling the Demonic

The devil is real and so are his demons. We should start here since one of the devil's greatest tactics is to feign his existence. He would love for you to not be concerned with him and live as though he doesn't exist. The less aware you are of him and his ways, the more easily he can subtly wreak havoc on your life in gradual increments.

On the flip side, let's not blow this out of proportion. The devil is a pawn on God's chessboard. While he can cause great deception, he is no match for the Almighty God. The way I see it, we grow the most from resistance. Without an enemy around, how then would believers grow? God simply uses the enemy as a source of opportunities for His children to rise up and fight battles they were born to win.

As we dive into some of the ways the enemy may have an influence in your life, and what you can do to remove the influence, I want to assure you that we are coming at this from a place of victory. I have no doubt you will win your battle against pornography or anything else, because the devil is defeated. He should not be ignored, nor should he be glorified. Let's understand that he has a role, but we have been given the authority to dismantle the influence he has in our lives and in the world.

Why Can't God Just Deliver Me?

When I first had the idea to create a program that would help men overcome pornography, I thought about sitting down with some investors to get startup capital. That was new territory for me, but I was bound and determined to get this program off the ground one way or another. The first potential investor I reached out to was a church friend. A much older, wealthier, church friend.

We went out for lunch and caught up. Then I mentioned that I had a new project I wanted to share with him. It was my first time doing this, so I honestly had no idea what I was doing. I explained my former struggle with pornography, the lack of resources available for Christians who are struggling, and that I had a revelation from God on how to help other guys find the same kind of freedom.

Anytime you start talking to somebody about pornography, you have to be prepared for any and every kind of response. Some people might have a struggle themselves, so they don't really want to dialogue. Others might find it uncomfortable to talk about sexual subjects in such an open forum. This gentleman is not a particularly expressive man, so I had a hard time getting a read on how he felt about what I was sharing.

"I think it's a genius idea. In fact, I think it's a God idea," he finally replied.

Wow! I was excited now. This guy liked my idea. Let's see if he'd put his money where his mouth was.

"I had a struggle with pornography as well," he continued. "A bunch of us were struggling in my small group. Then we had this amazing experience. Each of us, on our own, was delivered by God from pornography in a matter of moments. I had an experience with God in my house—he delivered me. I reached out to my other friends to tell them about it only to find out they got delivered too. All around the same time. It was amazing."

My heart sank. I was really excited for him, don't get me wrong. But I knew that if his experience of freedom was instant deliverance, it was unlikely he would invest in a project like mine that requires a process. That turned out to be true. We had a great lunch and he was very supportive of my idea, but he was not interested in investing.

I had to really confront myself after this experience because I wondered if maybe I was doing people a disservice by offering a systematic process for porn addiction recovery. Maybe it would just be better if I got really good at deliverance prayer so that people could be healed instantly instead of going through a process. That's when God spoke up (while journaling, of course).

God explained to me that people who go through a process are better off because not only are they free, but they understand how they got there. In doing so, they have a better chance at preserving their freedom and helping others achieve freedom themselves. There is immense value in the process, even if it takes more time and requires more effort. Someone who gets free from a deliverance prayer is only equipped with a prayer to preserve their freedom and help others get free. That's a pretty big difference.

You may be wondering why God hasn't delivered you yet. Why He won't just change your thinking and give you more strength to fight temptations and urges. Or why He won't reverse the effects of your difficult childhood that has created issues for you as an adult. You may think you're waiting on God, but just so you know, God is waiting on you.

Sometimes we have to go through a process because the growth that comes through the journey is more important than the end result. This is not always the case—I have heard many stories over the years of men who have been supernaturally delivered of pornography, drugs, smoking, swearing, anger, etc. It happens every day, and there is no reason it cannot happen to you. But it is not the only option, and in some ways, it is not even the best option.

So here's where this lands. The first option is to seek God for a supernatural work. Pray, fast, press in, and do whatever you can to have Him do an instant work. Yield to Him and cry out for freedom. It's not a guessing game to see if God wants you to live a life of integrity. He's made it clear that He desires this for you, so do not be afraid to ask Him to deliver you.

If that doesn't pan out, then consider yourself invited into a process. One that will require some effort but has even greater rewards. Rewards that go far beyond what any instantaneous deliverance could offer. You see, when you choose a process, you get the best of both worlds. Long-term freedom, along with the tools, capacity, and maturity to sustain it. I know of many people who have been set free of something in a prayer meeting only to have it crawl back a few weeks or months later. They had the reward of instantaneous deliverance but did not have enough development to sustain it.

We have already unpacked a lot of this process: Laying a good foundation with timeless principles; building emotional fitness; learning to overcome the past; discovering our identity; and aligning our beliefs with God. Now, it's time to uproot any spiritual strongholds that might be holding you back in your recovery journey.

Repentance

There is no freedom in Christ without repentance. To resolve damaged spiritual roots in your life, repentance must be part of the equation. If you had no need for repentance, then you would have no damaged roots.

We commonly confuse repentance with asking for forgiveness. They are not the same thing. If you make a mistake, asking for forgiveness is a very honorable thing to do. Commendable, even. But it is not the same as repenting. The Greek word for repentance is *metanoia*, which means a change in the mode of thought or feeling. That's pretty powerful. Repentance changes your thinking and how you feel about a situation or subject.

Now, the most important thing about repentance is that it should not be guilt-driven. We talked earlier about how guilt can play a useful role in your life by catalyzing positive change. But you cannot simply say, "Oh, God, I messed up again, and I feel terrible, and I'm so bad. Please forgive me." Guilt is a good motivator for forgiveness, but on its own, not a good motivator for repentance. When you feel guilty for what you've done, you should be seeking God's forgiveness. That's okay. But scripture tells us that repentance should be driven by something else.

Romans 2:4 says it is the kindness (some translations say goodness) of God that leads us to repentance.[68] Repentance should not be fear-driven. "You better repent or else…" doesn't really go a long way. It might instill some fear, and it might provoke people to make short-term behavioral changes, but in the long run, it won't have much impact. Instead, repentance is choosing to change our thinking and our feelings about a scenario or subject in response to God's immeasurable love and kindness toward us.

That's why we have worked so hard to deal with emotional baggage and sort out your identity, and it's the reason for all the journal exercises—so that you could have an experience with God's kindness that would lead you to repentance. Not out of fear of what could happen if you don't, but rather because you've seen His kindness and now you know that it's best for you to change your thinking, so you can move forward toward a better life of freedom.

While there may be times when we repent for something and it's forever dealt with, repentance is usually a continuous process. A process that you have already embraced so well throughout this book without even realizing it. Think about how much work you have put into changing your thinking and your emotional responses. You are right on track.

Now, if you believe that there are things in your life you need to repent for, you will find a script in the workbook to help you do the work of repentance. But remember, it's just a starting point. Repentance is continual change in our thinking and perceptions until they are aligned with God. It is ongoing. I find myself daily repenting for judgments, poor decisions, and ungodly thinking. I do not repent to obtain God's forgiveness. I repent that I may move closer to permanently removing these issues from my life.

Whether you need to repent for judging yourself, objectifying women, making porn an idol, neglecting your loved ones for work, choosing porn/sex/drugs/alcohol instead of God, or for whatever other reason, I highly recommend that you take a few minutes and go through the script.

Soul Ties

Human beings are social creatures. Research in just about any field (social psychology, neuroscience, physiology, physical therapy, medicine) confirms that we were not meant to do this thing called life alone.[69] We are made to connect with others. To form a connection with another person is a bond and we bond with various people in varying degrees.

You have a bond with your first-grade teacher. It's probably not that strong, especially at this point in your life. You have a bond with your best friend. It's likely quite strong—certainly stronger than the connection with your first-grade teacher!

The concept of bonding is important to understand when you are cleaning up your spiritual life. We are not simply physical beings. Think about the bond you have with a teacher in school. There is nothing physical about it. It's a psychological bond. An emotional bond. These connections are formed in invisible arenas of psychology and emotion. Similarly, bonds can be formed in the spiritual arena of life.

A great example of a spiritual bond is between a husband and a wife. We call that a covenant. A covenant is spiritually binding. God made covenants with His people throughout the Bible as well. These are sacred bonds that are anchored in the spiritual realm.

Most bonds you make in your life are not primarily spiritual, and perhaps not spiritual at all. The connection you made with your first-grade teacher likely had little spiritual depth. I was in Christian education most of my life, but the nature of my connection with my teachers was not particularly spiritual. It's not about the environment, it's about the nature of the connection. Conversely, I am a married man and have made a covenant with my wife. Our connection is very spiritual.

Where am I going with this?

Well…sex. Obviously. We are triune beings—body, soul, and spirit. After all, we are made in the image of a triune God. When you engage with someone on a sexual level, a bond is formed at a deeper level than just the physical. If someone tries to tell you they are having sex for purely physical reasons, they are lying. Physicality might be the primary driver, but it will never be the only one. It's not possible. Connections are also happening in the unseen arenas. We call these deeper-forming bonds **soul ties**.[70] Soul ties are made in various ways and various capacities. We won't be going into the details, but I want you to know that part of your journey to freedom will involve breaking unhealthy soul ties.

Most who read this book will likely have some sort of inappropriate sexual history—porn consumption, fornication, etc. I certainly made my share of mistakes along the way, and that's not even including my 15-year addiction to pornography, so I'm not coming at this from a "holier than thou" vantage point. The reason I'm tackling the subject of soul ties is that these activities form them. They are damaging and are holding you back. I do not want you to be bound by your sexual history so I must reiterate that you cannot break free from your previous sexual mistakes without breaking soul ties.

Damaging soul ties form when sexual interactions take place outside of marriage. Sexual interaction with another person physically bonds you on all three levels: body, soul, and spirit. The body bond is obvious. The soul bond is because sex is about an exchange at a soul level between two individuals. And the bond is also spiritual, because sex was designed as a spiritual practice for intimacy formation within a marriage. Sex is inherently spiritual.

Physical bonds are broken by distance. If you discontinue your sexual interactions with the other individual, the physical bond breaks, whether you were engaging with them in-person or watching them on a screen. The same is *not* true for your soul and spiritual bonds. Those bonds remain by default unless you do something about them.

When I was recovering from pornography, I began to analyze my viewing patterns. I was quite surprised to realize that there were a few categories and a few specific people that I gravitated toward. I had a few go-tos. The categories I viewed explained some of the fundamental needs that porn viewership was meeting for me. As an example, one of the most commonly searched subjects in porn websites is stepmom- and mother-related content.[71] Why do you think that is? Mother wounds are a real thing, my friends.

It made sense that I often had a few people in mind that I would regularly look up because that's what happens when a bond is formed. You naturally go back to the person you formed the bond with when needs arise. When I learned about soul ties, I immediately thought of the women that I had previous sexual experiences with. That was obvious. But it took me time to realize that I had also formed soul ties with the people I was regularly viewing online.

Damaging soul ties need to be broken. It's a critical part of moving on from your sexual past, and necessary for you to walk into healthy sexuality and full freedom. Sexuality is intricately woven into our sense of self. So as we work toward walking further in our godly identity, taking our thoughts captive, and leading holy lives, we have to be clear of all sexual clutter.

One of my first clients, Blake, was skeptical about the whole concept. After we batted around the subject for a while, he agreed that on his own time he would go through the soul tie script.

His word to describe breaking soul ties now? "Powerful." He realized that there were certain individuals that he had developed a much deeper bond with than he realized. Recognizing those ties and breaking them was necessary for his recovery from pornography. He also realized that because he had given of himself in these pseudo relationships, he was relinquishing resources that should have been used for real relationships. So not only did he experience the freedom of breaking the soul ties, he also freed up his heart to engage in more meaningful connections.

Some of you may relate to Blake's initial skepticism. The concept of soul ties is generally met with mixed opinions, so I'd like to offer you two choices. First, if you are ready to break soul ties, you can access the script in the workbook.

Second, if you feel unsure about all this, then I would suggest you talk to your spiritual authority about the subject. In a multitude of counselors, there is safety. Then I want you to ask yourself, "What do I have to lose?" In my opinion, there is little to lose and much to gain by going through the soul tie script. I'll let you decide what is best for you.

Holiness

Holiness is accurately reflecting the nature of Christ. Holiness goes far beyond behavior and far beyond reverence, though both are important in the discussion. Holiness is a matter of essence. It deals with the nature of a person. The goal in this life is that as we go further, we become more like Him. In doing so, we become more holy.

You'll notice in Revelation 4 that as the living creatures continually worship God, they do not declare, "Lovely, lovely, lovely is the Lord God Almighty." They do not say, "Worthy, worthy, worthy is the Lord God

Almighty." Day and night, night and day, these wacky-looking creatures (read the scripture and you'll see what I mean) boldly proclaim, "Holy, holy, holy is the Lord God Almighty."[72] Holiness is the essence of God. It's not a quality or characteristic that He possesses, it's His fundamental nature. Similarly, you and I are invited to walk in holiness. To embody the nature of Christ in such a pure and profound way that we reflect Him to everyone around in our intents, actions, and lifestyle.

Imagine that holiness is a person standing on two legs. One leg is called relationship, the other is called righteousness. For holiness to be functional, both legs must be of equal measure or there will be structural damage and eventually impaired function. A person whose physical legs are different lengths suffers from issues of alignment in the body. They may be limited in their mobility. They might be able to move, but not as effectively.

For you to live a holy life, you must walk in both relationship with God and the righteousness of God. If relationship is overemphasized, holiness becomes hyper grace. You do not have to look far to find these messages— they come from the people who explicitly or implicitly preach that you can do whatever you want, moral or immoral, because God loves you anyway. Few people preach this outrightly, but they tolerate sin behind closed doors because God's grace is sufficient. If God's grace is perfectly sufficient in someone's life, then there would be no sin in the first place.

This is a tricky subject because of course, we are talking about serious issues—sexual misbehavior is no joke. So is there grace for these experiences? No. There isn't. There is mercy for them.

Mercy is when you are pardoned from consequence. The wages of sin is death (Romans 6:23),[73] so in theory, our mistakes merit a pretty nasty consequence. However, the shed blood of Jesus pardons us from it. This is called mercy, not grace. People often mistakenly say, "There's grace for that," in response to someone's error or sin. Actually, there's mercy for it.

When we explored Principle #2 (Responsibility), we talked about the difference between an explanation and an excuse. These subjects nicely intertwine with the mercy–grace conversation. If we let mercy excuse bad behavior, we diminish standards and enable sin, side-stepping responsibility to do things differently in the future. This is where administering mercy incorrectly becomes problematic. However, having an explanation of why a mistake was made gives you an understanding of that mistake. And a good understanding should lead to compassion and mercy, enabling us to make improvements for the future.

Grace, then, is unmerited reward. It is divine empowerment. Grace is the ability to avoid sin—it's the basic premise of new covenant living. We are commanded to live holy lives and the grace of God makes this possible. His grace *is* sufficient for you because it empowers you to live, maybe not a perfect life, but a life worthy of Him. A life that accurately displays the nature of Christ. Without grace, we have no hope of achieving holiness. It is but a faint wish.

Holiness is not simply having a heart-connection with God. That is important. It is a must. It is quintessential in the discussion. Yet it is incomplete in itself. Relationship must be equally accompanied by righteousness. Doing the right, moral, godly thing in all circumstances at all times. A very difficult undertaking.

If, on the other hand, righteousness is overemphasized in our pursuit of holiness, it becomes religion. Holiness is then no longer about who you are, but what you do. There is no value for transformation. The primary concern is behavior, and where there are issues, behavior modification. This kind of thinking becomes shame-inducing and fear-based. Don't do XYZ, *or else.* Religion is just as dangerous as hyper grace. Both impair the believer from living a fluid, holy life.

To walk in true holiness, we must have a balance of both relationship and righteousness in equal measure. We simply cannot afford to only focus on one. As we grow in our connection with God, we become more like Him. In becoming more like Him, we act more righteously. As we act more righteously, we grow more connected to God. The cycle continues. It is truly a beautiful thing.

When you have a robust, dynamic relationship with God, righteousness is no longer a tool to gain His approval, it is a choice to protect your connection. You realize that the best thing you can do to honor and steward the relationship you have with God is to live righteously. This is incredibly powerful. Similarly, you grow in relationship with Him because you know that as you understand Him better, you will better understand righteousness.

I find that most Christians are very aware of the righteous aspect of holiness. We all have a moral compass, and we understand what is appropriate from a biblical perspective. If you are new to Christianity and do not have this understanding, I recommend reading Colossians 3 to give you a better idea.

The greatest void I witness in the men I work with and the greater body of Christ is the relationship part. You might think that is a bit ridiculous when you consider that *everyone* talks about "relationship" over "religion" (thanks, Jefferson Bethke).[74] But while many are trumpeting a message of relationship with Christ, few believers still understand what that looks like on a practical level. We love the theory of it, but how do you cultivate a heart connection with the living God?

The final section of this chapter will focus on the relational aspect of holiness. Not because it's more important, but because it's less understood. The standards for righteousness are easy to extract from scripture, as they are often overtly conveyed. The methods for cultivating relationship with God are not as obvious. They are subtle, nuanced, and implicit. In the next few pages, you are going to learn some practical ways to walk in a fruitful and dynamic relationship with God, achieving new levels of holiness in the process.

Intimacy with God

The idea of intimacy with God comes with mixed reviews. Intimacy is such a "feely" word. Can't we just say connection? Or relationship?

Of course we can. But should we?

When you are growing up, intimacy is meant to be experienced primarily through your parents. What happens when you become an adult? You can't keep going to Mom and Dad.

Well, you'll get married one day, right? And then your spouse will satisfy all your needs for intimacy. Ask anyone who thought that and then got married, and you'll realize how comical that thinking is. Your spouse is another imperfect human. If you think they will perfectly meet your core need for intimacy, you are sorely mistaken.

"Yes, Sathiya, but this is a broken world. *No one* can perfectly meet my core need for intimacy."

I agree. No one in this broken world can do that. What about someone who lives outside of your world? Does it not make sense that a perfect and eternal God can perfectly and eternally meet your need for intimacy? Remember, we are not talking about physical or sexual intimacy here. We are talking about the experience of being seen, known, and understood by another person.

This is why intimacy with God matters. Not something that is gushy and romantic, but a raw, transparent connection with God that holds nothing back. Much like the relationship King David had with God. When you read the Psalms, you see that David did not mince words. He had no problem expressing his feelings in the moment. Letting God see him. Know him. And understand him.

This is part one. Our conscious choice to let God see, know, and understand is only half of the equation. The other half, of course, is God's end of the deal. It's His conscious choice to be seen, known, and understood by you.

With time, your relationship with God will become sacred. Personally, I fiercely guard my connection and times with God. I am unwavering in my morning times with Him, but not because I feel obligated to or because I am fearful of the ramifications if I don't. The relationship has become precious to me and these are moments that I look forward to.

This kind of deep, personal, meaningful connection with God is available to you. And as a matter of fact, is essential for you. The kind of fulfillment and satisfaction you experience in a meaningful, personal connection with God outshines any human relationship you could have, marriage included, and it certainly outshines any lures that pornography, masturbation, or any other sexual temptation might offer. When God is your primary source of intimacy, everything else in your world is enough.

Psalm 23:1 says it best, "The Lord is my Shepherd, I shall not want."[75] When God is our primary source, we long for little else.

Collateral Reward

I will be honest: intimacy with God was a struggle of mine for a long time. I would hear stories of people who had incredibly deep and personal relationships with God, and I didn't get it. Admittedly, for much of that time, I also didn't want an intimate relationship either. I didn't see its value and didn't really understand it.

Eventually, after some spiritual growth and a better grasp on the subject, I reached a place where I saw its importance but still, I had no clue how to experience it. The crux of this season took place in England. Part of the curriculum at ministry school involved a missions trip. Teams are sent to all four corners of the globe for these glorious three-week outreach opportunities. Our team was blessed with the chance to experience the land of tea, crumpets, and phenomenal soccer (football, to be accurate).

While it was very exciting to go to England, our schedule was relaxed, to say the least. Other outreach teams from the school had full schedules, jumping from one thing to the next, but for our team it was the opposite. There was not a ton of work for us to do, so every day we were encouraged to spend time with God and do our devotionals to fill the open space in our calendars. It was disappointing to have such a slow schedule, but I am ever the optimist and decided to make the most of it. Little did I know then how much that decision would change my life.

It was about the midpoint of our trip. I was feeling desperate to experience God on a deeper, intimate level, while also trying to manage my boredom. So on a very average morning, I sat down to read the Bible.

Have you ever had that experience where you read something that you have read a hundred times, but suddenly it leaps off the page and you see it in a new light? That's what happened to me on this fateful day when I opened up to Matthew 6.

Jesus is in the middle of His Sermon on the Mount, sparing nothing and no one. The first 18 verses of Matthew 6 center on the spiritual disciplines, specifically doing good, praying, and fasting.

I have read these scriptures before. They are great, as they provide direction on how to behave appropriately in church settings, how to pray using the Lord's Prayer, and how to fast correctly. That was always my view of this passage. But suddenly, as I read Matthew 6 on this rather rainy and dull day, my heart came alive.

"Be careful not to practice your righteousness in front of others to be seen by them. If you do, you will have no reward from your Father in heaven. So when you give to the needy, do not announce it with trumpets, as the hypocrites do in the synagogues and on the streets, to be honored by others. Truly I tell you, they have received their reward in full. But when you give to the needy, do not let your left hand know what your right hand is doing, so that your giving may be in secret. Then your Father, who sees what is done in secret, will reward you."

—Matthew 6:1–4[76]

My takeaways from this passage have always been to do things with a good heart, not to be seen by men but to be seen by God, and always prioritize the private life. Don't let public rewards or social approval become a motivator for your spiritual acts. These are good takeaways, and truthfully, I have built my life on them. But there is another lesson embedded in this passage.

Doing good, or giving to those in need, is an invitation to have an experience with God. This is not just meant to be done in secret to keep it hidden, it is meant to be done in secret so that it is a personal experience just between you and God. No one else.

Also, did you notice that the reward is from the Father? It's not from God. It's not from the Lord. It's not from the Spirit. It's from the Father. Jesus frequently spoke about the Father, because of course, this is how He related to God. But here, He is explaining how we are to relate to God. He chooses to use the word "Father," a highly relational term. Remember that as we read on.

"And when you pray, do not be like the hypocrites, for they love to pray standing in the synagogues and on the street corners to be seen by others. Truly I tell you, they have received their reward in full. But when you pray, go into your room, close the door and pray to your Father, who is unseen. Then your Father, who sees what is done in secret, will reward you. And when you pray, do not keep on babbling like pagans, for they think they will be heard because of their many words. Do not be like them, for your Father knows what you need before you ask him. This, then, is how you should pray:
Our Father in heaven,
Hallowed be your name…"
—Matthew 6:5–9[77]

The layout of this scripture is very similar. Jesus explains what the hypocrites do when they pray. Then he urges us to avoid their example because they pursue public reward. Instead, pray privately. Make it personal—just between you and the Father. Invite Him in and no one else. And when you do, your Father who sees what is done secretly will reward you. Again, there is an implication in Jesus's instruction: Prayer is not about being seen or getting results. It is first about connecting with the Father.

Then, Jesus makes this wild statement: "Your Father knows what you need before you ask him. This, then, is how you should pray…"

Did you catch that? How many times do we pray to let God know our needs? God, please provide a new house. God, I need a new job. God, I need a raise. God, I'm really stressed, I need peace.

Jesus is saying, just so you know, the Father already knows your needs, which means if you are praying to simply make God aware of your needs, you are wasting your time. Why, then, would Jesus encourage us to pray if God already knows our needs? Could it be that prayer is more about developing intimacy with God than it is about producing outcomes?

Jesus invites us to experience prayer privately with the Father as a personal experience, where connecting with Him is our first priority, before we engage in any prayer itself.

Finally, Jesus says:

"When you fast, do not look somber as the hypocrites do, for they disfigure their faces to show others they are fasting. Truly I tell you, they have received their reward in full. But when you fast, put oil on your head and wash your face, so that it will not be obvious to others that you are fasting, but only to your Father, who is unseen; and your Father, who sees what is done in secret, will reward you."
—Matthew 6:16–18[78]

The message here is: Don't worry about being seen by anyone, except the Father. Jesus is redirecting you and me into the secret place with the Father to build intimacy with Him. To be seen, known, and understood in a way that will far exceed the intimacy we could experience with anyone else.

We have made the mistake of reducing spiritual disciplines to practices and behaviors when they are meant to be *facilitators* of intimacy. Similarly, we have mistaken the secret place as a breeding ground for public reward. Many Christians believe that if you spend enough time with God privately, eventually He rewards you publicly.

What if He *is* the reward? Could it be that as we adhere to Jesus's teachings and pursue greater intimacy with God in a private manner, we are rewarded by experiencing more of Him in the process? And anything beyond that is simply a bonus?

This is my personal approach to spiritual disciplines. I believe that while all disciplines have their value, ultimately, the reason we engage with them is to foster intimacy with the living God. Without this component, spiritual disciplines become rigid and rote. But the model Jesus sets in Matthew 6 makes it clear they are meant to be dynamic and engaging.

And that's not the best part.

In my own life, I can confess that I am much more like my wife after being with her for many years. When we first met, I was my own person. I did things my own way. But as our lives have intersected and overlapped more and more over the years, this dynamic has changed. There are things I do now that I clearly learned from her.

As an example, my wife is Jamaican. She speaks patois. She is therefore, by default, a hundred times cooler than I will ever be. Shaloma has done a great job of adopting Canadian culture while still preserving a decent amount of her Jamaican heritage (her Jamaican friends might disagree with that one, but this is my book and that's my opinion). In fact, you wouldn't really know Shaloma is Jamaican unless you paid close attention. Her accent is almost nonexistent and she speaks in clear English.

That is, of course, until she gets in a car. I don't know what it is about driving, but the slightest of deficiencies or delinquencies in other drivers on the road brings out a completely different side of my wife. Some call it road rage. I call it Shaloma's inner Jamaican. Driving is to Shaloma what anger is to the hulk.

I used to laugh at my wife's antics until one day I got cut off on the highway and my inner Jamaican came out. Patois, slang, and even a bit of an accent. I was spewing my frustrations at a Bob Marley level. Where did that come from? And more importantly, did I just become cool?!

No, still not cool.

But clearly, the time spent with my wife had begun to rub off on me. I can assure you that if I lived my life without Shaloma, there is no way I would respond like that to an incompetent driver!

This is the fruit of intimacy. Our relationship is flawed. We make mistakes. We have miscommunications and misunderstandings. But we get back up and try again. We spend time together, and in the process, I've become more like her and she has become more like me (she may road rage like a Jamaican, but she cooks like an Indian).

Similarly, the collateral reward of building intimacy with God is that we become more like Him. In spending time getting to know Him, and letting Him know us, we adopt His nature. His holy and righteous nature. And in the process, He starts to rub off on us. We start to embody His essence. This is the power of intimacy.

This pursuit of holiness does not happen without an intimate pursuit of the Almighty God. So finally, we're going to look at a few practical ways to walk this out.

The Disciplines

I want to say two things before we get into the disciplines.

Spiritual disciplines alone will not save you. I spoke with a pastor last week who has faithfully read his Bible and engaged in other spiritual practices every morning for the last five years. He is also hopelessly addicted to pornography. He has tried more programs than anyone else I've ever met, including some I had never heard of. The guy is severely impaired and equally diligent in his daily devotionals. Do the devotionals still help? You bet. In fact, I am scared to think of what his condition might be like without them. But clearly, on their own, they will not solve his problems.

Secondly, my greatest fear is that you will look at these six disciplines and lump them all in the same category, thinking you can pick the ones that suit you best and run with them. That is not how this works. Each spiritual discipline has its own flavor.

Each offers value to your relationship with God. Some may already be commonplace in your day-to-day life—that's awesome and I'm proud of you for having those in place. But understand that without having all six of these disciplines active, you are missing out on the other flavors. I personally believe the best-rounded relationships with God are those that can jump from one discipline to the next. Being able to engage and connect on several different levels is the mark of a robust relationship.

Lastly, please understand that doing the spiritual disciplines is not about how you feel. I know, I'm the guy who is teaching you how to get in touch with your heart and label your feelings, and now I'm telling you how you feel doesn't matter. Here's what I mean. Do not let how you feel stop you from engaging in a spiritual discipline.

It's called a *discipline* for a reason. Sometimes, it will not be enjoyable. Sometimes, you will not be in the mood. Do it anyway. You are not doing this for positive vibes and good feelings. You're doing this to become more like God and to cultivate intimacy in the most important relationship in your life so you can live a life of freedom. Sometimes this will come naturally and enjoyably, other times you will need to discipline yourself and force engagement anyway.

I encourage you to take stock as we go through these disciplines. Evaluate how well you engage with each one and think about what it might look like to increase or implement them in your life going forward.

The Word

The Bible is becoming increasingly important in our day and age. Many believers are Bible-illiterate. They do not understand its significance, and they do not know how to read it. The greatest value of the Bible is getting to know the Author. Each page contains valuable content that propels us into further connection with Him.

A few things you must know about the Word. Firstly, if you look to the Bible to help you, you will find solutions. I don't know where, because I do not know what your specific issue is. But the Bible is a potent resource, full of insights, guidance, and directives for godly living.

As you read the Bible, you will learn more about God. You'll start to discover what He is like and how He relates to His people. You'll start to see the importance of covenants, relationships, and why God cares about the things He cares about. The Word is a beautiful invitation into a greater understanding of God.

If you are not regularly in the Word, I want to encourage you to fix that. There are tons of apps, Bible plans, Bible studies, and other resources to help you get into the Word on a regular basis. Take advantage of them.

Prayer

Prayer is communication with God. The Bible does not specify that we must fold our hands or close our eyes, although these are things that I instinctively do because of my upbringing. The most important element of prayer is open lines of communication. Many reduce prayer to a laundry list of requests. "Please heal Aunt Gladys. I pray so-and-so gets a promotion, etc." It's very easy to come before an Almighty God and voice your concerns and requests, but prayer is so much more than that.

I personally view prayer through the same components as journaling: expression *and* reflection. You must have both. Prayer is not meant to just be you blabbing away. There's another person on the other end of the line! How often do you do all the talking during your prayer time? You were given two ears and one mouth for a reason. I find that prayer is the most impactful for me when I take time to listen after I'm done talking. These are the sweet places where the Spirit of God loves to speak. Don't reduce prayer to just your side of the deal.

Another great benefit of prayer is that it merges your heart with God's. I can't count the number of times I have come to God concerned about a particular situation, and as I voice my concerns and then listen, my heart toward the situation starts to change.

Prayer creates avenues for communication in both directions while unifying our hearts with God. Don't get me wrong, there is nothing wrong with having prayer requests and voicing your concerns, but do not forget the other parts. When you approach prayer this way, the act of prayer itself becomes very rewarding, and the outcome is a bonus. Sometimes our prayers get answered the way we want, and it is so sweet. Other times, they do not because God has something better. Either way, it's a win.

I strongly encourage you to integrate prayer into your regular rhythms of life. 1 Thessalonians 5 encourages us to pray at all times.[79] Without ceasing. It is impossible to get on your knees every moment of every day and pray, but what might it look like to steadily communicate with God throughout your day instead? Think about it, and evaluate how you can integrate prayer with your daily life.

Worship

Worship is not music. Worship is not tithing. Worship is not animal sacrifice. All of these are expressions of worship, but they are not the essence. True worship is any intent, utterance, or act that ascribes worth to God. The worth of God is the central, fundamental component of worship. We worship because He is worthy.

When you approach worship in this manner, God receiving the Glory He deserves becomes priority. Worship is meant to be a sacrifice, and it's in this place that it has the greatest impact. Modern worship mentalities center around self. Scriptural worship mentalities *sacrifice* self. The difference is dramatic. We must never make worship about ourselves and what we can get. Worship is no longer a sacrifice when your gain is a higher priority than His. Make His gain the priority, and the benefits of worship will naturally come.

There is something about beholding God in all His splendor that impacts the deepest parts of us. I can't explain why, but I do know this: Worship is massively important for your long-term success, freedom, and wholeness. When you make worship a regular part of your life, you will be amazed at the person you become and the things you accomplish. It might be through tithing your money or your time or some other resource. It might be through the way you parent your kids and treat your colleagues. It might be through regularly blasting worship music and letting loose in your bedroom. The expressions are not as important as the essence.

Find ways to regularly spend time worshiping God. Taking the focus off the cares of life and directing your attention to the infinite worthiness of God will have as much, if not more, impact on your well-being than any other strategy or discipline.

Fasting

I am shocked at how uncommon fasting is among Christians. In my own life, I have experienced things with God through fasting in a way that is so different from the other disciplines. It is one of my favorite flavors, if you will.

Examples of fasting are found throughout the Bible, each one offering its own insight. The gist is that fasting increases your desire for God and it accelerates outcomes. Fasting does not have to be flashy. In fact, it should be the opposite, as we learned in Matthew 6. I have learned that fasting is a great way to catalyze hunger for God. I let my physical hunger pangs remind me to turn my attention to Jesus and quickly pray, which takes me to my next point.

Fasting coupled with prayer is extremely powerful. When you can let your hunger pangs serve as a reminder to pray into a situation or a particular area of your life, the results are incredible. I can show you a list of things that have taken place in my life over the last few years because I fasted and prayed about them. If I had not fasted or prayed, they might have happened still, but not as quickly or as intensely.

I fast for 24 hours every week and have done so since 2017 and I have no intention of stopping. One of my spiritual leaders scoffed at the idea of fasting "only 24 hours" when many of the examples of fasting in the Bible are for three days, 21 days, and 40 days.[80] I asked him how long he usually fasts and his face went flush. That ended the conversation pretty quickly. As I said, fasting is commonly overlooked today.

Others have argued that eventually your body will acclimate to 24 hours of fasting and it won't even cost you much. That's a good point, but it's not *the* point. Remember that the goal of all spiritual disciplines, fasting included, is that we cultivate a connection with God. Fasting is no different. I love the days I fast because it gives me a chance to be more intentional about praying and redirecting my attention to Him on a regular basis. Eventually, I may fast for longer periods, but I'm more interested in consistency and longevity at this point (Principle #5).

Meditation

Meditation is very much coupled with the Word. You cannot meditate properly without first knowing the truth. In more recent years, this whole practice has become mainstream, but with so many forms of meditation out there it is hard to keep track.

For our purposes, here is what you must know. First of all, biblical meditation is not emptying yourself out and clearing your mind. That is eastern meditation and I do not recommend that approach. Biblical meditation is filling your mind with the truth of God.

Biblical meditation is equivalent to rumination, the way a cow digests its food. In case you aren't aware, a cow will chew its food, swallow it, regurgitate it, chew it some more, swallow it, and repeat the process a few more times. Mark where you are in the book if you need to puke a little before reading on.

Like any practice, you can start small with meditation. As little as five minutes of meditation is enough to make a difference, and as you get comfortable with five minutes, you can increase the length of your practice. If you want to get more into meditation, I'd highly encourage you to talk to a trusted spiritual leader about it. Make sure that the way you're practicing is aligned with the Word of God and not mixed in with some of the other mainstream methods that are similar but not biblical.

Stillness

While this is by far the least popular of the spiritual disciplines we're exploring, it might be the most important in today's world. Because we are overstimulated and incredibly busy, stillness feels impossible. Yet the Bible is clear that stillness leads to the knowledge of God: "Be still and know that I am God" (Psalm 46:10).[81]

Stillness is about taking time to slow down and to rest in the presence of God. There is honestly nothing like it. Life has its troubles, its chaos, and its stress. When you take time to simply quiet yourself, stay still, and welcome the presence of God, you begin to experience peace that surpasses all understanding.

I want to be a little more practical for this discipline because it is less understood than the others. To really maximize the impact of stillness, there are a few things you should do.

1. **Find a conducive environment.** Think about the time of the day, the distractions in the room, the lighting, etc. Where and when will you have the best chance of being still?

2. **Music helps.** Finding gentle music to play in the background can help a lot. There are tons of options. The workbook has a YouTube link to one of my unreleased instrumental albums if you are looking for a starting point. Some of my clients prefer music that is instrumental so that they are not distracted by the words, but that is not a requirement. Just find music that will help you stay still.

3. **Engage with God's presence.** This one is harder to articulate because there isn't a formula. The key to stillness is becoming aware of God's presence. Once you reach that point, anything can happen. But make sure you stay in a receiving posture. Stillness is not the time to pray or meditate.

4. **Receive.** In all other spiritual disciplines, we are doing something or initiating a process. With stillness, the goal is to receive peace

from God and possibly revelation. The main goal is quality time in His presence. It's that deep place of connection where you don't need to say anything or do anything, you can simply be around each other and experience connection as a result.

While stillness might be the hardest to pull off, I believe it is the most important discipline for us to engage in moving forward. If you want some help evaluating which disciplines you need to focus on in the season you are currently in, the workbook for this chapter will help you do exactly that.

CHAPTER 9

Secrets to Permanent Freedom

Therefore, if anyone is in Christ, he is a new creation; old things have passed away; behold, all things have become new.
—2 Corinthians 5:17[82]

I barely survived the first time I drove a car. There were several reasons. For starters, I was 15 years old and not allowed to drive legally. Secondly, it was a cold, Canadian winter night and roads were slippery. Thirdly, the car was a stick shift. Realistically, it would have been harder to *not* crash the car under these conditions.

A classmate of mine lived on a massive property. We'll call him Mitch. His parents owned many greenhouses, which is quite common in the area I'm from. When you grow up on agricultural properties, it's common to start driving the machinery at a pretty young age. Mitch had been driving vehicles around his property since he was 11 years old. He was seasoned. The rest of us had no idea what we were doing.

As rambunctious teenagers with nothing better to do, Mitch asked us if we wanted to do some driving. It was a no-brainer. Our vehicle of choice was a rather run-down 1980 Nissan Sentra. While the car was old and barely started, it was a stick shift and had four reasonably secured tires, so it was perfect for our purposes.

We had the time of our lives as everyone else took their turn. When it came to me, Mitch asked, "You want to try?" The idea of driving was thrilling since the only vehicle I had driven at that point in my life was a go-kart. But driving stick scared me. I had no idea how it worked. "Don't worry, I'll teach you," Mitch replied. I strapped myself in and away we went.

I've seen stables with fewer stalls. It took me forever to get the car into first gear. If you've driven stick, you know that this is the hardest part. Eventually, with some good teaching and even more luck, I got the car into first. What a thrill! I quickly hit my top speed in first gear at a whopping 10 mph. I was king of the world.

"Okay let's go to second gear," Mitch, instructed. Oh baby, here we go. Second gear is a breeze once you've made it into first. I had now doubled my speed to 20 mph and if I was not king of the world before, I definitely was now.

But as the saying goes, all good things must come to an end.

"Alright, start slowing down," Mitch calmly directed. "Slow down!" Mitch said with a little more intensity. "Press the brake!" Mitch exclaimed.

"I am pressing the brake!" Nope. I was not. I was pressing the clutch. At the last second, I realized my error, found the brake, and slammed it. The car slowed down momentarily and then hit a patch of ice. We slid to the end of the row, across the country road, and onto the neighbor's property, coming within inches of hitting a tree.

A brief silence marked the moment as we took in what had happened. Then we all burst out laughing. Mitch looked at me and calmly said, "I'll drive back home." Yeah, good call.

When I turned 16 and could legally drive, I was eager to redeem the experience. For the most part, the excitement of being able to drive legally overpowered any fears or doubts I had from driving that Nissan Sentra. I picked up driving pretty quickly and got my license.

However, 11 years later, I hit a snag when I bought a car with a manual transmission. Why manual? Because it's cool. Everyone knows if you can drive stick shift, you are automatically a bit cooler.

My first day with the car was an experience, to say the least. I had my dad come with me to pick up the car because he knew how to drive stick properly. I signed the papers, handed the keys to my dad, and he stepped into my new car to drive it to the training ground—the same parking lot where he taught me to drive when I was 16 years old. In some ways, it was beautifully nostalgic. But in most ways, it was downright ugly.

The good news was that I had watched hours of YouTube videos on driving stick. Couple that with my previous experiences and I was basically an expert.

After 45 minutes, the car had moved a grand total of -3 inches and smoke was coming from the hood.

"I've made a terrible mistake," I thought to myself.

My dad agreed and suggested we take a breather, so back to the house we went. I watched more YouTube videos, threw up a couple of prayers, and carb-loaded. I needed all the energy I could get. About half an hour later, we went back to the parking lot to try again. This time, I got it. Again, the thrill of being in first gear hit me. It was just like old times, minus the beater car, icy conditions, and illegalities. Eventually, I felt comfortable in the parking lot so we hit the streets. I wanted to get the car checked out by my mechanic, so we made our way toward his shop.

When you are learning to drive stick, red lights become the enemy because it means you have to stop, and if you have to stop, you then have to get back into first gear. I'll be honest, the first few stoplights were nerve-wracking, but eventually, I got the hang of it. "Driving stick isn't so bad," I thought to myself. Oh, Sathiya. Still so much to learn.

We reached yet another red light. No big deal! That was until I looked in the rearview mirror and noticed a police cruiser directly behind me. My confidence plummeted. After what felt like five minutes of waiting, the light turned green. No matter how hard I tried, I could not get the car into first gear. My brain was too scrambled from the pressure. I was convinced the cop was going to give me a ticket for being a horrible stick-shift driver! The light turned red again and the car had not moved a millimeter. I looked in my rearview mirror again and noticed the siren was on now.

I rolled down the window as the cop made his way to me. He took a quick peek inside and gently asked, "Someone learning how to drive stick?"

"Yessir," I sheepishly replied.

"Alright, no worries. If you can't get it at this next light then let your old man drive, okay?"

"Yessir," I replied again.

My dad and I chuckled as we both breathed a sigh of relief. Thank God the cop was nice. The light turned green and I got the car into first gear first try. My nerves settled and we were back in business.

We reached my mechanic who was thrilled to see us. Our mechanic runs his shop out of the garage of his home. So rather than pulling into a lot, handing the keys over, and sipping coffee while your car is fixed, you have to pull the car into his garage while he directs you to ensure you're properly aligned with the hoist.

This is normally not that big of a deal, and even for a novice stick-shift driver like myself, all I had to do was align the car properly. There was just one problem. I had to get back into first gear again, and now in front of my mechanic. The pressure was back on. I would rather have had the cop behind me!

I started up the car, released the clutch, and stalled. Again, and again, and again. Frustrated and embarrassed, I rolled down my window ready to tell my dad, "You just drive it in." But before I could open my mouth, I heard Dad's voice gently, but confidently saying, "Keep going, son! You can do it!" That encouragement was all I needed. I put the car into first gear, pulled the car in, and handed over the keys. What a relief! The saga was complete.

That evening, I drove my car back to my place, which was over two hours away, without stalling it once. I certainly had my share of blunders over the next few weeks, but with time, I grew quite confident and now drive stick like it's second nature.

The words my dad uttered to me then are the same words I say to you now: Keep trying, you can do it. I don't know where you are in your journey to freedom. Maybe you're at square one, or you're almost there and need one last push. Maybe you're somewhere in the middle and still figuring things out. The road is not easy. You will stall. You will think you have something figured out only to fail again. You may encounter unplanned challenges along the way. Stay the course. Keep trying. You can do it.

I want to leave you with a few best practices to get the most out of the system we've explored that will ensure long-term freedom. These are seldom discussed in a recovery context, but I've found them to be crucial for the success of our clients. I also wanted to conclude a few recovery stories that were initiated at some point in the book but left incomplete.

Know Your Season

One of the biggest mistakes I've made in my own life is ignoring the season. There are seasons that mark our current realities, and if we do not identify them, we will live chaotic and aimless lives. When we are aware of our season—the changeable stages and phases of life—then our next aim is to identify the priorities of that season. This gives us fluidity to move through life, enabling us to make adjustments should unexpected situations and challenges arise.

It would be impossible for you to apply everything in this book immediately. In fact, I even discourage the men I work with in my program from applying every single thing they learn. Instead, the goal is for them to identify their season, pinpoint the priorities of that season, and focus on the concepts of the program that will serve those priorities best. This is a much more effective way to live and is key for long-term success.

A great example is the spiritual disciplines. We have talked about six different disciplines that can help you cultivate intimacy with God and ultimately live a healthier spiritual life. A balanced life would include a little of each of these. Pray and worship every morning. Read your Bible on lunch breaks. Focus on meditation and stillness in the evenings. Fast once a week. Who's going to do all of that consistently for the rest of their life? Probably no one.

Instead, ask, "What is my season? What are the priorities of my season? Which of these spiritual disciplines will serve those priorities the best?"

I was speaking on this topic to a group of young adults at a camp. Most of them had given up their summer to help hundreds of children encounter God, something that I find highly commendable. I did a little Q&A after my talk and one young woman said she didn't understand how to set her priorities.

So I asked, "What season are you in?" She was totally blank. Had no idea.

"Okay, well has God spoken anything to you about this season? Have you noticed any recurring themes or topics coming up? Is there a particular area you are focused on right now?" I continued.

"Oh!" she exclaimed, "Well one of my main goals over the summer is to grow in my relationship with God. University life has been really hard on me spiritually and I want to go into next semester on a strong foundation."

"That's great! So what have you been doing daily and weekly to invest in your relationship with God?"

Another blank stare. "I haven't done anything. I've made the kids my priority and then any free time I have is usually spent with my peers."

"Any idea how you could alter your routines to strengthen your relationship with God?"

"Well, I could get up a bit earlier in the mornings to spend time with Him. I always find this so invigorating, but I have a hard time waking early. I've also wanted to study a few books of the Bible. I could dedicate an evening every week toward that."

By the end of this conversation she sounded a lot more optimistic. And while she was just a young woman still finding her way in life, her experience is one that we can all relate to.

How often do the cares of life consume us until we realize that we've lost sight of our true priorities? When you try to live a balanced life, you will experience this feeling regularly. Instead, observe the season. You might have to do some digging. Some journaling with God. Some prayer time. Some listening and learning. It's worth it to find out what season you're in and to identify the priorities that match it.

Spending your evenings reading God's Word and praying will always be good things. But there might be seasons where you will have to cram that in in the morning because you have other priorities, like parenting or starting a business, and you need your evenings to do those things. Nothing wrong with that, just make sure God is in it. Don't settle for your own good ideas.

Without identifying the season, you will foolishly look at other people in different seasons and compare. Remember Raj? The guy who quit his job and rather than passively exiting, decided to speak up honestly because he knew he had something to share?

Raj has had one primary priority as he's gone through my DeepClean system: to cultivate emotional fitness. In addition to signing up for my program, Raj has also been seeing a counselor. About two months in, the counselor noticed a dramatic change in Raj's emotional well-being. He was emotionally agile, and able to identify and process his emotions with remarkable maturity. The fruits of his investment were starting to appear.

As I'm writing this, Raj has been free of porn for six months after struggling with it daily for almost 15 years. His exact words are, "I have been free at different times, but never this long and never with this much ease." This is the power of knowing your season and its priorities, adjusting your life to match them.

With a "balance" mentality, Raj would be tempted to compare himself to some of the other guys in the program who are stronger in this area and might feel discouraged because he is behind them. That would evoke a sense of needing to catch up and wondering if something was wrong with him for not having emotional fitness already. But with a "seasons" approach, Raj is able to focus on *his* priorities and not feel any shame about them. As a result, he's experiencing unprecedented levels of freedom.

Celebrate Small Victories

As men, we tend to be hard on ourselves. We demand perfection or we believe that our work is never good enough. This is a dangerous mentality because it will rob you of lessons learned from current success and the ability to increase or enhance what is working so far. So please heed these words: You must celebrate small victories to experience long-term freedom.

I'm not sure what it is about this concept that is so uncomfortable. For me personally, by nature, I will not celebrate anything until it is grandiose, spectacular, and worthy of applause. That's just my tendency and I'm learning that many men are wired similarly. It feels almost belittling to celebrate small victories.

Here's the thing. Celebrating small victories is an important part of staying encouraged along the way and of giving yourself the necessary compassion needed for the journey. We are playing the long game, so we must plan accordingly. If you can only celebrate when you reach your destination, you are going to become burnt out and jaded. You might still achieve the destination if you have enough brute strength and willpower, but you will not enjoy the process and your relationships will suffer along the way.

Celebrating small victories is a glorious opportunity to marvel at the progress you make and reset yourself for the next leg of the journey. It also gives you a chance to invite loved ones in to celebrate with you and relish the moment. This practice was particularly impactful for Phil—he's the guy who moved twice in a month and used his external circumstances to justify looking at porn and masturbating.

I have pushed Phil to celebrate small victories again and again, even though this is the exact opposite of his nature. When he first started Deep-

Clean, he would slip a few times a week. So when he only slipped once in a week, we celebrated! And when he started to go a week or two without slips, we celebrated. And as his progress furthered, we continued to celebrate. It didn't negate the fact that he still had work to do to reach his end goal, rather it commended the steps he was actively taking and progress he was making.

Reflecting on his journey, his exact words are, "God has used this time to develop my character and my emotional stability. I'm not acting out because I'm frustrated or annoyed anymore. Celebrating small victories along the way has helped me appreciate my progress and stay the course while pursuing new levels of freedom."

I want to encourage you to take a moment right now and reflect on how far you've come. Think about the person you were one, three, or even five years ago. Are you the same person? Have you learned any new life lessons? Are you closer to any of your goals now than you were back then? It's crazy how quickly we forget how far we've come. I guarantee if you do this and take a minute to reflect on how much you've grown and matured even in just the last few years, you would be proud of yourself.

Imagine if I decided to never drive a car again after my first experience. That would be reasonable considering my pathetic first attempt at driving stick! But it would have robbed me of a vital life skill. My dad's words, "Keep trying, you can do it," are words that I needed to hear in that moment at the mechanic's to keep me going. To help me realize that if I have put the car in first gear before, then I can do it again! And again, and again. Now, I don't even have to think about it.

This is why you celebrate small victories. As you identify areas where you've grown, it reminds your brain of what you are capable of. If this is how much you have grown in the last year, then how much more will you grow in this year ahead? Celebrating small victories not only gives us an appreciation for our past and how far we've come, it also encourages us to pursue greater heights in the future.

Ever-Growth

Humans are made to grow. Period. This is not a matter of opinion or some philosophical conjecture, it's a proven principle. When we are stagnant and we don't feel like life is moving forward, we become miserable. It's not because we are miserable people, it's because we are not experiencing the very thing we are fundamentally wired for—growth.

When prospective clients want to join my program, the implication is usually that they are no longer growing in their pursuit of freedom and they cannot take it anymore. We hate stagnancy, and for good reason. This is God's design. Scriptures say that we go from glory to glory, faith to faith, everlasting to everlasting, etc. We have scriptures like Haggai 2:9 that say, "the glory of this present house will be greater than the glory of the former house."[83] God's heart is always that things improve, develop, and grow.

So how on earth do we become stuck? If growth is so important, why wouldn't it happen naturally and continuously for us? There is one reason, and if you can learn to reverse this common pitfall, you will experience continuous growth. The pitfall I'm referring to keeps people stuck in their jobs, stagnant in their close relationships, disconnected from God, and feeling hopeless about their future. It's not what you think it is. It's not the devil or complacency or anything like that. It is much more covert. Hidden. It can be a good thing in the right context, so sometimes we falsely assume it's good in all contexts.

How do we become stuck?

Comfort.

Your greatest catalyst for growth is a willingness to confront discomfort. All growth exists outside of your comfort zone. For you to learn, to experience more freedom, to become a new and better man. For you to kick pornography for good and have healthy sexuality and to experience true intimacy in the relationships that mean the most to you, you will have to go outside of your comfort zone. Little can be achieved within it.

You will more than likely make mistakes, but that's part of the process.

Remember Jim? The guy who cheated on his wife with escorts, got caught, confessed everything, and entered a 12-step program only to fall again 18 months later? How uncomfortable is it to reach out for more help after you've completed a 12-step program unsuccessfully? How much discomfort would you experience confessing yet another time that you need help and that you're willing to spend your hard-earned dollars to get it? Jim had to humble himself. He had to face reality and confront the most uncomfortable option in his dire situation: reaching out and getting help. Again.

Jim is approaching a year of freedom from porn and masturbation, but it's different this time because he has resolved the roots of his issue. Because of his extensive history, he will have to continue to work hard. Implementing best practices, regularly guarding his heart, and ensuring he confronts the small discomforts essential to achieving steady freedom, like opening up to friends and journaling on a regular basis. If you confront small discomforts regularly, you will avoid situations where you are forced to face great discomforts later on.

I know that you read this book so that you could grow and learn. You want to become a better man. You want to walk in your calling. You want to untangle the sin that so easily entangles. You want to be a better husband, either now or when the time comes. There is no way you've read this far so that you could carry on living a boring and stagnant life. Read this carefully—the growth you long for exists on the other side of your comfort zone. You will have to confront discomfort to achieve long-term freedom.

The New Man

You have never been closer to freedom than today. Every day leading up to now has given you experience, insight, and opportunity to become the man God has made you to be. I know this journey is difficult. I know it's challenging. I know that sometimes things feel like they are going backward even though you are putting in every effort to move forward.

My greatest encouragement to you is to keep going and to find a program that you can commit to. Those who dabble or chronically consume information without any application are the ones that stay stuck and disappointed with their progress. If you want to get free of porn, find a coach and a system that you can stick with. If you wanted to get in better physical shape long-term, wouldn't you reach out to a personal trainer who can help you get there? At the very least you would get a gym membership. You cannot afford to simply know how to get free from pornography, you must *act* on the knowledge, and nothing facilitates this better than a proven program. If you believe DeepClean might be what you're looking for, please visit my website www.sathiyasam.com/coaching.

Let me take this moment to remind you that God is for you, not against. You do not have to twist His arm to attain freedom in life. He is more excited about your freedom and success than you are. It doesn't mean there won't be challenges along the way, but it does mean that He will be there to see you through so that you can move forward into the fullness of the life He has called you to lead. With heaven on your side and a proven system, it is hard to not get the results you want.

The time is now. Remember Principle #3 (Freedom Bookends). You have deep-seated reasons that drive you in this life. You have lofty visions of what you want life to look like one day. My friend, I have no doubt in my mind you can fulfill all these things. I don't need to know you or your story to have full confidence in you. That's because everything you've learned in this book has helped the young and old, rich and poor, educated and uneducated, Christian and non-Christian, the single and married. There is no person too far from the grace of God—you are not the exception.

In case you need a little more encouragement, read Appendix A where I've profiled more stories of guys just like you who have taken the concepts of this book, diligently applied them, and achieved phenomenal levels of freedom. Their stories are inspiring and regularly remind me why God is so passionate about liberating men from the grips of pornography and sexual misbehavior.

Wherever you are in your journey, I am cheering you on. I believe in you. I am for you, and I challenge you to not settle for a mediocre life. You were born for greatness, and if you earnestly apply what you've learned in these pages, I'm confident you will uncover just how great you really are.

Many times I am asked, "What's the greatest part about living a life of freedom?" That is an easy one: the security. Proverbs 10:9 says, "he who walks with integrity walks securely."[84] I would pay any price necessary for the security I now have in myself, my close relationships, and my spirituality. It's hard work, but it's worth it.

Keep trying, you can do it.

More Success Stories

In case you need an injection of hope, I've provided some more client success stories. These are stories of ordinary men who have achieved extraordinary results for three simple reasons:

1. The grace of God

2. Their diligence

3. The system

Struggling with sexual misbehavior can feel lonely. Whether it's porn, masturbation, infidelity, fornication, or anything else, we generally feel isolated and even ostracized for our shortcomings and wonder if there is anyone else out there who feels the way we do. I am wildly passionate about bridging this gap so that anyone struggling can find safe places that provide healing, which is why all my programs come with group coaching and a tight-knit community.

These stories may encourage you along the way and help you to see that you are not the only one. Some of these guys come from pretty rough situations, which is why I am so confident in the content of this book. If they can experience freedom against all odds, you can too.

Make sure you read these stories to seek inspiration. If you catch yourself comparing or feeling worse about your situation, then I would put the book down. This section is meant to be inspiring and to fuel your desire for greater success in your life. Enjoy.

Blake

From religious shame to porn recovery coach.

Yes, this is the same Blake from Chapter 8. His story is too good to not share. When Blake came to me, he had been struggling with porn on a daily basis for over 20 years. When you have a problem that has lingered for that long, you wonder if this is just how life will be until you die. That was Blake's mentality. He was riddled with religious shame because he was strong in his faith but had this hidden sin.

When we started working together, Blake said his number one goal was to reach a place where he could help other guys get free. He felt called to church leadership and ministry, but the idea of serving in that capacity was unbearable because of his problem.

Blake had to address some underlying issues. He had a few very faulty beliefs and he was emotionally immature. He was not insensitive per se, but he lacked the necessary skills to manage his emotional life. There were also a few damaging experiences from his past that he had not fully resolved. Experiences that marked him and negatively shaped his sense of self. We went through some major forgiveness in these areas as well.

While these aspects were all impactful, I will never forget seeing Blake after he had finished the Identity section of the program. He was a new man. Something had clearly changed. He was handling himself with more confidence and poise. While I was one of the first people to witness the change in Blake, I was not the last. People started coming up to him at church and asking for his advice on their struggles in life. No prompts or anything. His inner leader was coming out and people were taking notice. He began to get much more involved in heading up church ministries and was offered the chance to join the preaching rotation. Blake had changed so much that his new form commanded opportunity.

Amazing as this all was, Blake's true desire was to help other men get free of porn. And I'm happy to say that he does this today. Blake has joined the DeepClean team as a jack-of-all-trades. He does group coaching, individual coaching, and a whole plethora of other things that help men get clean, free, and confident.

Raj

Recovering from the past, learning to love himself.

Raj sent me an email one day that coaches like me dream about receiving. Rather than trying to paraphrase his story and experience, I've decided to include the email in its fullness. No edits.

"Sathiya, I just wanted to send a bit of encouragement and let you know how much I appreciate DeepClean. Not only have I not looked at pornography in over 6 months, but I have seen SO much healing in so many areas of my life as a result of this program.

"I think one of the most significant skills I have gained from this is the ability to manage my emotions well and pinpoint traumatic experiences in my life to be able to process the pain, as well as forgive who I need to forgive. I had no idea that I was driven by so much anger, resentment, sadness, and rejection.

"I've also been digging into attachment theory over the past few weeks and I realized that I have been well on my way since digging into Deep-Clean to change my attachment style from fearful-avoidant to secure without even knowing what those were. I know this because the quality of my relationship with myself, as well as others, has drastically improved.

"I feel more satisfied in my relationships and for the first time in my life, I am beginning to love myself. I see myself as someone who is inherently valuable and is a blessing to other people instead of someone who is just a bother. And on top of that, it's easier for me to form romantic relationships. I don't feel like I'm going blindly into dates anymore and I'm able to evaluate whether someone should be pursued, rather than if they like me.

"I just started Stage 5 today and I am so excited for what the rest of the course has to offer. If I could, I would fly to Canada today to give you a huge hug and buy you a steak dinner. Thanks for everything you've done in this course, Sathiya. You're the man."

Raj is a machine. He is plowing through this system and experiencing unprecedented levels of freedom in record time and the best is still to come for him. Freedom is momentous, it takes a lot of work to get the ball rolling initially, but once the wheels are in motion it's hard to slow down.

Nicholas

Accountant with a hidden life gets in touch with his
inner self and bolsters his marriage.

When we first connected Nicholas was exhausted mentally, withdrawn spiritually, and disconnected from his meaningful relationships. His greatest fear: breaking down. He was so overwhelmed by his struggle with porn, he feared it was only a matter of time. Breaking down would naturally have major implications for his career, marriage, and young children. And as ironic as it may sound, porn was the only thing that was (temporarily) keeping his life afloat.

Nicholas was caught in the classic pattern of viewing porn, feeling guilty, vowing not to do it again, and then relapsing not too long after. He had tried multiple accountability tools, and while they helped enforce some self-control, there was always a workaround when he was tempted enough. He needed to get to the root of his issues.

When I asked Nicholas to identify the most impactful part of his time in DeepClean, he said "Digging deeper into the thoughts and feelings that underpin my behavior, beginning to understand how they affect me, and how I can gain ownership over them." It's amazing how far a little self-awareness can take you. This was by far his biggest growth point as Nicholas started to become much more attuned to his internal life. From here, things really started to take a positive turn.

"I find myself less drawn to these things to medicate my negative emotions. I can't say that I'm not tempted, but I'm better equipped to handle those temptations than before. I also have a better perspective regarding God's unconditional love for me, which helps me combat my fears of failure and rejection that would often lead me into porn use."

Nicholas can also open up to his wife more now that he has a better understanding of his internal world. And by improving his marriage, Nicholas is also changing the course of his children's lives. Reaching a place of sexual health is not just for you, it's for your loved ones and your lineage.

Howard

Executive pastor rediscovers himself, explodes with freedom.

Howard was stuck. As an executive pastor, he had nowhere to turn with his struggle. He knew it had to be addressed, but he kept putting it off. After almost *four decades* of struggling, he had had enough. Howard desperately needed help.

Howard's exact words were, "When I signed up for DeepClean, I had no idea what was in store for me on this journey. All I knew was I had a problem and Jesus was clearly saying to me, 'Do you want to get well?' as he did to the paralytic man at the Pool of Bethesda."

Of all my clients, I don't know if anyone has been more diligent than Howard. He has embraced the methodologies of DeepClean with incredible vigor and his results speak for themselves. After struggling two to three times a week prior to the program, Howard finished the course going over 100 days without a single slip. And that's just scratching the surface. Howard learned to identify emotions, harness intel from his past, process pain and forgive others, uproot false beliefs, and identify the true role of spiritual warfare in the process.

During Howard's initial strategy call with me, he mentioned that while he had "adulted" well—held a steady job, owned cars, owned a home—he always felt like a little boy. Near the end of the program, after so much hard work has been done, we do a little label exercise to signify the transformation that has taken place. It's essentially ripping off an old label that you used to wear and replacing it with a new identity statement that was received from God. Howard took off the label of "Little boy" and took on a new label of "Strong man of God." He truly is a new man.

Today, Howard still attends the coaching calls, and is an active voice and leader in multiple porn recovery spaces. His story of radical transformation is nearly unparalleled, not only because of the behavioral change he underwent but because of his ability to adopt a new dogma that focuses on matters of the heart. At his stage of life, an accomplishment of this magnitude is nothing short of impressive. He is an inspiration to many men already and his story will continue to propel many more men to freedom in years to come.

Bradley

From shameful skeptic to journal fanatic

Bradley came to me anxious, nervous, and confused. He had a consistency issue and was terrified of getting married one day because he knew his problem with porn would interfere. A question I love asking clients when they book their first call with me is, "What has been the cost?" It's a basic question, but a real eye-opener for them when they start to count how pornography has impacted the emotional, mental, relational, financial, social, spiritual, and vocational parts of their life.

Bradley was living under constant pressure from his parents to achieve at a high level and get married. This was costing him his well-being and it strained his relationship with them. Bradley was also turning to porn and masturbation to manage stress. He had no other coping mechanisms. Lastly, Bradley was angry. He was mad at himself for struggling so much and he was mad at God for not delivering him of his addiction.

Bradley's words of wisdom? "Admit you need help. Everything else follows after." My favorite part about Bradley's story is that he hated journaling. He doesn't like writing things down so he resisted the whole idea. One day, I could tell he was an emotional volcano ready to erupt at any moment and he had no idea how to dissipate the tension. I asked him why he wasn't journaling. It was clearly going to help him.

At first he pushed back with all the classic excuses—writing isn't my strength, what's the point, etc. Then I realized he hadn't even tried it. He resented the idea of writing things down so much that in his mind it wasn't even worth a shot! Unbelievable.

After some godly coercion (aka coaching), Bradley agreed to do 10 minutes of journaling in our session, following the methodology outlined in Chapter 3. He didn't give much of a response, but I could tell it went better than he was expecting. When Bradley graduated DeepClean, he said that by far the most impactful part of the program was journaling. He hardly goes a day without it now. Funny how that works!

As a matter of fact, around the time Bradley completed DeepClean, a girl that he was seeing broke things off with him. He said normally he would have used porn and masturbation to medicate, and he would have lashed out at others as an outlet for his anger. But this time, he had his journal. He digested his emotions. Processed the pain. And reached a place of peace and health. It didn't make the ending of the relationship enjoyable or easy, but it allowed him to handle the experience in a powerful and healthy way.

Sometimes the things we resist the most are the things we need the most. That proved to be the case for Bradley, who is a stronger, more mature man after completing DeepClean. While his most recent relationship didn't pan out, he has never been better positioned for a long-term relationship because he has done the hard work now.

Unleash The Man Within Podcast

Find out more at www.sathiyasam.com/podcast

Principles, tools and insights to increase your integrity and confidence.

- Five (5) episodes per week packed with deep content in a light-hearted way

- Guidance for resolving root issues

- How to advance your calling

- Interviews with leading experts in men's health

- Learn from real-life client examples

AVAILABLE ON ALL MAJOR PLATFORMS

DeepClean Coaching

Resolve the roots. Restore your relationships. Fulfill your calling.

Stop guessing how to get free. DeepClean helps men overcome pornography addiction using a proven, systematic process. The same process that each client mentioned in this book used to get free.

All DeepClean programs provide you:

- **Life-changing Content** in easy-to-understand terms with practical applications that you can put to use immediately.

- **World-Class Coaching.** Receive expert guidance through the entire process until you are completely free. Group coaching calls are hosted on a regular basis. You can attend them for the rest of your life if you choose to.

- **Tight-Knit Community** of men around the world pursuing freedom just like you. Don't do the journey alone. Receive the support, camaraderie, and encouragement you deserve.

Find out more at www.sathiyasam.com/coaching

Acknowledgements

Writing a book is something I have wanted to do for many years now. To finally reach this point is a dream come true and one that I will be celebrating for many years to come. Like any large-scale project, there were so many people that have made this happen.

For starters, I want to thank my gorgeous wife Shaloma. Thank you for the support, encouragement, and sacrifice that you provided throughout this entire project. You love me so well and I couldn't have done this without you by my side. This book is just as much mine as it is yours. I love you.

As Dr. Joe Martin put it – I come from "good stock". Mom and Dad, thank you for setting me up for success in life. You are the best parents a guy could ask for and I long to have a similar impact on my kids. Also, it has been fun learning from each other as we write our books at the same time - excited to see where God takes the final products.

Priya & Jaya, you guys make life worth living. I'm grateful to have the two of you as my siblings to enjoy life together, including – relentless teasing of Mom and complaining about Dad's cell phone usage. Yeah, I'm ready to go.

To my groomsmen – Matt, Kenny, Joey, Jake, Taylor & Keith – thanks for your friendship all these years. This book would not have happened without your belief in me. Let's have a "meeting" asap, I'll give the speech.

Andrew Hildebrand & Steve Gay, I don't know if I've ever seen God orchestrate the coming together of a group more clearly. Without our mastermind, I'm not sure this book would have happened when it did. Thanks for pushing me out of my comfort zone, enlarging my vision for Deep-Clean and putting up with my dietary quirks. Celery waters on me next mastermind.

A huge thanks to the Book Launchers team who has given me an unbelievable self-publishing experience! Special shoutouts to Julie Broad for killer self-publishing advice and my author concierges Marta Kowitz & Elissa Graeser.

To my assistants, Kris & Ann. You have helped me with the book in more ways than one. Thank you for looking after many behind-the-scenes elements, including the workbook. You've given the readers a spectacular experience beyond the book itself. Secondly, thanks for looking after so many logistical and operational aspects of DeepClean to free up time so I could focus on the book. You have added incredible strength to our team.

Andrew Blackwood, your counselling over the years has been monumental in my health and the success of my marriage. Thank you for your warm, yet direct, guidance. To call you and your beautiful family good friends now is a true honor and one that I do not take lightly. See you at the beach.

To Steve & Sandra Long and Ben & Sarah Jackson, thanks for allowing me to get DeepClean off the ground while working at the church. Your mentorship, kindness, and support have meant the world. I miss working for you guys!

Jonathan & Alice Clarke, thanks for being true friends these last few years while also guiding Shaloma & I through so many different seasons and stages of life. You guys have given us so much support, including while this book was being written and developed. Love you both dearly!

To Drew Boa, Shawn Bonneteau, Garrett Jonsson and Dr. Joe Martin, thanks for the phenomenal work you are doing in the porn recovery space. I am so grateful to have trustworthy colleagues that I can glean from as we continue to push for a society where sexual integrity is the norm.

Endnotes

1 Ross Benes, "Porn Could Have a Bigger Economic Influence on the US than Netflix," Yahoo Finance, June 20, 2018, https://finance.yahoo.com/news/porn-could-bigger-economic-influence-121524565.html.

2 David Schultz, "Divorce Rates Double When People Start Watching Porn," *Science*, August 26, 2016, https://www.sciencemag.org/news/2016/08/divorce-rates-double-when-people-start-watching-porn.

3 Chiara Sabina, et al., "Rapid Communication: The Nature and Dynamics of Internet Pornography Exposure for Youth," *CyberPsychology & Behavior* 11, no. 6 (2008), https://doi.org/10.1089/cpb.2007.0179.

4 Proverbs 20:11 (New Living Translation)

5 Luke 6:45 (New King James Version).

6 Proverbs 4:23 (NLT).

7 Matthew 7:24–27 (English Standard Version).

8 Proverbs 25:28 (NLT).

9 Proverbs 16:32, (NKJV).

10 Proverbs 21:5 (NKJV).

11 Proverbs 29:18a (King James Version).

12 Proverbs 6:6–8 (NKJV).

13 Melissa Healy, "The Surprising Thing the 'Marshmallow Test' Reveals about Kids in an Instant-Gratification World," the *Los Angeles Times*, June 26, 2018, https://www.latimes.com/science/sciencenow/la-sci-sn-marshmallow-test-kids-20180626-story.html.

14 Ibid.

15 B.J. Casey, et al., "Behavioral and Neural Correlates of Delay of Gratification 40 Years Later," *Proceedings of the National Academy of Sciences of the United States of America* (PNAS) 108, no. 36 (September 2011), https://www.doi.org/10.1073/pnas.1108561108.

16 Proverbs 13:11 (ESV).

17 Scott Weiss, "The Power of Consistent Saving and Compound Interest," Mahopac Money, accessed June 3, 2021, https://mahopacmoney.com/2019/04/28/the-power-of-consistent-saving-and-compound-interest/.

18 Matthew 6:19-21 (New International Version).

19 Hilary Jacobs Hendel, "Ignoring Your Emotions Is Bad for Your Health. Here's What to Do About It," *TIME*, February 27, 2018, https://time.com/5163576/ignoring-your-emotions-bad-for-your-health/.

20 Da-Yee Jeung et al, "Emotional Labor and Burnout: A Review of the Literature," *Yonsei Medical Journal* 59, no. 2 (2018): 187–93, https://doi.org/10.3349/ymj.2018.59.2.187.

21 Mila Kisina, "Unresolved Feelings and Suppressed Emotions in Addiction," Genesis, accessed June 3, 2021, https://www.genesisrecovery.com/unresolved-feelings-in-addiction/.

22 "Netflix Revenue 2006–2021 | NFLX," Macrotrends, accessed June 3, 2021, https://www.macrotrends.net/stocks/charts/NFLX/netflix/revenue.

23 Psalm 6:6–7 (NKJV).

24 Terence Y. Mullins, "Jesus, the 'Son of David,'" *Andrews University Seminary Studies* 29, no. 2 (1991), https://www.andrews.edu/library/car/cardigital/Periodicals/AUSS/1991-2/1991-2-02.pdf.

25 Matthew 6:8 (NKJV).

26 Léa Rose Emery, "What Modern Arranged Marriages Really Look Like," *Brides*, updated August 11, 2020, https://www.brides.com/story/modern-arranged-marriages.

27 Reggie Ugwu, "Brené Brown Is Rooting for You, Especially Now," the *New York Times*, April 24, 2020, https://www.nytimes.com/2020/04/24/arts/brene-brown-podcast-virus.html.

28 Jill Suttie, "How to Listen to Pain," *Greater Good Magazine*,

February 17, 2016, https://greatergood.berkeley.edu/article/item/how_to_listen_to_pain.

29 Steve Safigan, "Shame Resilience Theory," Positive Psychology News, May 16, 2012, https://positivepsychologynews.com/news/steve-safigan/2012051622128.

30 "Guilt," GoodTherapy, updated November 21, 2019, https://www.goodtherapy.org/learn-about-therapy/issues/guilt.

31 "Squatter camp," Your Dictionary, accessed June 3, 2021, https://www.yourdictionary.com/squatter-camp.

32 Drew Boa, "How To Fall Asleep Without Porn," Husband Material, November 16, 2020, https://www.husbandmaterial.com/blog/how-to-fall-asleep-without-porn

33 Darlene Lancer, "How to Raise Emotionally Healthy Children," PsychCentral, May 17, 2016, https://psychcentral.com/lib/how-to-raise-emotionally-healthy-children#1.

34 Emily M. Cohodes et al, "Development and Validation of the Parental Assistance with Child Emotion Regulation (PACER) Questionnaire," Research on Child and Adolescent Psychopathology (2021), https://doi.org/10.1007/s10802-020-00759-9.

35 "Sweet Brown on Apartment Fire: 'Ain't Nobody Got Time for That!'" KFOR Oklahoma's News 4, April 11, 2012, https://www.youtube.com/watch?v=ydmPh4MXT3g.

36 James Herbert, "Kobe Hate-Listened to 'Don't Stop Believin'' for Two Years after Celtics Loss," CBS, December 26, 2015, https://www.cbssports.com/nba/news/kobe-hate-listened-to-dont-stop-believin-for-2-years-after-celtics-loss/.

37 Kendra Cherry, "How Freud's Pleasure Principle Works," Verywell Mind, May 8, 2020, https://www.verywellmind.com/what-is-the-pleasure-principle-2795472.

38 Ian Leslie, "The Scientists Who Make Apps Addictive," *1843 Magazine*, October 20, 2016, https://www.economist.com/1843/2016/10/20/the-scientists-who-make-apps-addictive.

39 Lucy E. Cousins, "Are There Downsides to Always Trying to Be Positive?" HCF, February 2018, https://www.hcf.com.au/health-agenda/body-mind/mental-health/downsides-to-always-being-positive.

40 Matthew 6:15 (NKJV).

41 Colossians 3:13 (NKJV).

42 Luke 3:22 (NKJV).

43 Luke 4:3 (NIV).

44 Matthew 4:4, Christian Standard Bible.

45 Matthew 16:6 (ESV).

46 Leslie Riopel, "15 Most Interesting Self-Compassion Research Findings," Positive Psychology, February 27, 2021, https://positivepsychology.com/self-compassion-research/.

47 Matthew 22:37–9 (NKJV).

48 Matthew 6:22–23 (NLT).

49 Proverbs 18:21 (ESV).

50 Psalm 138:3 (NIV).

51 Romans 8:1 (NKJV).

52 John 10:10 (NKJV).

53 James 4:7 (NIV).

54 Proverbs 23:23 (NIV).

55   Matt Simon, "Fantastically Wrong: What Darwin Really Screwed Up About Evolution," *Wired*, December 17, 2014, https://www.wired.com/2014/12/fantastically-wrong-thing-evolution-darwin-really-screwed/.

56   Hebrews 4:15 (NIV).

57   "Core Belief Magnet Metaphor," Psychology Tools, accessed June 4, 2021, https://www.psychologytools.com/resource/core-belief-magnet-metaphor/.

58   1 Corinthians 2 (NIV).

59   1 Corinthian 15:33 (NIV).

60   Eberhard Fuchs and Gabriele Flügge, "Adult Neuroplasticity: More Than 40 Years of Research," *Neural Plasticity* (2014), https://www.doi.org/10.1155/2014/541870.

61   "Neuroplasticity 101," Brainfutures, accessed June 4, 2021, https://www.brainfutures.org/neuroplasticity-101/.

62   Matthew 7:24-28 (NKJV).

63   Matthew 23:43–5 (NLT).

64   Proverbs 24:3–6 (NKJV).

65   Luke 6:45 (ESV).

66   Matthew 16:16 (NKJV).

67   Matthew 16:17 (NKJV).

68   Romans 2:3–5, Evangelical Heritage Version.

69   Jed Magen, "Loneliness Is Bad for Your Health," The Conversation, February 26, 2018, https://theconversation.com/loneliness-is-bad-for-your-health-90901.

70   Sandra Luck, "Nine Symptoms of Soul Ties You Can Recognize," Soul Connection, accessed June 4, 2021, https://www.soulconnection.net/symptoms-of-soul-ties/.

71   "Pornhub's Annual Report: Can You Guess 2019's Top Searched Porn Terms?" Fight the New Drug, December 17, 2019, https://fightthenewdrug.org/2019-pornhub-annual-report/.

72   Revelation 4, (NIV).

73   Romans 6:23 (NIV).

74   "Jefferson Bethke, 'Why I Hate Religion, But Love Jesus || Spoken Word,'" YouTube video, January 10, 2012, https://www.youtube.com/watch?v=1IAhDGYlpqY.

75   Psalm 23:1 (NKJV).

76   Matthew 6:1–4 (NIV).

77   Matthew 6:5–9 (NIV).

78   Matthew 6:16-18 (NIV).

79   1 Thessalonians 5:17 (NKJV).

80   "Fasting," Open Bible, accessed June 4, 2021, https://www.openbible.info/topics/fasting.

81 Psalm 46:10 (NIV).

82 2 Corinthians 5:16-18 (Lexham English Bible).

83 Haggai 2:9 (NIV).

84 Proverbs 10:9 (NKJV).

Made in the USA
Monee, IL
22 December 2024

316ed1c6-26d4-4c15-80c5-f3d951c2be5aR01